Slow Boat
—— through ——
Germany

Avonbay on the Main at Karlstadt.

Slow Boat
through
Germany

HUGH McKNIGHT

Adlard Coles Nautical
London

For the boating pioneers who travelled there before us, and especially:

Henry M Doughty, 1841–1916
Cecil Scott Forester, 1899–1966

BY THE SAME AUTHOR

Canal and River Craft in Pictures, David & Charles, Newton Abbot, 1969.
The Canal Enthusiasts' Handbook (with David Edwards-May), *1970–71* and *No 2*, 1973, David & Charles, Newton Abbot.
A Source Book of Canals, Locks and Canal Boats, Ward Lock, London, 1974.
The Guinness Guide to Waterways of Western Europe, Guinness, London, 1978.
The Shell Book of Inland Waterways, David & Charles, Newton Abbot, 3rd ed, in preparation for 1994.
Waterways Postcards 1900–1930, Shepperton Swan, Shepperton, 1983. Winner, Prix du Livre Cartophile.
Cruising French Waterways, Adlard Coles Nautical, 2nd ed, 1991. Winner, Thomas Cook Guide Book Award.
Slow Boat Through France, David & Charles, Newton Abbot, 1991.

Published in 1993 by Adlard Coles Nautical,
an imprint of A & C Black (Publishers) Ltd,
35 Bedford Row, London WC1R 4JH

Copyright © Text, illustrations and maps, Hugh McKnight 1993

First edition 1993

ISBN 0-7136-3778-1

A CIP catalogue record for this book is available from the British Library.

Set in 11 on 13pt Monophoto Photina by Selwood Systems, Midsomer Norton and printed and bound in Great Britain by Butler & Tanner Ltd, Frome and London.

While every effort has been taken to ensure the accuracy of this book, neither the author nor the publishers can take responsibility for any accident or damage arising out of any error of commission or omission.

Contents

Preface   vii

1   Rhine   1
2   Neckar   23
3   Lahn   32
4   Moselle   43
5   Eastwards to the Elbe   70
6   Elbe and Havel   85
7   Berlin   96
8   Mecklenburg Wonderland   109
9   Return to the West   126
10 Main   139
11 Rhine–Main–Danube Canal   155
12 Danubian Epilogue   174
    Appendix 1   Cruising in Germany   182
    Appendix 2   Selected Bibliography   194
    Index   197

Maps

    Waterways of Germany   vi
    Rhine   3
    Neckar   27
    Lahn   35
    Moselle   51
    Rhine to Berlin   74
    Greater Berlin   98
    Berlin to Mecklenburg   111
    Mecklenburg Lakes   121
    Main to the Danube   144

The waterways network of Germany: 1 Ems-Jade C. 2 Nordgeorgsfehn C. 3 Küsten C. 4 Hunte. 5 Die Schlei. 6 Stör. 7 Warnow. 8 Elbe-Havel C. 9 Havel. 10 Havel-Oder C. 11 Oder-Spree C. 12 Warthe.

Preface

Readers of *Slow Boat Through France* will know that our plans for extensive exploration of the canals and rivers of mainland Europe came to fruition in June 1985. It was then that our 11 m twin-engined steel cruiser *Avonbay* saw England for the last time, reached Calais after a somewhat worrying crossing of the Channel, and embarked on a series of holiday journeys extending from Paris to Alsace and Belgium to the Mediterranean. But it was only a matter of time before our horizons broadened eastwards to Germany. At this point, even the most enthusiastic crystal-ball gazer could never have predicted the fall of communism, resulting in a reunified German nation with a waterways network totalling 7133 km and providing direct links with exotic destinations that included Poland, Bohemia and Austria.

Long experience of inland navigations ranging from Great Britain to Sweden gave us the degree of confidence necessary to tackle the River Rhine, one of the world's most challenging waterways, and a river that carries more freight than any other route in Europe. Entering from France, there is no approach to the German interior that avoids the Rhine. Quite rightly, boat-handling qualifications are obligatory for this and other German canals and rivers (see Appendix 1, page 186).

Reflection on the events of this century naturally made us wonder what kind of reception we would receive in a country then little known to British boaters. Would we be greeted with dislike and derision? Several times during the first two years of my life I came close to annihilation by the Nazi bombs that rained on our home, west of London. *Avonbay*'s co-owner, John Humphries, had experienced life-threatening situations during the war as a young officer in the Royal Navy. How would we adapt to long periods where our day-to-day survival depended on establishing cordial relations with the locals?

Fortunately, my family history has some German connections. During the First World War my mother was educated at a north London grammar school where the pacifist headmistress reacted to the outbreak of hostilities by substituting German lessons for French! Standards must have been high, for decades later I was to acquire an informal and elementary grasp of the language almost without trying. When we decided to head for Berlin and the lost world of the Mecklenburg Lakes in east Germany, this provided a useful basis for communication, enhanced by 12 one-hour private lessons.

My mother's youngest sister Marjorie (who was prevented with some difficulty from joining the Freedom Fighters during the Spanish Civil War) found herself working with the British Army of Occupation after the Berlin Airlift. Regular gift parcels of German hand-painted wooden toys were one of the delights of my early childhood. To their great credit, my grandparents raised no objection when Aunt Marjorie unexpectedly returned to England married to a charming German engineer named Hein and set up home in Hampstead. They led an extremely contented life for the next 25 years until Uncle Hein died. Many of his tools are still in daily use on board our boat. Long-standing German friends included Charles Gérard, proprietor of H$_2$O, our favourite winter mooring on the French canals at St Jean-de-Losne. Thus Germany was unlikely to be a problem for us.

As a holiday home, *Avonbay* is owned jointly with former Inland Waterways Association chairman John Humphries and his wife June. Throughout our travels, we three formed the basic crew, often joined by one or more of the Humphries girls: Evelyn, Amanda (and husband Charles) and Diana (with assorted friends). Several years after her eightieth birthday, my mother was on board for a cruise up the Lahn: her first visit to Germany since seeing the Kaiser under house arrest in the Netherlands all those many years before. Marine engineer and surveyor Jim Macdonald and his wife Mig have regularly accompanied me: apart from their boating expertise and companionship, Jim's great attribute is wizardry with all things mechanical. I could never have contemplated rebuilding the port engine in the space of a single morning on the Mittelland Canal!

This book describes cruises made between 1986 and 1992, a period that includes momentous events in recent German history. Some German routes still await exploration, but I believe that we have already travelled many of the most attractive and worthwhile navigations. As far as I can ascertain, ours was the first UK-registered pleasure boat to reach Berlin (on her own keel) since before the Second World War. A year later, *Avonbay* became the first motor cruiser to complete an inaugural run through the new Main–Danube Canal.

Much inspiration came from earlier boating explorers, whose published accounts accompanied us on our own travels: among them are H M Doughty, C S Forester and that great friend of all European waterway enthusiasts, Dr Roger Pilkington. Others who helped in a variety of ways include Heidi and Wolfgang Banzhaf, Sir Michael and Lady Henrietta Burton, our German teacher Dennis Cook, Charles Gérard, Norman Halfar, Lord Harvington, Caroline and Michael Hofman, Henry Nagel, Tobias Poensgen, Alfred Soler and Lawrence Talbot. I would like to express a particular debt of gratitude to the members of numerous yacht clubs and the owners of several German marinas where commercial transactions were coupled with a display of genuine friendship. Some sections of this book were first published in *Motor*

OPPOSITE A Rhine steamship poster of 1897.

Boat & Yachting, and its editor, along with those of *Motorboats Monthly* and *Waterways World*, generously supplied me with origination facilities for some of my colour photographs which appear as illustrations. Janet Murphy of Adlard Coles Nautical has allowed me an unusual degree of freedom in the content and design. The select company of advertisers whose products and services enliven the final pages are all known to me personally, and I wholeheartedly encourage readers to use them.

Thanks are due to Dr Roger Pilkington for kindly agreeing to my use of two extracts from his *Small Boat Through Germany*; and to Messrs Bachman & Turner for permission to quote from Merlin Minshall's *Guilt-Edged*.

References in the text to 'West Germany' and 'East Berlin' apply to the situation before reunification. Thereafter, I have used 'east Germany' and 'west Berlin'. It is necessary to differentiate between the two halves of this country, where a startling contrast in conditions and lifestyle will inevitably linger for many years.

While *Avonbay* was cruising, £1 (UK) was roughly equivalent to 3DM (German). Since then, the British pound has been devalued.

Now it's time to fire both engines, check that the German courtesy flag is fluttering at the starboard crosstrees, cast off the mooring lines, and set out to discover some of the most exciting and beautiful navigations in Europe.

Hugh McKnight
The Clock House
Shepperton-on-Thames
TW17 8RU England

Note:
Rather than provide translations throughout the text, the meanings of certain German words used are explained below.

Alte Brücke	old bridge	*Ratskeller*	town hall cellar, often used as a restaurant
Bootsclub	yacht club		
Bürgermeister	mayor	*Schiffshebewerk*	barge lift
Gastarbeiten	foreign workers (frequently Turkish or from Eastern Europe)	*Schloss*	castle
		Sportboot	pleasure boat (not necessarily a very fast one)
Hafen	harbour		
Haltes nautiques (French)	moorings with facilities	*Sportbootsschleuse*	pleasure boat lock (of restricted dimensions)
Hauptmarkt	main market (square)	*Stein*	stone
Hebewerk	barge lift	*Südliches*	an area around Ochsenfurt on the Main
Kurhaus/-saal	spa building	*Maindreieck*	
Lahnschiffe	River Lahn barge	*Under den Linden*	'Under the Limes' (a Berlin street)
Landbrot	traditional country-style bread		
		Verboten	forbidden
Polizeiboot	police launch	*Wasserpolizei*	water police
Rathaus	town hall	*Winter Hafen*	winter harbour

1 Rhine

Father Rhine, on an early 20th century Liebig card.

Second only to the Danube in length, the Rhine is Europe's leading river highway, navigable for 885 km from the little town of Rhein-felden, upstream of Basle, to its confused estuary on the North Sea coast at Rotterdam. Serving Switzerland, France, Germany and the Netherlands, by far the greatest part of its course lies alongside or within German territory. This is a waterway that pleasure craft must confront with a degree of caution, yet given a reliable boat, adequate common sense and only occasionally nerves of steel, travelling the Rhine is within the ability of most would-be waterways explorers.

I tend to regard it as an unavoidable stage in the process of reaching other more rewarding and less demanding navigations. The inescapable fact is that, short of being lifted overland, no boat can reach the German interior from France, Belgium or the Netherlands without making a coastal passage of careering down the Rhine. We on *Avonbay* are *inland* boaters and regard the second of these options as the most practicable.

The map shows how connections are made several times with the French network in Alsace; with the Moselle, for Luxembourg and France; and from the eastern bank into the Neckar, Main (leading to the Danube), Lahn and, through the Ruhr, into the heart of Germany to Berlin, the Baltic, Poland and the Czech Republic.

Avonbay's golden-plated rule, sometimes to be broken *in extremis*, is to work *downstream*. This saves time and fuel that would otherwise be wasted by trying to force against the current. Moderately powered displacement cruisers will find upstream passages either tediously slow or impossible; travelling south up the Rhine Gorge, between Lahnstein and Bingen where flow is strongest, is an option that *Avonbay* can never consider, except perhaps under tow. There, we just have enough power to pull into a harbour, but to make acceptable upstream progress would require a stillwater speed of at least 12 knots. Never should the might of this river be underestimated. It is very different from ambling along the Upper Thames.

Once in a while, you will read press reports of shipping disasters in the Rhine – of 3000-tonne barges colliding in fog, being swept on to shallows, or even exploding under impact. And these are craft handled by professionals with a lifetime's training. Pleasure boats should *never* take chances with the Rhine. Quite reasonably, all in charge of motor cruisers on the German Rhine, no matter what their nationality, must carry some proof of qualification (see Appendix 1). This rule is regarded very seriously by the *Wasserpolizei*. On one occasion, we were boarded in midstream and asked to produce our Royal Yachting Association Helmsman's (Overseas) Certificate of Competence. Had I not carried one, *Avonbay* would have been escorted to a harbour and presumably impounded. Doubtless, there are financial penalties for failure to comply. Craft in excess of 15 tonnes may only be handled by skippers qualified to a degree that is well beyond the scope of most pleasure boaters.

The brochures of the Rhine passenger vessel companies would have you believe that the entire waterway is a scenic delight. In reality, this is strictly true only of the 60 km Gorge, upstream of Koblenz. Here, castles perch on clifftops, high above little towns of brightly painted buildings. Elsewhere, the Rhine varies from deserted willow-covered shingle banks to scenes of heavy industry. Not that scenery will be uppermost in your mind: almost always, commercial traffic is so dense that the helmsman must maintain continuous concentration, preferably aided by one crew member keeping a constant watch astern. Most other vessels are faster than *Avonbay*, so it is vital to know what is about to overtake and give it sufficient space. There have been times when a dozen upstream barges are matched by a similar number working downriver. Often, we have counted three freight vessels alongside us simultaneously.

Wash created in a busy reach can be considerable, especially with a head-on wind. When the fore-end of a laden 2000-tonner disappears for several seconds in clouds of spray, it doesn't take much imagination to visualise what *Avonbay* is having to cope with! On one journey between the Lahn and the Dutch border, our wipers were almost continuously in use for two days, clearing water from the windscreen. The ship's bell rang repeatedly as we rolled. While some barges tend to continue day and night, pleasure craft are ill-advised to run after dark; in any case, I find that a spell of five hours at the wheel is quite enough for one person. It is then time to pull out of the thoroughfare into a congenial yacht harbour to rest for a while, and gather the required nervous energy for the next onslaught.

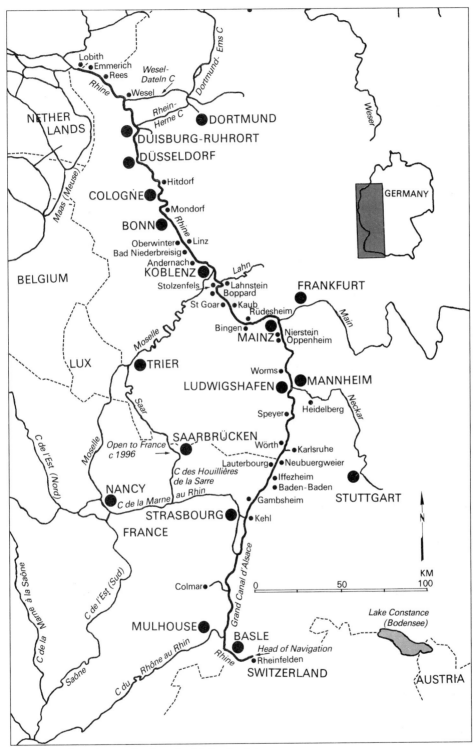

The Rhine from Switzerland to the Netherlands.

We always carry charts of the waterways we travel, although this is rarely essential from a safety viewpoint. However, they are *vital* on the Rhine: otherwise, there is no way of knowing in advance where the buoyed channel lies or the whereabouts of tranquil marinas when you decide that it is time to halt.

Before starting, the boat should be prepared as if for a sea voyage: mooring lines stowed so that they cannot be washed overboard and the anchor made ready for instant use in the event of engine failure. We have yet to find ourselves in this situation – indeed, I even doubt the ability of our anchor to hold in the fierce current of the Gorge. At times like these, I am thankful to have twin engines. Crockery, bottles and other movable objects should be stowed with care – a galley full of broken glass is clearly a hazard.

Small craft are expected to stay well clear of their large freight-carrying companions. In my experience, the barge skippers are invariably considerate, provided you maintain a straight course, keeping close to the starboard side of the channel. Upstream commercial traffic and passenger ships will frequently cut corners, either to save themselves distance or to avoid the strongest currents. The technique is known as 'blue-flagging'. Any intention of taking the 'wrong' side of the fairway is indicated by displaying a blue board with flashing white light at the centre. Pleasure boats are not expected to respond in similar fashion, but I find that it is wise to oversteer somewhat, so that there is absolutely no doubt as to which course you are taking.

In recent years we have travelled the entire navigable Rhine from Switzerland to the Netherlands twice, as well as making additional, shorter, journeys over parts of its course. With more than one competent (and qualified) helmsman able to share the steering, huge daily distances can be covered, for there are no locks to impede progress from Iffezheim (K334) all the way to the North Sea (K1030).

But enough of warnings: had I known a quarter of what I now know about the Rhine when we made our first hesitant journey in 1980, we might never have left the safety of small canals. As co-founders of the France-based Blue Line hire fleet, we derived no financial gain but had free use of a boat for several weeks each summer. This time, a single-engined Bermuda cruiser, originally designed for use on the Norfolk Broads, was on offer. We decided on a nearly impossible itinerary from Burgundy and via the canalised Doubs, the Grand Canal d'Alsace, Strasbourg, Nancy and the Canal de l'Est back to St Jean-de-Losne. This prodigious distance bristled with locks and was to be completed in slightly less than three weeks. 'Grand Canal d'Alsace' is, in fact, nothing less than the canalised Rhine, equipped with vast locks, heroically wide concrete channels and, in places, portions of near natural river that pour down from the distant Swiss Alps. We chose to avoid potential complications over German regulations by staying determinedly within France, although I do not recall that we appreciated then that competence qualifications might be demanded.

Travelling with the stream, we were not keen to moor overnight on the

Rhine, and we escaped instead to the calm of the Canal du Rhône au Rhin at Rheinau. Although probably this was the first hire cruiser to sample these waters (and I would hope that few have since followed our example) we were largely ignored by lock keepers, who anyway conducted all negotiations in German. It was to be a very long and hot day. Much of the journey was spent crashing violently in the double – or even triple – wash of the huge barges that were making for or arriving from the Swiss port of Basle. Totally unsuited for such treatment, our little boat took all this punishment remarkably well – until a wall-mounted and heavily stacked food cupboard collapsed rather suddenly on to the galley floor.

Our next experience of the Rhine came only a few months later, when June, John and I were guests of Lord and Lady Harvington for three weeks on their splendid new Nelson 42, *Melitina*. We ascended the Rhine Gorge from Koblenz, travelled on to Mainz, and then followed the course of the Main and Main–Danube Canal to Nuremberg. Eleven years in advance of the canal's completion, *Melitina* there resorted to the autobahn, in order to complete her extraordinary cruise through the Danube as far as the Black Sea. We were willing guests, but navigational worries remained the concern of our host. *Melitina*'s top speed of around 20 knots gave us a considerable advantage up the Rhine, easily outstripping all craft with the exception of police launches. Thus we unknowingly acquired a totally false degree of confidence, feeling that our newly purchased *Avonbay* would take everything easily within her stride during her first exposure to Father Rhine in 1986.

Slow Boat Through France describes our exciting progress upriver to Basle and Rheinfelden, where speed was reduced to an unimpressive crawl. That account tells of our meeting a Swiss Customs officer of dubious moral character and leaves the reader wondering what happened to *Avonbay* then, before she reappeared on the French Moselle a year later. In fact, in the summer of 1986 we navigated the Rhine as far as the Neckar, explored that river to Plochingen and back, then continued to Mainz for a cruise up to distant Bamberg. The boat wintered in Frankfurt and restarted her travels the following Easter with a passage down the Rhine Gorge, followed by a run up the Lahn. August 1987 was reserved for our return to France, via the Moselle.

Avonbay's next Rhine encounter came in 1990, when we tackled the lower river from Koblenz to the Netherlands. We were to return 11 months later, cruising the Strasbourg/Ruhrort section as the first stage of our long journey eastwards to Berlin. Finally, unexpected opening of the Main–Danube Canal through Bavaria in 1992 prompted us once more to travel between Strasbourg and Mainz. For us, navigating the Rhine is rather akin to boating on a runaway escalator: hence all these downstream trips, followed by more relaxing southward journeys through Belgium and France. As our Rhine explorations have of necessity been somewhat fragmented, the description that follows is an amalgam drawn from several years. I have concentrated on special highlights rather than attempting to describe all the places and attractions of a great river; these have been fully covered elsewhere (see Appendix 2, page 194).

Used with difficulty in Roman times, the Rhine was obstructed by no fewer than 62 individual toll points, established in the Middle Ages between Basle and Rotterdam. Most castle strongholds now seen in the Gorge were erected by robber barons with the aim of plundering passing traffic. Teams of men or horses would struggle to haul cargo against the stream; few navigational improvements were attempted until Johann Gottfried Tulla reduced the torrential upper section, Basle to Mannheim, into something approaching a proper inland waterway. Until his taming programme of the early nineteenth century, more than 2000 islands littered a meandering water course, often several kilometres in width. By 1874 freight ports had been established in Karlsruhe, Strasbourg, Kehl and Basle; steam tugs hauled barges in long trains and the river had been shortened by as much as 82 km. Tolls were gradually abolished with the creation of the Central Commission for Rhine Shipping, an international body formed under the Mannheim Shipping Act of 1868. Representatives of Germany, France, the Netherlands, Belgium, Switzerland and (rather surprisingly) Great Britain continue to administer a waterway that now carries more freight than any other comparable route in the world and is regularly used by over 12 000 vessels.

Constant dredging aims to maintain a deepwater channel from Switzerland to the North Sea. Earlier obstacles have long been removed: notably over 80 rocky reefs in the length immediately downstream of the Bingen Loch. Mid-twentieth-century building of the Grand Canal d'Alsace, Basle to Iffezheim, resulted in ten massive duplicated locks, each with associated hydroelectric plants. Undoubted navigational advantages have only been achieved at the expense of serious side effects, not least of which is the possibility of catastrophic flooding in the reaches downriver. More canalisation and further locks may have to be planned. It remains to be seen if the long-considered scheme to canalise the Swiss portion, 150 km to Lake Constance, involving some tunnelling work, will ever be carried out.

Often, *Avonbay*'s flirtations with the Rhine have started in Strasbourg, that most Germanic of all French cities. Negotiation of the Canal de la Marne au Rhin involves nothing more taxing than passing from Lorraine to Alsace through the Niderviller and Arzviller tunnels, floating down to the valley of the River Zorn in a remarkable inclined plane boat lift, playing with a series of descending radar-controlled locks, and finally turning into the River Ill when we have reached the headquarters of the European Parliament. Our favoured Strasbourg mooring on the Quai des Pêcheurs is within easy walking distance of timbered houses in La Petite France quarter; sitting on deck, the illuminated wedding cake spire of the cathedral provides our night-light. Unfortunately, these moorings have lately become full with converted barge restaurants. No spaces remained on our most recent visit, so we breasted up with a deserted cruiser flying a German ensign and soon had welcomed two boatfuls of Italian holidaymakers, who tied on to us.

A little before midnight, our unknown neighbours boarded their boat, noisily talking English with American accents directly outside my cabin window. They appeared to be four or five young girls. One fell into the water amid hysterical laughter, so sleep was impossible until they had themselves retired at 2 am. Five hours later I was woken by insistent tapping on the cabinside: 'Hugh! Are you there?' Grumpily, I presented myself at the saloon doorway to discover that the leader of this jolly party wanted me to autograph a book. I complied as gracefully as circumstances permitted and decided that there are times when it is preferable to travel *incognito*.

With fuel and water tanks filled, we present ourselves at the Écluses Nord, suffer an anticipated delay while a railway bridge is swung aside, and head down a short cut to see the Rhine's murky waters rushing past the exit. Our bow lookout signals that all is clear (ie that no barges, especially downstream runners, are within 500 m). I advance the throttles and we surge forward into the great river. Effectively, this is goodbye to France, although two locks and another 50 km of river are to intervene before each side of the Rhine lies within Germany.

The pilot guides indicate numerous basins where pleasure craft can lie safely for the night. Each Rhine voyage introduces us to new yacht clubs, but quite often we use those we have previously found to be friendly havens. One good one, on the French shore at K335.4, is a tranquil pool off the Iffezheim weirstream. On our first visit in June 1991 no club members appeared to demand a fee. When we returned in July of the next year an air of clubhouse bonhomie was so intense that my offer to part with the expected 9DM was waved aside with the suggestion that payment could wait until later. As it was still early evening, I cycled into the nearby village, passing en route some abandoned French Customs buildings. A stream of cars poured over the bridge connecting France with Germany. Months in advance of the 1993 relaxation of trade barriers, this border no longer appeared to exist and, for car travellers at least, the two countries had merged into a single nation.

The French don't seem to be very enthusiastic Rhine boaters, for none were to be discovered here. We had arrived at the Motor Yacht Club Baden-Baden e.V., which was filled with German cruisers who conveniently ignored a quirk of geography and occupied territory on the west bank of the Rhine. I returned to the boat minutes before the oppressive weather suddenly erupted into a violent storm. Within seconds, our deck was peppered with hailstones the size of small marbles. Then the sky cleared again, thunder retreated over the hills, and we knew that the next day would bring another glorious heatwave. Presumably this storm had sent the locals scurrying for home, taking with them any chance of exacting payment from the British explorers.

Running our engines at 2000 rpm – which is about three-quarters of their potential maximum – gives *Avonbay* a canal speed of around 12 kph. From Strasbourg to Iffezheim, this had increased to about 16 kph. Now, below the taming influence of locks and weirs, we timed our progress against the bank-mounted distance markers and noted a very respectable 24 kph. This is quite acceptable until it is time to stop. And stopping was obligatory at K354, where the German authorities have their Neuburgweier Customs station.

The first time we exported the boat here, advice had been sought from the German Chamber of Industry and Commerce in London. That august body's opinion, accompanied by a £50 invoice, led us to suppose that there were no punitive regulations then in force, although whether or not we might be charged Value Added Tax on *Avonbay*'s estimated worth 'will always be a matter for the discretion of the Customs Office at the border'. We had no intention of parting with that sort of money, so we were more than pleased to be able to entertain a boatload of off-duty German Customs officials with wives and children when they came on board the previous evening at the French Lauterbourg harbour (K349).

Safe arrival in Neuburgweier *Zollhafen* entailed crabbing out of the river's flow, engines briefly at maximum speed, while we heeled over at an alarming angle. Once inside, throttling hard astern only just prevented us from colliding with a bright-green Customs launch to which we were expected to make fast. Formalities were few, for although we had liberally dispensed alcohol the night before, our friends had remained sufficiently alert to recognise us now. All earlier forebodings vanished when we were told that *Avonbay* could remain in *Deutschland* for as long as she chose.

My next visit, five years later, came early in the voyage to Berlin, when I was crewed by Mig and Jim Macdonald. All went according to plan until it was time to leave. Some distance downriver, a huge white Köln–Düsseldorf hotel ship was surging into the stream, blue-flagging on our side of the channel. Normally I would have waited until it had passed, but as we hovered in the basin exit I realised that we were preventing a Customs launch from entering. We certainly had no wish to be apprehended for obstruction. Jim was steering. Making a split-second executive captain's decision, I yelled to him: 'Go for it!' Instantly, the current grasped our hull and we hurtled sideways downriver at 10 or 11 knots, realising with alarm that the hotel ship was making much greater headway than expected. High on the other vessel's bridge, I glimpsed a startled helmsman; he then appeared to increase speed. We escaped a head-on collision by perhaps five seconds. Consideration for Customs launches subsequently declined in our list of priorities. The resulting turmoil produced nothing more serious than a broken egg cup as *Avonbay* rolled violently, but we had come frighteningly close to disaster.

Not all Rhine problems end so happily, though. Several years earlier, a retired British couple who were clients of mine launched their trailed cruiser on the middle Rhine at the start of a planned voyage to the Danube. The culmination of this adventure was to be a reunion with a group of school-friends in George's Hungarian homeland. For several days Mindy had been uncharacteristically anxious, but knowing how her husband had been looking forward to the trip she kept these fears to herself. Within hours of setting out up the Rhine, their little boat burst into flames. Unable to extinguish the fire and worried at the probability of a bottled gas explosion, the pair had no alternative but to jump into the river. Fortunately, Mindy's previous apprehension had already prompted her to wear a lifejacket. Clinging on to long lines attached to their blazing cruiser, they were swept a considerable distance downriver, until they eventually ended up on a rocky shore. Other vessels had meanwhile alerted the fire services, but by then their plastic boat was blazing from stem to stern. 'What we salvaged would hardly have filled a garden wheelbarrow,' George told me some months later, producing a metal spanner that had been badly distorted by the heat. 'We lost almost everything: clothing, money and passports. Amazingly, out of all the belongings assembled for a cruise of several months, the only thing worth keeping was my copy of *Cruising French Waterways*. I have heard of waterproof books, but never ones that can survive such a conflagration!' I do not believe that the cause of the disaster was ever known for certain; that little boat was, however, fitted with an inboard petrol engine.

Coming past the Neuburgweier Customs harbour in 1992, we nearly didn't bother to stop. After all, road traffic was crossing the border quite freely. Nevertheless, we did pull in to ask whether this procedure was still required. 'Certainly,' came the reply, followed by the briefest inspection of our passports. It must be strange to be in a job whose *raison d'être* has disappeared.

On one occasion, we made a non-stop run from here to Bingen; at 173 km this constitutes an inland cruising record for *Avonbay* that is unlikely to be broken. Not once did the hard-worked engines give us the slightest cause for concern. Nor, with a continual procession of freight carriers, passenger ships, pleasure cruisers and even rowing boats and canoes, was there ever time to become bored. Gradually the bleak surroundings became more interesting: partly drowned willows beyond Wörth; campers on a gravel beach; and several floating bridges moored to the banks. These are presumably retained for military use; fortunately, we have never found one obstructing the channel, which would result in us having somehow to turn to face the flow.

Speyer, K399, with its copper cathedral dome, passed quickly on the port side. Then there was a power station at Neckarau with a rare collection of working locomotives which are periodically charged with steam, rather than carrying their own boilers. Fuel refineries, a factory containing small mountains of some bright-yellow chemical and dozens of barges announce arrival at the Ludwigshafen/Mannheim complex, around the junction with the River Neckar. These are the second busiest docks on German inland waters. Conditions are becoming distinctly rough!

It was in Mannheim that we experienced our first and only Rhine sighting of a British cargo boat. Named *Claudia W*, she was quite the most uninspiring, rust-streaked vessel I have yet to meet on a European waterway, scruffier by far than any craft encountered in east Germany. Her tattered red ensign was faded pale pink, yet somehow she presented a brave sight, deeply laden and making good progress upstream. Registered in Gibraltar, she very possibly made regular runs both on the North Sea and the Mediterranean. But what a poor advertisement for the once proud British merchant fleet! We waved and received a cheerful reply from the crew.

During our first run through the city of Worms, we found – much to our surprise – that we were gaining on a 3000-tonne capacity container ship. Most commercial craft waste little time in pulling away from *Avonbay*. This container ship's controls were mounted on a telescopic bridge which, when raised, allowed the captain a view of all traffic, provided it was at least 400 m ahead. But as this leviathan approached road and railway crossings, her wheelhouse subsided until the helmsman could see nothing but the steel side of the nearest container stowed on deck. We hoped that he was not suffering from acute amnesia, for he appeared to be effectively steering 'blind' for prolonged periods. Meanwhile, a police launch, presumably in radio contact, buzzed around the ship, warning of approaching hazards. Beyond the city, there would be no more overhead obstructions until the outskirts of Mainz, 48 km downriver. The container ship soon piled on speed and began to draw away from us.

No longer required as escorts, the *Wasserpolizei* directed their attentions to us, requested that we turned to face upstream, and neatly made fast to *Avonbay* in midriver! We had never before been boarded in such a manner. At such times you worry what regulations you might have transgressed. I was too surprised to photograph the event, and anyway suspected that they might be slightly camera-shy. There are moments when you instinctively know better than to take pictures of German officials or installations. One of the police stepped on board with a business-like request for papers. Control of both boats was now in the hands of our uniformed friends. Passports, registration document and insurance certificate were inspected in laborious detail, and then it was time for my RYA 'driver's licence' to be produced. Fortunately, this was considered acceptable proof of our competence. That we had successfully negotiated the Thames Estuary, the English Channel, toiled through several hundred French locks and braved the Rhine for nearly 300 km from Switzerland, would perhaps have been more telling evidence of our ability to cruise through Worms! Almost as an afterthought, they asked where we had come from. 'London,' we replied. When their response was 'What? In that?' it was difficult to be sure if their reaction was one of admiration or horrorstruck disbelief. Politely, we were wished a good journey and the *Wasserpolizei* roared off, rather pointedly demonstrating that their engine room contained considerably more horses than *Avonbay*'s.

Surroundings started to improve at Oppenheim (K470) as the river widened and the first vineyards appeared on the slopes of Nierstein. Seeing the great tracts of hillside devoted to wine production, it is almost impossible to believe that all the resulting alcohol can find a market. Rhine wine is a leading industry of this part of the river, remorselessly consumed in thousands of waterside drinking establishments. Hock is the favoured white wine of *Avonbay*'s owners, drunk in liberal quantities in England as well as when boating on the Continent. We therefore had more than a passing interest in the serried ranks of vines. This is perhaps a suitable point at which to mention that the German water police introduced random breath tests for inland boat skippers in 1992; no longer are prosecutions only made where craft are navigated in a dangerous manner.

We have cruised through Mainz no fewer than five times, mostly with our sights set on the River Main, joining the Rhine at K497. Only once have we explored the city, which boasts pleasantly central moorings in the *Winter Hafen*. But within reach of the Rhine Gorge, greater attractions beckon. Half-submerged tree-covered islands create twin navigation channels at the upstream approach to Rüdesheim, the river's leading tourist town and the closest approach to the Costa Brava that you are likely to discover in Germany. As the nearest pleasure craft harbour lies 2 km upstream, one single investigation of Rüdesheim has been enough to reveal that the town is cheerfully brash, noisy and populated by rather aggressive beer-swilling youngsters. More to our taste is the Bingen *Hafen* (opposite, K527), to be entered cautiously once you have checked that the Rüdesheim car ferry is not about to emerge. We have overnighted here several times and eaten at

Container ship on the Rhine at Worms. Note the telescopic bridge.

an agreeable floating restaurant (a novel vegetable was deep-fried parsley) before summoning up the courage for a high-speed descent of the Gorge the next day.

One pleasant excursion is to take the ferry to Rüdesheim town centre and there board a cable car which glides over vineyards to the Niderwald Monument, a key site in the history of modern Germany. Towering over the river, this 37 m-high statue of Germania (a Teutonic version of our own Britannia) was erected to mark the formation of the German Reich after the Franco-Prussian War of 1870–1. Boating enthusiasts, while impressed by the sheer grandeur of this large young lady, will enjoy even more the splendid panorama of the Rhine, looking down on to the Binger Loch and an ever-present congestion of barges passing through the turbulent narrows. The German *Loch* means 'hole', and in this context is very different from the familiar Scottish word.

Long before I had arrived here in a boat, I found myself in Rüdesheim and was tempted to make a tour of the Gorge by light aircraft. Here, surely, was an opportunity to take a unique series of photographs. The fare for a 15-minute flight was steep – more so, when I realised that the elderly single-engined machine would be taking off from a sloping grass field which terminated on the edge of a cliff. Fortunately, I didn't know at the time that the loss of light aircraft accounts by far for the majority of aeronautical disasters. Before take-off, I explained my photographic requirements to the pilot, an ageing relic from the Second World War Luftwaffe. We zoomed thrillingly low over hillsides, castles and barges. It was only when we returned to land that I was informed: 'You must now surrender your film for processing under government control. All pictures not considered to endanger national security will be sent to you.' Had I known this beforehand, I would not have bothered to buy a ticket. I handed over one roll of film from the several I had exposed, paid a processing fee, and (almost inevitably) heard no more. My other 'illicit' pictures were a little disappointing. The Rhine Gorge appears to photograph best from the deck of a boat or when standing on *terra firma* high above the valley.

Exciting though the experience is, to pass through the Gorge in a small boat is probably not the best way of appreciating the numerous small towns and dozens of castles. Known in German as the *Gebirgsstrecke* ('mountain stretch'), the 62 km length from Bingen to Koblenz has nearly 40 castles, in varying states of ruin and restoration – more than in any comparable place on earth. Full exploration could take a week by car, driving down one bank and returning via the other; a train journey provides yet another perspective.

Even in times of low water the river's current is fast, with boat-shaped marker buoys heeling over as if at any moment they will be dragged from their anchorages. Sightseeing stops are a near-impossibility, for the only two official yacht harbours at Lorch (K539.8) and below St Goar (K559) are not easy to enter and offer little space for visitors.

Remaining close to a line of buoys on the starboard side, we were fairly safe from other traffic – although the echo-sounder frequently showed how near we came to touching bottom. Beyond the channel, vicious rocks break surface; not infrequently, violent back eddies create unexpected havoc with the steering. This has to be the most action-packed and exhilarating section of inland waterway in Europe.

The point of no return comes off the mouth of the unnavigable River Nahe, shortly followed by the Gothic *Mäuseturm* ('Mouse Tower'), once used as a signal station at the head of the Binger Loch. Until they were blasted away, rock-strewn shallows dictated that cargoes were unloaded to be carried overland past this most treacherous reach. Legend has it that Archbishop Hatto of Mainz seized a group of starving beggars and imprisoned them in a barn which was then fired. 'Listen to my mice squeaking,' he cried joyfully. Whereupon, a swarm of rodents chased him to the Tower and ate him alive!

During *Avonbay*'s first descent in driving rain one spring, my German publishers Heidi and Wolfgang joined us. It was comforting to know that they produce the leading Rhine chart book. Ahead, one of half-a-dozen upcoming 2000-tonne cargo ships was displaying her blue board, indicating that she wished to pass on the 'wrong' side, starboard to starboard. I started to steer for the centre of the narrow channel. 'That is not necessary,' assured Wolfgang. I believed him. As the great barge bore down on us, it held its course, almost brushing the line of buoys; it was now too late for us to swing to port. The barge hooted angrily, its powerful airhorn reverberating off the steep hillsides. 'Don't worry,' said Wolfgang as the barge flashed its searchlight repeatedly. We surged past, with barely 2 m of water between the boats. 'They think they own this river!'

On through Assmannshausen, unusual in that the wine produced is red, and there were castles glowering down on us at every turn. The most extraordinary of them is Pfalz (K546), upstream of Kaub. Situated on a rocky island at the foot of terraced vineyards, its whitewashed walls and slated turrets are reminiscent of a great battleship. First recorded in the early fourteenth century, it was erected by King Ludwig the Bavarian and was admirably placed for toll collection.

The narrowest part of the Gorge is a bend known as *die Schere* ('scissors'), below the Loreley Rock. Now that the base of this towering cliff has been reshaped to accommodate a highway, it has lost some of its former grandeur. Small wonder that barge skippers wrecked on this dangerous corner began to invent legends of malicious Rhine maidens who lured passing boats to their doom. Nowadays, such disasters are less likely to happen, for a complicated array of traffic lights warns craft of approaching ships. Probably the significance of these signals is fully explained (in German) in one or all of the pilot books, but I have never understood their precise meaning – relying instead on Wolfgang's insistence that downstream boats are quite reasonably given priority. However, it is also helpful to be able to stay close

OVERLEAF *The Rhine at St Goar in 1878, by T L Rowbotham.*

to the stern of another (hopefully) knowledgeable vessel along this stretch.

June had prepared a rather splendid buffet lunch in the saloon, comprising many varieties of sausage and other locally procured specialities. We apologised to our guests that today was the one day when we could not moor up to eat. 'I think,' volunteered Heidi, 'that maybe we could get into the St Goar *Hafen*. The opening is quite wide.' This seemed a good, if chancy, idea. *Avonbay* swung round to face the current, but we could only just manage to keep her stationary relative to the bank. The rocks around the harbour mouth looked menacing as we edged closer, aiming for the upstream end. By the time we were in slack water, we were still 12 m from the downstream rocks. Success!

St Goar (K557) was a good choice for our lunchtime break and we have since stopped there on another occasion, ignoring the fact that the harbour is normally reserved for maintenance craft and other official boats. High above, Burg Rheinfels looks down on the little town; it was once the most powerful of the Rhine castles and although now largely ruined we found it to be a romantic structure, with extensive cellars, spiral stairways up to the towers, and a local history museum containing navigation relics. For those in search of quality souvenirs, it is necessary to head for a shop displaying what is described as 'the largest cuckoo clock in the world'. Within is a treasure-house of traditional musical boxes, miniature rooms furnished in amazing detail, beer *Steins* and a host of other unmistakably German tourist material.

No bridges span the Gorge: instead, car ferries provide road connections from time to time. When seeking a suitable long-stay mooring on the lower River Lahn, having left *Avonbay* in Frankfurt for the winter, we arrived in Boppard (K570) and, after a good lunch overlooking the river, decided to cross to the other side. That year, our 6-litre S3 Bentley was making her first visit to Germany. We thought it would be a novel experience to take her on the ferry, designed for eight or ten vehicles. The crewman responsible for positioning cars on board clearly was unused to such large automobiles, waved us into a parking space that blocked all access for other customers, and consequently delayed the sailing for a full ten minutes. Admirers gathered round our two-tone green car, loudly exclaiming: 'It was in just such an *Auto* that Herr Hitler used to travel!' There was little point in reminding them that the *Führer* was in fact more often seen in a convertible Mercedes.

When the yellow stone extravaganza of nineteenth-century Stolzenfels Castle ('Proud Cliff') appears to port, we know that our journey through the most spectacular part of the river is nearly over. Much rebuilt by Friedrich Wilhelm IV (later King of Prussia), Stolzenfels was visited by Victoria and Albert. Opposite, the mouth of the River Lahn offers a welcoming mooring in Oberlahnstein. But during *Avonbay*'s 1991 voyage we had no reason to halt, and instead pressed on for three more hours until we had reached Oberwinter. That day, we managed to cover 112 km from Bingen and could easily have done more but for a two-hour midday break in St Goar. It will be apparent that Rhine boating encourages us to tackle considerable distances in a short space of time.

On the second Saturday of August, the annual 'Rhine in Flames' is staged, with the river floodlit from Braubach (K581) to Koblenz, junction of the Moselle. Fireworks and bonfires add to the spectacle, which we are determined to visit one year. The dates of 11, 12 and 13 May are regarded as important ones in Koblenz, for then, legend claims, *die Eisheiligen* (the 'Ice Saints') Mamertus, Pancratius and Servatius arrive in the area. Should they bring warm sunshine, the October grape harvest will be good. Cold weather – or, worse still, a spring frost – foretells disaster at this critical time.

Speed on the river is now reduced, rarely exceeding 4–5 kph between here and the Dutch border. Traffic levels, however, tend to increase, making for moderately rough conditions much of the time.

Stolzenfels Castle and Rhine traffic from the mouth of the Lahn.

Unknown and unapproachable towns pass in rapid succession: Andernach (K612), with a sixteenth-century roofed crane, last used to load barges in 1911; Bad Niederbreisig (K624), an elegant spa; and Linz (K630), whose baroque gabled waterfront buildings are painted in a variety of pastel colours.

On one occasion, Oberwinter (K639) provided our overnight halt at a small commercial marina with floating stages. Mig, Jim and I dined at a converted barge restaurant where a young and cheerful waitress knew enough English to offer a choice of two draught beers: 'We have a nice beer and a nasty beer! Which will you try?' Naturally, we selected the 'nice' beer, although I have since wished that at least one of us had sampled the other one!

Bonn, rather unkindly dubbed Germany's 'Capital Village', is now threatened by a return of administration and government to Berlin. Catching sight of a union flag flying from the roof of the riverside British Embassy, we determined to visit the town, only to discover that no one has ever bothered to equip it with moorings. June and I had no alternative but to continue 6 km to a basin in the little suburb of Mondorf, where we telephoned for a taxi. Since 1949 Germany has been run from Bonn on a temporary basis; few people then suspected that this role would continue for more than forty years. We arrived in the attractive pedestrianised centre and, like so many other visitors, sought out the birthplace of Ludwig van Beethoven. This sixteenth-century timber building, now surrounded by shops, contains many small rooms displaying musical instruments and other relics of the great composer. Back at the boat, our basin was a peaceful contrast to the Rhine: beyond a line of poplars, the nearly constant 'chuffing' of ships' engines lulled us to sleep.

The main attraction the next day would be Cologne (Köln) at K687, to be reached by mid-morning. On hearing that we planned to stay for only a few hours, the Rhinauhafen officials waived any mooring fee. In fact, we soon realised that it was not a very agreeable place to lie for the night. Several hundred pleasure boats shared the gloomy high-walled basin with commercial shipping. Even though we were a long way from the Rhine, a heavy wash continually rocked our pontoon. Furthermore, there was an oppressive roar from road traffic. For all that, a shore excursion was obligatory to discover a little of what had in the Middle Ages been Germany's largest city when it was surpassed in Europe only by Paris and Constantinople.

Severely damaged during the Second World War, Cologne has restored much from the past. We made our way on foot to the great Gothic cathedral, slowly built from the fourteenth to the sixteenth centuries and finally completed in 1880. English newspapers were on sale in the nearby main railway station; even more useful, a Thomas Cook travel shop contained a specialist nautical book store. En route for Berlin and the east, I found here several elusive navigation charts for waterways beyond the Elbe as well as noting (with pleasure!) that some of my own publications were on display. One final pleasant task was to fill our drinking-water tanks. We could now boast that we carried nearly 400 litres of Eau de Cologne! In the late afternoon, *Avonbay* nosed back into the river. Driving rain and very poor visibility made me doubt the wisdom of making further progress that day. Notwithstanding this being July, barges were showing navigation lights by 6 pm. Some 18 km downstream, conditions had deteriorated so much that we agreed on the urgent necessity of finding somewhere for the night – almost anywhere in fact!

So it was that one of our most friendly Rhine harbours was discovered entirely by chance: the elongated basin at Hitdorf (K707), shared by three yacht clubs. Rain was falling so heavily by then that the windscreen wipers could only just maintain a safe view forward. Several figures, pulling on oilskins, appeared on a pontoon. Not only did these cheerful people help us moor, but they insisted we joined them in their little clubhouse, where a large barrel of Köln beer had just been broached. We accepted a glass of this and then had great difficulty in refusing an invitation to join them for a party. Gargantuan quantities of food were already spread out on tables. Half an hour in their convivial company had been welcome, but this feast might well continue until after midnight – which would place an intolerable strain on our conversational abilities. Far better that we should make our excuses and leave now, before it was too late!

When we cast off in the morning, all was quiet ashore; our merry-making friends had departed for home at about 2 am. Out in the channel, metre-high waves thrown up by the barges gave us quite the roughest conditions we had experienced since our Dover–Calais crossing five years earlier. Almost continuous clouds of spray flew over the wheelhouse. It was a pity that the water was so contaminated: *Avonbay*'s decks would have benefited from this violent cleansing. Heading northwards towards the Ruhr, an intensely industrialised region known to the Germans as their *Kohlenpott* ('Coal Bucket'), we had expected surroundings to become gloomily squalid. However, this was far from the case. Even in the heart of Düsseldorf, flocks of sheep grazed at the water's edge, a sight that we found doubly strange as lamb is almost unobtainable in most German butchers' shops. Once past the extensive commercial docks, we searched the chart for a suitable lunchtime stopping place, selecting the aptly named Paradieshafen, surrounded by trees at K749. Our reception at this yacht club was so agreeable that I was happy to be able to make a return visit in 1991. We had already settled in for the night when we were intrigued by a Swedish motor sailer repeatedly running aground in the entrance, before managing to slide into the harbour and moor alongside us. We realised we were lucky to have arrived without touching bottom, as her draft was identical to ours. Ingrid and Magnus were medical students, homeward bound from the Mediterranean. We pooled ingredients for a meal in our saloon, and when it was time to leave next day, we gladly accepted the suggestion that the motor sailer should re-enter the Rhine first.

In these reaches of the lower river, inland shipping is joined by even larger coastal traffic. Frequently, we registered depths up to 12 m. As the waterway widened, there was ample space for container barges to lie in pairs at anchor. Yacht harbours no longer contained just motor cruisers: the North Sea coast was sufficiently close to encourage boaters to keep their sailing craft here too. Within two hours of leaving Düsseldorf, we found ourselves at Duisburg-Ruhrort, Germany's leading inland port. This is a maze of docks on the east side of the Rhine, based around the navigable River Ruhr and the Rhein–Herne Kanal.

On pulling into the Eisenbahnhafen (K781), we were welcomed at the Ruhrorter Yacht Club, a thriving establishment with clubhouse precariously perched on concrete supports alongside a fuelling depot. 'Hello, *Avonbay*!' called out one boatowner, delighted to meet a vessel whose travels he had followed in the pages of *Motor Boat & Yachting*. Here, pleasure cruising coexists happily with the serious business of freight transport. Close to our mooring, a yard contained stacks of shiny new barge propellers, each so large that it could only be moved by crane.

Erected on parkland overlooking the Rhine, a tall barge mast was dressed with strings of bright flags, a tradition we had noted in many waterside towns. Dealers in over-priced junk were holding what was ambitiously described as an 'Openair Antiques Fair'. Typical of items on offer was a valueless modern beer bottle (empty) from Burton-upon-Trent, priced at 6DM! Unlike many tourist haunts where *Avonbay* had called, Ruhrort is a real

Duisburg-Ruhrort, Germany's leading port, depicted on a souvenir plate. The town's waterway history is admirably recalled in its Inland Shipping Museum.

working town. It is a place intersected by noisy trams, flourishing shops and cheerful beer houses.

Four days earlier, when we were in the Bad Ems marina on the Lahn, Germany had beaten England in the semi-finals of the football World Cup. Although this is not a sport we normally follow with great interest, our boating neighbours were so excited and full of praise for England's performance that it was difficult not to catch some of their enthusiasm. It was Sunday, 8 July 1990, and all the Eisenbahnhafen locals had deserted their boats to watch the final on the clubhouse television. Periodic waves of applause drifted down to our mooring as we finished dinner on board. There were shouts of wild excitement when Germany defeated Argentina. Within minutes, the town was filled with blaring car horns and spontaneous demonstrations of delight – which were soon accompanied by police sirens. Ruhrort had a famous victory to celebrate: and this was one night when decent standards of behaviour were forgotten. On reflection, it was just as well that England had not got to the final. Win or lose, we might easily have been the target of unruly conduct.

Some 77 km of German river remained before we would reach the Dutch frontier. This section was treated as a $4\frac{1}{2}$-hour non-stop run, as we noted how the windswept landscape already had an unmistakable look of the Low Countries. Emmerich, Gateway to the Netherlands, was our final German town, a place with the feel of a seaside resort. Customs launches patrolled, ready to inspect passing ships, many of which lay at anchor. We located a pleasure boat harbour in a lake beyond a great suspension bridge, paid for our night's mooring, and received a key to the otherwise impenetrable gate. Thankful that *Avonbay* carries bicycles, we skirted a chemical works and soon arrived in the town centre. All along the riverside promenade, coachloads of elderly ladies were emerging from cafés after an afternoon devoted to the consumption of mountainous cream cakes. Our carefully selected Yugoslav restaurant served excellent large steaks and had picture windows directly overlooking the Rhine. Smugly, June and I watched a procession of boats crashing through the waves, rather grateful that for the next 12 hours our travelling home would remain tranquil in her sheltered harbour. When it was time to pay the bill, we collected a handful of coins, made reasonably sure that it slightly exceeded our debt, and poured the lot on to the tablecloth. Our need for German currency had ended.

Outside, the streets were filled with a travelling fair that had features quite unlike those of fairs in Britain. Six Shetland ponies ambled dejectedly round a sawdust ring, providing rides for sad-faced little children. Brightly coloured sweets, fatty fried objects and an entire roast pig catered for sudden attacks of hunger. We watched one family consume food as if they hadn't eaten for days before climbing into a horrendous 'fun-ride' that comprised a 12-seat car at the base of a pendulum. Once in motion, it swung in ever-increasing arcs, eventually completing full circles to the evident terror of the passengers trapped inside. The showman in charge displayed a well-rehearsed technique of faking a breakdown at the very moment the gondola was inverted high in the air. 'Bitte, do not worry,' he cried over a public-address system. 'Wir haben ein kleines Problem. We'll soon have you down!' The roast-pig eaters screamed for mercy. Any mildly alarming moments during our Rhine cruise paled into insignificance against all this!

Questioning of the locals revealed that we had to clear Customs at Lobith, a small Dutch town at K863. Directed by notice boards, we steered into a basin where all convenient berths were occupied by official launches or other private craft. Keen, as always, to comply with any legal requirements, we secured Avonbay to some dangerously decayed wooden staging and walked to the nearby Customs offices. The German formalities were few, and merely required the completion of a simple form which then had to be presented to Dutch officials across the corridor. The Dutch questions were far more searching, culminating in a declaration as to the quantity of spirits we carried. Not sure if a search of our alcohol store would follow, I hesitated. I knew that our stocks had mounted up. 'Maybe you have 5 litres?' the officer helpfully suggested. 'Yes,' I agreed. 'That would be almost exactly right!' Thankfully, the interview was over.

Out in the river, a floating supermarket was crammed with bargemen's requisites: everything from tinned food to steel cables, drums of tar and navigation charts. We purchased a jumbo-sized container of Dutch Brasso, enough for our extensive polishing needs for the coming year.

Ahead, the great waterway broadened to 500 m in width, then divided into several channels leading to Amsterdam, Rotterdam and the North Sea. We turned south towards Tilburg and the border crossing into Belgium. Avonbay had completed her exploration of the German Rhine.

2 Neckar

Proposed electrical haulage on the Neckar, 1908.

After the Rhine Gorge, Heidelberg must be the best-known tourist attraction on any Germany waterway. Cruising there and on to the limit of the beautiful River Neckar was one of our earliest expeditions, with a return run being made in August 1986. Some 202 km of deep navigation, suitable for 1350-tonne barges, with 27 locks, was created between 1921 and 1968. Before this, the Neckar, although canalised in parts, was a shallow and unreliable route. It was used with difficulty by horsedrawn craft until the arrival in 1878 of the first of seven steam-powered *Kettenschiffe* (chain ships), 45 m × 6.5 m and drawing a mere 0.47 m. Operated by seven-men crews, they remained in service until 1935. They achieved an average upstream speed of 4.5 kph, and hauled on a continuous welded chain laid along the river bed for 115 km between the Rhine and Heilbronn. When the *Kettenschiffe* met in mid-river, the chain had to be released and recovered with grappling hooks after they had passed each other.

Arthur MacDonnell, writing in his *Camping Voyages on German Rivers* (1890), doesn't seem to have been an admirer of these curious tugs, judging from his description of his meeting with one at Neckarsulm:

> These vessels, which are a kind of tug of surpassing ugliness, ply between Heilbronn and Mannheim, being similar to those employed on the Moldau and Elbe between Prague and Hamburg. From both ends, which are shaped alike and are flush with the water, they gradually rise to the centre, where the funnel and machinery are situated. Along a groove running down the middle, from stem to stern, passes a thick iron chain, which otherwise rests in the bed

of the river and the ends of which are fastened at Heilbronn and Mannheim. An arrangement of cogwheels drags the monster slowly upstream by clutching and passing down the chain. There is nearly always a long string of barges behind. The rattling, grating, rasping, panting and whistling called forth by the process is probably the most diabolical combination of sounds hitherto invented by the human mind. Anyone hearing it for the first time feels an almost irresistible impulse to firmly fix a finger in each ear and make a bee-line at the top of his speed straight across country regardless of obstacles. Fortunately the human ear seems to grow accustomed to anything in time. What other theory could explain the fact that these vessels have crews? Possibly, however, only those who have been born deaf take employment on them.

No sooner had the new port of Stuttgart been opened to receive its first barge in 1958 than traffic congestion prompted duplication of all locks between there and the Rhine. Fifty years before, detailed plans were drawn up to build a canal from the upper Neckar to join a proposed Danube Lateral Canal between Ulm and Dillingen. Some 112 km long and reaching a height of nearly 500 m above sea level, the Neckar–Donau Kanal would have had the loftiest summit in Europe, requiring three substantial tunnels, eight ship lifts, fifteen locks and ten aqueducts. After the Second World War, the scheme was resurrected in modified form, and included a link to Lake Constance, head of the Rhine in Switzerland. The likely completion date was put at 2035. Even if construction does begin it will only be of interest to future generations of waterway explorers.

Leaving the Rhine at Mannheim, we had to travel a considerable distance past floodbanks and heavy industry before we arrived at the first lock in Feudenheim, consisting of three chambers side by side. We expected the river to be beautiful, but any charms it had were concealed for most of the 24 km to Heidelberg, with much of this section being artificial channel. Compensations were, however, to be found in the little towns of Ladenburg, Neckarhausen and Edingen, with glimpses of the Odenwald forest to port.

We reached romantic Heidelberg on a hot Saturday afternoon, when thousands of bodies were bronzing themselves on riverside lawns below the Philosophers' Way. The town is built of red sandstone, so the rambling castle ruins, the Alte Brücke and elegant waterfront villas appear to be reflecting a perpetual sunset. Barely wider than the Thames at Richmond, the Neckar here is alarmingly congested, with laden freighters, passenger craft, private pleasure cruisers, rowing boats and canoes all competing for space. Finding no room on a long quay in the town centre, we dropped back several hundred metres and hovered off the *Motorbootclub* Heidelberg. Soon members were rearranging their craft so that we could come alongside our own pontoon. The 48-hour stay with use of water and electricity was free, a welcome – but sadly unusual – event in Germany. Our new friends assured us that we were the first British vessel to arrive in the city that summer. Their warm welcome certainly contributed to the success of our visit.

Heidelberg Castle from the Neckar, 1878, by C Whymper.

Heidelberg is well known as home of Germany's oldest university. Elizabeth, daughter of England's James I, lived here after her marriage to Frederick V, Elector of the Rhineland Palatinate. Their youngest daughter, Sophia, was mother of George I, who brought the House of Hanover to Britain.

Avonbay subscribes to the view that while castles, museums and ancient churches are sometimes worth investigation, a more rounded impression of any new town is to be gained by relaxing on deck or engaging in shopping expeditions. We indulged in plenty of each activity, and found a very agreeable restaurant in the courtyard of the town museum. We also had enough time to write postcards and catch up on some boat maintenance. One of the few disadvantages of keeping *Avonbay* permanently abroad is that the quest for discovering new waterways leaves too few moments for smartening up the paintwork or doing running repairs.

Although the Neckar has great charm for almost all of the 160 km between Heidelberg and Stuttgart, we were to find that the first two or three days of our upstream cruise offered the finest scenery. Numerous castle-topped crags provide constant interest, together with car ferries, appealing villages of brightly painted half-timbered houses and, further on, terraces of vineyards. Moorings can be difficult to find, for bank protection is more often in the form of loose rock than vertical quays. Like much else in Germany, the construction of public landing stages is beset with punitive regulations: hence the metal certificates found on rowing club jetties, declaring them fit for nine people to congregate at once. This seemed to be a rather strange number until we realised that it must refer to the crew of a racing eight and their cox! Few German towns feel inclined to cater for the passing private cruiser; useful lessons could be learned from Chambers of Trade and Commerce in even the smallest of French towns where provision of *Haltes Nautiques* ensures a constant flow of customers to shops and restaurants. Such boat club harbours as do exist are often located in the countryside: this is fine for their members, but less convenient for visitors. Sometimes we would consult timetables and chance lying on passenger-boat piers. We now consider anchoring overnight in a river used by large barges only as a last resort. When we tried this on the Neckar, we dragged a couple of hundred metres after the first freighter of the day woke us up at 6.15 am. Signs proclaiming *Anlegen verboten* ('No mooring') proliferate.

That year, waiting for locks was very time-consuming, as keepers were reluctant to work the great chambers for a single pleasure boat, and chose to keep the lights at red until the arrival of a barge with which we could share. Fortunately, these appeared at regular intervals. What did surprise us was the very small number of cruisers in use; during the out-and-back run of over 400 km, we encountered fewer than 50. Unable to understand why so many remained on their moorings in mid-August, we were told – none too convincingly – that the boating season was nearing its end. Advance notification of our arrival at locks, using the VHF radio, was helpful, although my German was then rarely up to understanding the reply received! Key words to use are *berg* (upstream-bound) and *tal* (downstream).

Excellent navigation markers – poles and buoys – showed where the deepwater channel lay. Following normal convention, red was left to port, green to starboard. If in doubt, we merely reminded ourselves that as we were rising, lock by lock, we were 'coming in from the sea'.

Neckarsteinach (K38) is notable for no fewer than four castles. Mooring is possible on a wall near a mural on the Schiff Hotel. This brings to mind memories of the long-vanished horse-drawn traffic, showing a team of three animals hauling a sailing barge upriver. Another *Schloss* in Hirschhorn (K47) is protected by ancient fortifications built up the steep slope of a hill. Down at water level, several cruisers lay on a convenient quay, beyond which a

The Neckar Navigation.

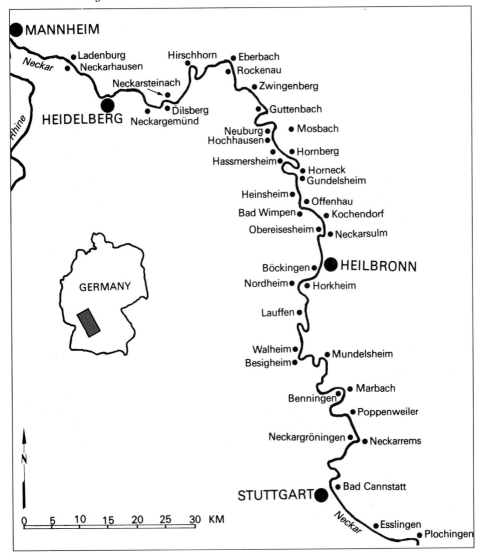

score of little houses peeped over a flood wall. Now the Neckar flows round a 300° loop, with a road tunnelling through rocky cliffs at each end of the meander. We negotiated Hirschhorn Lock with a 1111-tonne Dutch fuel barge named *Marina*. Her English-speaking skipper consulted his chart when we asked for advice as to a suitable night's mooring. 'Eberbach is the best place on the whole river,' he said. 'That's where we shall stop.' Some 10 km farther on we duly made fast, ahead of him and another barge. In the gathering dusk, floodlights illuminated an ancient tower and courtyard.

Early morning brought clouds of mist, swirling low over the peaceful river. Surrealistic barges, searchlights gleaming, parted the whiteness that rapidly closed behind them, leaving nothing but an ever-fainter rhythmic thudding of their powerful engines. This is a magic time of day, when I can sit up in bed, draw the curtains, and look out beyond *Avonbay*'s narrow sidedeck to savour yet another fresh view. (When we have arrived after dark, our surroundings often produce an element of surprise when we awake the next day.) Fresh coffee is percolating on the stove (my cabin serves also as ship's galley). Already there is enough warmth in the sun to burn off the droplets of dew on deck. Confident of a hot day, dressing is confined to the bare essentials as we anticipate the pleasures of a further day's discoveries. No static country cottage could ever compare with the adaptability of our mobile *maison secondaire*. Soon we are gently being rocked in the wash of six dawn-starting Neckar ships. It is time to be off.

When I first started inland cruising, guides to every waterway did not exist as they do today. Sometimes I feel that a sense of challenge is missing when every shop, restaurant and water point is clearly indicated on the chart. But no publication is infallible and sometimes discoveries can still be made. We found a useful supermarket alongside Rockenau Lock (K61.4) and what appeared to be a possible mooring by the ferry in Lindach (K63), neither of which were on the chart. Another ferry at Zwingenberg (K66) seemed to serve no purpose other than to link the little town with a camping site on the opposite bank. As we drew closer, we were surprised to see that

A horse-drawn barge in a waterside mural at Neckarsteinach.

the boat contained a horse and cart, suggesting that Germany's 'economic miracle' had not completely destroyed farming methods from another age.

Gradually the valley widened and became less hilly and the red rock of Heidelberg was replaced by limestone. Several small towns and two locks brought us to Burg Hornberg, a proud fortress of golden stone set high above vineyard terraces. In the early sixteenth century this became home to Götz von Berlichingen, the 'Knight of the Iron Hand', immortalised by Goethe for his part in the Peasants' Revolt. Learning that the *Schloss* had become a restaurant/hotel, its massive central tower and surrounding lesser turrets seemed ideal for an excursion. The prospect of refreshments would compensate for the 4 km uphill walk through the vines. But, yet again, there was no suitable mooring. Coming downstream a week later, though, a conveniently placed maintenance barge made the visit possible. After a crew change in Stuttgart, I was now accompanied by June and three girls, none of them enthusiastic hikers. The grumble-filled trudge under a blazing sun eventually brought us to the Hornberg summit. Knowing better than to suggest an immediate tour of the building, I ordered cold drinks and ice creams all round and, in response to a unanimous demand, telephoned for a taxi to take us back to the boat. Disastrously, the service was so slow that we had hardly finished eating and drinking when our taxi arrived. Consequently, Schloss Hornberg retained its secrets. Small wonder that I subsequently lost interest in providing educational trips for *Avonbay*'s young ladies!

Through the village of Hassmersheim (K88), long associated with inland shipping and still supporting the Vogel-Speidel barge works, we passed round three sides of the cream-painted Schloss Horneck. Beyond Gundelsheim Lock, one of the Neckar's most impressively situated towns appeared on a clifftop. This is Bad Wimpen (K100), a resort dating from Roman times and now dominated by its thirteenth-century Blue Tower. A tripping boat already occupied its jetty at the foot of a chalky outcrop. Clearly, we could not pause there. Instead, I calculated that mid-afternoon on a Tuesday was as good a time as any for risking tying to a rowing-club stage. The closest approach on foot to Wimpen was via a steep zig-zag path, first crossing a railway track and then climbing upwards through dense woodland. Dozens of ornate wooden houses set at haphazard angles, a handful of shops and a memorable view of the river made our efforts well worth while. German ice creams never fail to amaze. We ordered the smallest on offer in a café, but we each got two huge scoops of chocolate ice, sitting in a bed of whipped cream, topped with further cream and decorated with streams of chocolate sauce. When we eventually descended to the boat, we were relieved to discover that there were no irate oarsmen gathered on their landing stage.

Industry intrudes a little at the approach to Heilbronn (K113), a city of busy wharves and the NSU car works at Neckarsulm. Few historic buildings survived the Second World War; as the waterway is largely contained in an artificial channel, we decided that there were many more appealing places that deserved our attention. But, once more, we needed a stopping place for the night. So we cautiously entered an original portion of the old Neckar navigation at K110; when a yacht club promised by the chart failed to materialise, we made do with a derelict workboat. Next morning, no one could be found to lock us through the 4.5 m-wide Wilhelmschleuse, so we turned to rejoin the through route. Crumbling banks with untrimmed trees were tell-tale signs that this backwater is largely ignored by visiting boats.

Forest-covered hills were now replaced by cornfields, orchards and terraces of vineyards. In the wider, less restricted valley, many lock approaches were up sections of canal. Traffic lights control a blind run-in to the lock at Lauffen (K125), with a series of yacht clubs in the succeeding reach. The skies were busy with helicopters sweeping low over the vines, dumping clouds of poisonous spray. In Besigheim (K137) we took on water at no charge from the Walter boatyard and arrived that evening in Benningen. What at first appeared to be a scruffy drinking house served us a splendid alfresco dinner, at very reasonable cost, at a table shaded by lime trees. Delicious Neckar wine accompanied this feast.

Passage through the locks was sometimes a tedious affair, with Pleidesheim keeping us waiting for 90 minutes. It was possible that the keeper had not seen us, so I resumed communication by VHF, a vital skill that greatly improved in subsequent years. Beyond Marbach, birthplace of Schiller, a depth-sounding operation at Poppenweiler Lock caused a further delay before we were at last admitted to the chamber in the company of a barge filled with dredgings. Stopping for lunch in Neckarrems was made possible by joining six small cruisers on landing stages in the mouth of the little River Rems.

On the return voyage, a bankside restaurant at the outskirts of Stuttgart seemed an agreeable place to stop for the night. *Avonbay* aroused much admiration among the other diners, including one British client who had emigrated to Germany in 1971. He told us that he had travelled widely over European canals and rivers in his small motor cruiser. Fifteen years away from home had left him with a curious accent, making us initially think he was a native German with a better than normal grasp of English.

Time had run out for Evie and John, so we arranged for a safe place to leave the boat alongside the lock island at Cannstatt. During the day that June remained on board alone, catching up on domestic chores, she received regular visits from the crew of a police boat, who were delighted to have found a friendly British cruiser that could be relied on to dispense coffee and whisky. The rest of our party boarded a tram on the Mercedesstrasse to take a train from Stuttgart to Frankfurt airport. There, we collected Amanda and Auriole who had flown from London to join *Avonbay* for the second part of the cruise up the Main to Bamberg. My supervision of this complicated crew-changing exercise was clouded by the realisation that Stuttgart's airport would have provided a much easier connection with England. By late afternoon, though, the new arrivals had joined a crew comprising June, Diana and me. Thereafter, when lock keepers and other boaters commented

The crew of a Neckar freight barge.

(as they frequently did) on the all-female nature of my companions, I was never sure if they were expressing envy or offering their condolences!

Cannstatt's keeper asked if we intended to explore the Neckar's uppermost 19 km and four locks to the end of the line at Plochingen. He should have known better than to pose such a question to us waterway enthusiasts! In spite of assurances that these highest reaches were unusually attractive, we were to find little scenic interest. But for one factor, the journey was hardly worth making. At Untertürkheim Lock (K186.5) I climbed to the glass-sided control cabin to present the ship's papers. Entry was made slightly difficult by the profusion of magnificent potted pelargoniums and other plants arranged on shelves in spaces not filled by television monitors or switchgear. 'You intend to proceed to the final lock of Deizisau, *mein Herr?*' I was asked. I explained that British inland waterways travellers were incapable of turning back while there remained locks to navigate. To do otherwise would be as unthinkable as cruising to the Pontcysyllte Aqueduct without continuing to Llangollen and the Horseshoe Falls of Llantysilio. 'In that case, I would be most grateful, *bitte*, if you could take this gift to my friend at Deizisau Lock,' he replied, handing me a fiercely impressive column-shaped cactus, bristling with evil white needles. *Avonbay*'s unusual freight was duly delivered several hours later, to the evident surprise of its recipient.

Our return down the Neckar was accomplished in three days, renewing an acquaintance with barges that we already regarded as old friends. *Deus Tecum*, *Klara*, *Eros* and a host of others would continue to trade on this lovely river long after we had moved on to waters far away. As we prepared to leave the final lock, upstream of Mannheim, and suspecting that we might be slightly intimidated at the prospect of rushing down the Rhine to Mainz, the skipper of *Jacob Götz* wished us a good run and presented us with a miniature lifebuoy woven in red and white wool. Embroidered around the centre were the words *In Gottes Namen Güte Fahrt* ('In God's Name Good Journey'). With this talisman hanging in the wheelhouse, we felt confident of a safe passage.

3 Lahn

A 16th century German river barge.

If there is a prettier navigable river than the Lahn in the whole of Europe, I have yet to find it. Now devoted exclusively to pleasure boats, this little waterway boasts everything you could wish for: a succession of chocolate-box towns and villages; adequate overnight moorings precisely where you want to stop; and superb scenery, mostly in thickly wooded gorges with open meadows alongside the uppermost reaches. There are several ancient castles, a patch of vineyards, scores of historic half-timbered houses, and lock keepers who always seem genuinely pleased to see a boat!

Under the influence of the Dukes of Nassau, the Lahn was made navigable for shallow-draught vessels in the 1590s, using crude flash locks built into the weirs. Improvement works in 1808 created a more reliable trade route between the Rhine and Limburg; and in 1810, further upstream to Weilburg. The present locks date from 1846–59, although several were bypassed during the improvements of 1925–8 (the old cuts can still be seen, and now serve as pleasure boat moorings). For 68 km, from Lahnstein to Steeden, the 12 electrically operated locks are designed for 180-tonne barges, with chambers measuring 34 m × 5.34 m.

For many centuries the valley was an important mining area, with lead, silver, iron, slate and marble being produced in huge quantities. In the early part of this century, 200 000 tonnes of iron ore were extracted annually at Weilburg. These activities have largely ceased, as has all barge traffic. The last loads of marble from a quarry near Diez were carried down the river in 1971.

Under normal water level conditions, boats drawing up to 1.6 m can, in theory, travel for several kilometres beyond Limburg; we found that *Avonbay*'s 1.3 m was several times closer to the limit than I should have liked. Bridges generally provide an air draught of at least 3.5 m.

Perhaps uniquely in Europe, a further 81 km of navigation between Steeden and Giessen, equipped with a dozen fully operational DIY locks, are only available to cruisers of extremely shallow draught – certainly no more than 0.5 m. The greatest use of this section is made by canoes and long-distance rowing pairs and fours. Germany's sole canal tunnel can be found at Weilburg, approached from below by a two-rise lock staircase.

To arrive at Lahnstein, junction with the Rhine, is like leaving a motorway for a country lane. On *Avonbay*'s first visit, as we hurtled through the Rhine Gorge in torrential rain, no more welcoming sight could have greeted us than the floating stages of a boatyard several hundred metres up the Lahn. On the far side of the great river, the cream crenellations of *Schloss* Stolzenfels beckoned from a wooded cliff-face perch. Today, we could draw breath and appreciate our surroundings. On yet another visit, we planned to leave the boat for several months a short way up the Lahn at Bad Ems. Ploughing against the Rhine current for 6 km between the Moselle at Koblenz and Lahnstein was a somewhat nervous exercise in slow motion. At times our speed fell to a mere 4 kph. In similar conditions, several months later, the downstream return run was all over in a quarter of the time. Every pleasure cruiser will always be glad to turn into the calm and safety of the Lahn.

Initial reminders of past industry linger in the river's lowest reaches, but even here the terrain is dramatic with craggy hillsides, thickly covered with beech and other deciduous trees. On our first exploration, several days before Easter, the only greenery was provided by newly burst willow buds. A layer of fine silt on the banks and debris caught in branches, showed how the Lahn had recently risen by well over a metre. A fairly powerful flow remained even now, especially immediately below the weirs. Needless to say, we navigated with care.

Between April and October, lock keepers are on duty 9.30 am–6.30 pm, weekdays; 9 am–7 pm, Sundays and public holidays. Traffic lights – or indicators similar to old-fashioned railway signals – tell approaching craft whether chambers are ready. A further, extremely misleading, sign is an arrow, pointing in each case to an unnavigable weirstream. Painted on a background of red and white horizontal stripes, this sign is designed to warn of danger. In most countries other than Germany, the intention would be precisely the opposite: to advise all craft to head in that direction!

Not knowing quite what to expect, we approached our first lock, Lahnstein, dead slow. A smiling keeper lowered two fixed ropes with which we were to moor, returned to his control console to raise the paddles, and we started a gentle ascent. As a similar procedure followed at the other locks and it was all so effortless, I had no misgivings about returning for a mid-summer cruise in *Avonbay*, although effectively single-handed. Throughout, a 12 kph speed limit (obeyed by all our fellow travellers) ensures that Lahn cruising is a relaxed and sedate affair.

We pressed on upriver, passing locks at Ahl and in the little town of Nievern, noting that while there are seldom deepwater quaysides, small jetties appear from time to time. Often only a metre in width, these are more than adequate for holding boats off the unfriendly piles of rock which serve as bank protection. Frequently, a village council representative or boatyard employee would appear clutching a book of tickets if we wished to remain overnight. Erection of these simple mooring structures, comprising a pair of upright poles connected to the shore via a planked walkway, was obviously an excellent investment. Early in the season, we always found moorings when and where we required them. High summer, though, brings a degree of congestion, with boats moored three or four abreast. In the latter period, then, there is much to be said in favour of anchoring off and reaching the bank with the ship's dinghy.

A long canal follows Ems Lock, off which is a perfectly delightful marina, created by the Kutscher family. For us, the only drawback was that no English was spoken, but we soon established a form of rapport with the owners. *Avonbay* has now been left in their care for two long periods, to our complete satisfaction, and we certainly intend to return. The little basin holds perhaps 30 craft. Landscaped moorings, a barbecue area and, since the summer of 1990, a stylish new clubhouse, all seem contrived to keep clients on their moorings. When we have been there, few boats are deserted, whether on weekday evenings or at weekends. There was always much jolly activity, from cleaning hulls and superstructures to sunbathing in open cockpits. Whereas when *Avonbay* is in commission it is unusual for us to remain 24 hours in the same place, I suspect that many of the Bad Emsers rarely (if ever!) move. On our first day aboard after driving from England in early July 1990, it was therefore something of a surprise to see at least a dozen boats being prepared for a great expedition. Engines were noisily tested, crates of food and drink loaded, windows and paintwork polished, dogs and children gathered up. Around teatime, the exodus started. One after another, the brave voyagers waved farewell to their less ambitious neighbours and disappeared from view up the lock cut. Where were they bound for, this band of explorers? Up the Moselle, through French Alsace and back down the Rhine? Perhaps downriver to the Netherlands and the meres of Friesland? To our amazement, all returned less than three hours later: the annual cruise was over! No wonder our tales of boating to Berlin, Nuremberg, Switzerland or the Mediterranean are sometimes greeted with polite incredulity.

Bad Ems is a small but very representative example of a particularly German species: the spa town. Even in Roman times, it had been noted that springs bubbled from the ground at an unusually high temperature. Because these waters were found to be rich in bicarbonate of soda and chloride of sodium, they were considered to be curative for a vast number of complaints. Far from the coast, inland Germany had hit upon a money-making alternative to the seaside holiday. By 1823 an annual 1200 patients arrived to take the cure. This had increased to 12 000 in 1906, with the back-up of an infrastructure that comprised an eighteenth-century *Kurhaus*, fashionable hotels, an onion-domed Russian church for the Czar and his family, and a row of elaborate villas bearing such names as *Schloss* Balmoral.

Strict rules of etiquette dictated the form of each day: Karl Baedeker's *Rhine* for 1906 advises: 'the waters are drunk chiefly between 6 and 8 am ... *Kaiserbrunnen* (83° Fahr.) [28° C] is the pleasantest'. *Kesselbrunnen*, served at 46° C (115° F), might have been a little too hot for some tastes. In his *A Mirror of the Duchy of Nassau* (1842), the Rev W Phelps notes 15 distinct disorders that would benefit from a course of Bad Ems treatment. These included loss of voice, gout, rheumatism, tubercles of the lungs, spitting of blood, scrophula, chronic eruptions of the skin, congestion of the liver and (somewhat guardedly) 'female complaints'. When a patient had drunk copious amounts of the water, he would then need to be immersed in it. Suites of private apartments were reserved for this purpose; the Royal *Kurhaus* was also fitted out with special 'gargling rooms'.

When not being subjected to medical treatment, visitors would take walks through the surrounding woods, enjoy the river from the deck of a steamer, or gather on the flower-filled waterside promenade. The *Kursaal* of 1839 was long renowned for its musical entertainment and the strains of Suppé, Lehár or Smetana can still be heard drifting across the river on summer evenings.

Above all, a century or more ago, the important thing was to be *seen* in Bad Ems; it attracted everyone who was anyone, from monarchs downwards. It was here, on 13 July 1870, that Kaiser Wilhelm dispatched his famous Bad Ems telegram to the French ambassador Benedetti: thus was started the

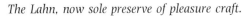

The Lahn, now sole preserve of pleasure craft.

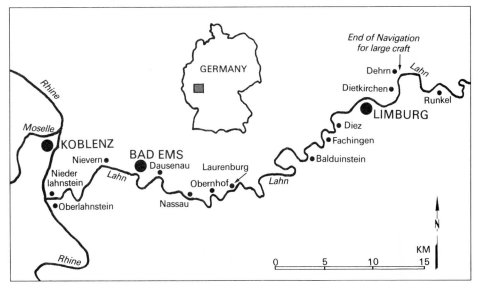

Franco-Prussian War, which ended with a sizeable part of France being in German hands for the next 45 years.

Today's patients are most likely to have been recommended to visit Bad Ems by their GPs, for as a holiday resort it is decidedly Bournemouth rather than Blackpool. The most exciting diversion is a brief trip to the rack-railway that claws up a hillside behind the main street. *Avonbay* found an agreeable mooring opposite the *Kurhaus* within a few steps of the Russian church. We dined in the leading hotel, finding little evidence of health-farm methods in the huge Germanic portions of meat and vegetables. At an adjacent table, a middle-aged woman was feeding her ancient and exceedingly frail relative. To our relief, this gloomy duo departed without recourse to stretcher or other medical attention.

The Kutscher boating empire extends far beyond its marina. In addition to collecting mooring fees in the town centre, it operates a sizeable fleet of rowing boats and launches. One of these takes the form of a giant swan named *Hugo*, cunningly propelled by a pedal-powered paddlewheel.

Always keen to try out a new experience, I persuaded our youngest crew members, Diana and Auriole, to join me in a visit to the public swimming baths, which are fed by natural spring water at 31° C (88° F). Stern female attendants prowled the changing rooms, ensuring that we first showered and then donned plastic caps before contaminating the indoor pool. This was connected by a water-filled corridor to an open-air swimming area, from which clouds of sulphurous steam rose into the chilly April sky. Notices strictly warned against 'jumping', 'diving' and 'interfering with other customers'; we had no intention of indulging in such activities. Most swimmers appeared to be of an age where a sudden fright might have induced a heart attack.

Beyond a lock lies the fortified village of Dausenau. Like virtually every inn along the river, a onetime bargemen's drinking house claims to be the original of the 'Wirtshaus an der Lahn', popularised in a German song. Doubtless, the inhabitants of Lahnstein and a handful of other towns would not agree! Little buildings peep over a high wall of grey stone, while near the town's towering gateway an old oak bears an iron plaque (itself of considerable age) proclaiming it to have stood for a thousand years. Once there were seven towers: the second remaining one leans at a Pisa-like angle and looks liable to crash one day on to the busy road beneath. On this warm day in spring there were clusters of blue and white violets on the ramparts, while in a camping site opposite tents were being erected in readiness for the Easter weekend.

Green marker buoys suggested we should make a wide sweep round the next bend and we soon arrived at Nassau, where there is an excellent deepwater mooring on the left, just upstream of a 1926 iron suspension bridge. The dukes of this seemingly unimportant town provided progeny who were to ascend to the thrones of Germany, the Netherlands and, as William of Orange, England. There's an inhabited *Schloss* and two ruined hilltop towers; a convenient railway station (the Lahn is particularly well served in this respect); and some useful shops. A local speciality, sold in white bottles bearing a blue sailing barge design, is orange Nassau liqueur. What really caught our eye was a butcher's delivery bicycle, a heavy machine, painted black with fat tyres. The wicker basket at the front was filled with a tempting selection of sausages.

The wildest reach so far encountered now took us up to Hollerich Lock, situated none too easily on a sharp bend where the weir cascaded forcefully at right angles to our path. The keeper complimented us on our (thankfully!) faultless approach, heaped praise on *Avonbay*, and suggested that she was surely a converted police launch. On learning that Bruno Zimmer was a qualified barge skipper, his kind remarks became even more welcome. He spoke good English, saying that for his next holiday he would like to hire a boat on British canals: 'A boat just like yours!' We supplied him with the addresses of several firms, but it somehow seemed tactless to tell him that few craft of *Avonbay*'s build and character are available to rent. We filled our drinking-water tanks, meanwhile admiring the surrounding landscape that is designated as some form of nature park. Yacht club moorings on the

Butcher's display in Nassau.

weirstream side of the lock island would be ideal for a short stay in this beautiful spot.

Schloss Langenau appeared to port, shortly after K112. Comprising a medieval keep and a somewhat later half-timbered mansion, we discovered this now to be the sales office of a wine producer. On the return downstream, we stopped in nearby Obernhof for one night, enjoying an excellent meal in the Lahn Café, surrounded by dramatic photographs showing the valley deep under flood water in 1984. As well as being a busy riverside resort with rowing boats and electric launches, this appears to be the only place that produces Lahn wine. We bought two half-cases from Ernst Haxel, finding it similar to a Rhine Liebfraumilch. As it was decidedly drinkable, little remained to take home to England!

Being a short river, the Lahn provided some of our most relaxed cruising ever. By the time our first return run was completed, we had stopped in virtually every town or village en route. Every single one merited exploration. Upstream of Kalkofen Lock, avoiding action had to be taken to prevent us being drawn on to piles protecting a power station intake.

After an agreeably unambitious cruise from Bad Ems, and attracted by a deepwater concrete quay, we stopped for the night in Laurenburg, a quiet little place where vegetable growing seemed to be the chief preoccupation. Here an elderly village *Frau* charged us a 5DM mooring fee, a habit that some will regard as a modern version of the Rhine's robber barons' practice of stretching chains across the navigation in order to exact 'taxes' from passing vessels. In this case, the cost was trifling and came with ten minutes of conversation as the lady told how her boating enthusiast son had lately rented a cruiser on the Shannon, a river where German hirers far outnumber those from the UK.

Dinner in the Schiff Hotel provided a further chance to inspect photographs of the Lahn floods together with a collection of early twentieth-century portraits of Prussian soldiers. Sensing that these proud individuals had most likely fought in the First World War, it seemed wise not to ask questions about precisely who they were.

The navigator is faced with a potentially hazardous situation at K98.5. On an acute blind turn (hooting advised) a hydroelectric plant creates a violent discharge across the fairway. While admiring the skill and cunning of the engineers who erected this obstacle in 1930 – making excellent use of a substantial fall in levels between here and the intake, two locks and 7 km upstream – we did consider that some sort of deflector was urgently needed to prevent the torrent from crossing our path at right angles. Further reminders of the river's capricious nature were provided at the lonely Schiedt Lock. Here the keeper's cottage stands well above the reach of winter flooding, while steel barriers protect the lock-operating gear from sheets of ice that might come crashing down on a swift current. We entered the Cramberg Loop, and by the time *Avonbay* had arrived at the next lock she was barely 500 m from the power station that had so brusquely swept us to one side an

Our mooring below the great castle of Diez.

hour earlier. Had this been a modern waterway, a canal tunnel would have been dug through the cliffs to connect each end of the meander.

A long-disused lock cut opposite Balduinstein now sheltered an assortment of small cruisers. We found an agreeable place to lie on the quayside, opposite, walked through a low arch beneath the tracks of the Bad Ems–Limburg railway, and made a brief investigation of the castle ruins. High above, another *Schloss*, this time a nineteenth-century rebuild, dominates the hilltop skyline. Back at the riverside, an elderly villager stopped to admire *Avonbay*. He had been a prisoner of war in Buckinghamshire in 1946–7, where he was employed as a gardener. Like many English-speaking Germans of his generation, he retained fond memories of his enforced stay in Britain.

Industry briefly intrudes at Fachingen, noted for its bottled mineral water; half a million jars were exported by barge in 1842. At K85 comes an extensive water-filled quarry. Our keel had made unexpected and violent contact with rocks on the river bed, so we were proceeding dead slow until our confidence had returned. Thus there was ample opportunity to stand on the wheelhouse roof, gazing over this historic site where the famous Lahn marble had once been mined and loaded (via now-derelict chutes) into *Lahnschiffe*. It has since become a private water park, devoted to water skiing, swimming and camping, conveniently situated on the outskirts of Diez. This sizeable town, which quickly became a particular favourite of ours, is dominated by a massive spiky fortress of the kind that inspired fairy stories of the Brothers Grimm. Built by the Counts of Diez, it had by the middle of the nineteenth century become, in the words of the Rev W Phelps, 'a penitentiary for condemned criminals of the worst description, who are kept to hard labour. Here they are constantly employed in the manufacture of articles of clothing for their own use; but the great business is the working of marble from the adjoining quarries. ... Here monumental tombs, tablets and head-stones, columns, chimney pieces, slabs, tables and small ornamental work are manufactured.' Today, convicts have been replaced by youth hostellers.

Downstream of an ancient stone bridge with tollhouse and cutwaters shaped like old boots, we found a floating landing stage, where, free of any payment, we could join two small cruisers and lose ourselves in a maze of narrow streets, packed with half-timbered houses. We approved of Diez, stayed there for one night, and gave June another rest from galley duties by eating ashore at the waterfront Imperial Hotel.

Further reminders of the Royal House of Orange come with a view of a vast and handsome baroque palace, glimpsed through the trees. This is the late seventeenth-century Oranienstein, a *Schloss* with richly decorated stucco ceilings and now occupied by the German armed forces.

Although rocky outcrops are still to be seen, especially where riverside houses in Staffel have gardens dotted with huge boulders, the valley of the Lahn now broadens into lush meadows. Limburg and the final lock of the 'large gauge' waterway lie ahead, with the seven terracotta and white-painted towers of a great cathedral visible from far off. A complicated structure in Romanesque Gothic, it dates from the mid-thirteenth century; external decoration to recreate the medieval appearance was applied as recently as 1968–72.

There's much to see in Limburg, so we lost no time in staking our claim to a quayside beyond the junction of the lock cut and weirstream, within a short distance of an old road bridge, a pair of waterwheels and the slightly forbidding fortified walls of a thirteenth-century *Schloss*. Visually, this is one of the outstanding urban riverscapes of Germany. Even as early in the year as Good Friday, we found an animated scene with the comings and goings of a passenger launch, racing craft from the nearby rowing club, the activities at a well-filled camping site, and the soporific rushing of water cascading over a pebble-strewn weir.

Avonbay *at anchor in Dietkirchen.*

unexpectedly open into café table-filled squares where fountains trickle and tourists (us included) consume prodigious quantities of beer. A lofty autobahn viaduct soars above the river with surprising elegance. Here we watched the sun sink behind the cathedral's dark silhouette, and then saw it ascend through a river mist the next morning.

Less than half the canalised Lahn had been explored; we now turned our attention to a final 4 km of navigation, only admitting defeat when we started to ground beyond the former cathedral of St Lubentius, on its clifftop site in the village of Dietkirchen. As the yacht club moorings were very congested, *Avonbay* was coaxed through a last kilometre of fast-flowing shallows to Dehrn, to take advantage of a drinking-water supply at the *Bootsclub* Limburg. Our discovery of the lovely Lahn was over; this was definitely the end of the line for large craft.

On our next visit I am determined to take a car to Giessen to spend a couple of long summer days working through the elusive 12 upper locks by dinghy. Now, however, it was time to turn in the narrowing stream, point our bows downriver, and return towards the mighty Rhine.

4 Moselle

Beilstein, from an engraving of 1858.

When we made our first ascent in August 1987 of the Moselle from the Rhine at Koblenz to the far-off reaches that flow through France, it was in the knowledge that such a journey had only become possible as recently as 1964, when canalisation was completed. 'Moselle' in English and French, 'Mosel' to the Germans, 'Musel' in Luxembourg – this is a river inseparable from wine production. Hardly a kilometre of the 242 km where it passes through Germany is not devoted almost exclusively to vineyards.

Navigated from Roman times, horsedrawn barges struggled through shallows where the depth was frequently no more than 0.45 m. From 1841, steam-powered passenger boats maintained a service between the Rhine and Trier, frequently suffering serious damage when they were driven on to rocks. *Patterson's Guide to the Rhine and its Provinces* (1901) mentions that the upstream run could be completed in two days at a cost per passenger of 7.5 marks or 5 marks, according to class; it was possible to make the downstream journey in just 11 hours (10 marks or 6.6 marks). By 1905, 6 million tonne/km of freight was carried annually, compared with 4045 tonne/km on the Rhine.

Parts of the upper, French, reaches were canalised between Metz and Nancy during the 1860s, while a further length, Metz to Thionville, was equipped with locks by 1932. Initial work to improve the German Moselle at Koblenz came to a halt in 1939. An international consortium, comprising Germany, France and Luxembourg, reached agreement for full canalisation after the Second World War. Work began in 1956, and in the remarkably short space of eight years ten locks had been constructed in Germany with two in Luxembourg. The large-capacity waterway is now extended through France to Neuves-Maisons, south of Nancy, and there are plans to take the line still farther to link up with the River Saône.

The German Moselle Navigation was engineered with environmental foresight well in advance of its times. Rather than spoil the exceptional beauty of the steep-sided valley or threaten any of the world-famous vineyards, virtually no canal cuts were created, even though there are several places where 10 km loops might have been bypassed by excavating a channel of only a few hundred metres. All lock and weir structures are designed to intrude as little as possible on the landscape; thus open weirs are all but invisible, especially to vessels running with the stream. A close watch on the chart is essential.

Avonbay had been slumbering for some weeks on the Lahn at Bad Ems. There were awesome complications on the drive from England when my Volvo developed automatic gearbox problems. June, Diana and I arrived with frayed nerves and the prospect of having to find a repair agent whose bill eventually amounted to nearly 50 per cent of the car's (heavily discounted) original purchase price. German breakdowns are best avoided! I was more than ready for some trouble-free and relaxed boating. We whistled down the lowest part of the Rhine Gorge, turned to port at *Deutsches Eck* ('German Corner') by the plinth of a now-vanished equestrian statue of Kaiser Wilhelm I, and sought a quayside mooring in the city of Koblenz. Opposite, on the far shore of the Rhine, the great fortress of Ehrenbreitstein glowered from its hilltop: this is a castle so extensive that in the mid-nineteenth century it could contain 14 000 troops with all supplies necessary for a four-year siege.

Koblenz moorings are potentially difficult, as no one has laid on facilities specifically for passing cruisers. On this occasion, several *péniches* and three large passenger ships were tied on the town wall. It was unclear if we had any right to join them. However, the only objection came from a sullen fisherman who considered he had a greater claim to his seat which we had stupidly mistaken for a cast-iron bollard. Returning here several years later, we were not actually requested to move on by a hotel ship, but its great bulk was manœuvred so close as it entered a vacant space astern that a split-second decision was made to get out of the way without delay. In the dark, an alternative berth was selected on the inhospitable facing shore, far from city facilities and restaurants. Even here was deemed unsuitable by the crew of a police launch that came alongside at midnight, in spite of our having hung up a riding light. We moved yet again. All these problems can be avoided by buying space at one of several yacht clubs (K4), beyond the first lock. Needless to say, these are far from the city centre.

After a bouncy night in *Castrum ad Confluentia*, we admired the Electoral Fortress alongside our promenade before exploring the city and returning much later laden with supermarket plunder. Koblenz Lock (K2), although equipped with two chambers, kept us waiting a full hour. Pleasure craft are regarded as an inferior species, and placed below freight and passenger vessels in locking priorities. At this stage we had not even considered using the 3.4 m-wide *Sportbootsschleuse*; when prompted by an even longer delay to work through a similar one at Trier, *Avonbay* came dangerously close to becoming wedged as the water gushed in. For us, there is no alternative to the big Moselle locks. Unusually for Germany, a charge is levied on pleasure craft working through on their own. In 1990 this amounted to 9DM for our 11 m boat, requested at the majority of locks; as it was then Easter, there were fewer passenger craft in operation and waiting for barges could have been very time-consuming. In the summer, there is normally sufficient traffic to avoid making payments.

Once clear of the city, the Moselle soon shows itself to be an exceptionally lovely river. Numerous little towns, mainly devoted to wine production, line the banks, surrounded by endless vineyards and wooded hilltops. Many have ancient castles. Winningen (K11) is typical, and although all mooring jetties are reserved for passenger craft, there is a useful harbour in an arm (K12). Unexpectedly, the current running against us was quite strong, so *Avonbay*'s speed at normal engine power barely exceeded 7 kph. Heavy rain during the next 48 hours brought mild flooding and a further slowing of our progress. Such conditions are unusual here, for the river is generally considered to be easy navigation as well as being more than adequately buoyed.

Most Moselle castles occupy commanding positions, perched high above the water. Gondorf (K19) is an exception, for the *Schloss* – built between the fifteenth and seventeenth centuries – stands directly on the riverbank. Comprising a collection of structures connected by a red-painted wooden gallery, it is intersected by a main road. Although we were slower than most other traffic, we would frequently arrive at locks just as barges and cruisers were entering – all rather hare and tortoise stuff! So it was at Lehmen (K21), a single chamber with a very fierce weir alongside. Oberfell (K23), a bright town of restaurants and numerous flags, and Alken (K24.5), with clients' landing stage outside the Anker Hotel, both looked tempting. Knowing we lacked the necessary time to explore everywhere, we decided to keep shore excursions to one or two each day, so investigating a smaller number of locations in depth.

Provided you seek permission to use one of several jetties at Moselkern (K34), a short taxi ride will take you much of the 6 km to the amazing Burg Eltz, possibly the finest of all Germany's castles and currently one of the country's top ten tourist attractions. Grouped around a courtyard, Eltz rises cliff-like from the surrounding forest and consists of various sections added between the twelfth and sixteenth centuries. Not unlike Ludwig II's Neuschwanstein, this is, however, genuine medieval architecture. I had never before seen its equal. The slated roofs, spiky turrets, outbreaks of half-

OVERLEAF *Cochem's impressive waterfront.*

timbering and precipitous walls must surely have been the inspiration for some of the Brothers Grimm's fairy tales. I can easily imagine Rapunzel letting down her golden hair from an upper window, all 20 ells of it. (That converts to nearly 23 m – I have just checked the length against the original text!) Rapunzel would not have been a welcome guest aboard *Avonbay*, where the daily washing of young ladies' hair is already an extravagant drain on domestic water supplies! With Rapunzel in the bow cabin, it is unlikely we should ever be able to disconnect the hose.

After a further lock at Müden (K37), we seized our opportunity to stop at the Mosel Boating Center Yachthafen in a wash-free inlet beyond the little town of Tries (K40). I am sure that if I had not sought out the harbourmaster, our stay would have been free. As it was, we were relieved of 22DM for one night – as much as we had been charged in London and Paris. The nearby village was pretty enough, but could hardly offer the same level of attractions as London or Paris!

Our next objective was Cochem (K53), the town most widely featured on Moselle travel posters. Delighted to find a central quay on the opposite, Cond, side where 20 cruisers were already tied up, directly facing the massive nineteenth-century castle restoration, we decided to stay for three nights for a total charge of 28.80DM. This would give us ample time ashore and, with luck, the dismal weather might improve. There are few things I dislike as much as travelling up a beautiful waterway for the first time and admiring the scenery through a curtain of rain.

We ate out at the adjacent Hafen Hotel and made trips by pedestrian ferry into the narrow streets of the old town, squeezed between vine-covered hillsides and the river frontage. As befits one of Germany's leading tourist destinations, the locals were exceedingly friendly, with many shops remaining open throughout the weekend. Several legends circulate, however, pointing to the extreme dim-wittedness of the Cochemites. One concerns the case of a velvet-coated creature apprehended burrowing under the town's defensive walls. Perhaps the mole was working for enemy agents who could then place explosive charges in his tunnels. Accordingly, the fearful burghers put the animal on trial, found it guilty, and imposed a sentence whereby it was to be buried alive! All very quaint and mildly insulting to the people of the district, we thought. It has to be admitted that I spent much of our stay in an abortive search for examples of crass stupidity!

Soon after dusk, there was a loud explosion as a volley of rockets was fired across the river. For the next 15 minutes we were treated to a grandstand view of the castle being 'consumed' by flames, as the structure was illuminated by a succession of flickering orange and red floodlights. An even more alarming display for the tourists was the mooring technique of the large tripping boats. As if 'dancing' to amplified music, they made a series of rapid 360° turns in the narrow channel, sometimes coming within 2 m of us.

OPPOSITE *Burg Eltz, perhaps Germany's finest castle (1843).*

During the late 1870s a railway was constructed up the Moselle valley. According to one contemporary account, its chief object was the rapid transport of up to half a million troops to the then German frontier city of Metz, in the event of another Franco-Prussian War. The line survives, fortunately hidden underground at Cochem, where it passes through the 4235 m Kaiser Wilhelm Tunnel. Diana and I boarded a train in order to collect our guest Auriole from Luxembourg Airport. This otherwise efficient operation was nearly spoiled as we came close to missing the last return service of the day.

Setting out once more on the boat, speed fell to just 6 kph, giving us ample time to appreciate the magnificence of the Moselle, which remained outstandingly attractive all the way to Trier. Beyond Fankel Lock (K59.5), what was eventually judged to be the river's most picturesque town appeared to port: Beilstein (K61). Occupying a waterside cleft in the hills, several dozen small wooden houses jostled for space beneath the Burg Metternich. The charm of the place instantly made us want to stop. Yet again, this seemed an impossibility. One of the few Moselle towns never seriously damaged by fire, Beilstein remained engraved on our memory. When driving through the district several years later, it was the obvious lunchtime halt. Perhaps our expectations had been too great, for we had seen all we needed to within five minutes. In reality, the village is best viewed from the deck of a boat.

One of the earliest English accounts of a journey down the Moselle is contained in Michael Quin's two-volume *Steam Voyages on the Seine, the Moselle & the Rhine with Railroad Visits to the Principal Cities of Belgium &c, &c*, published posthumously in 1843. Travelling aboard one of the two recently introduced 180 hp paddle-wheelers, Quin greatly enjoyed his journey, even though 'our progress was so rapid, that it seemed as if we were about to strike against an impenetrable mass of huge rock'. Accompanied by a young male companion, he experienced a narrow escape from the clutches of a German woman whose 'bust and her features bore every trace of the epoch at the wrong side of forty ... I had no hesitation in setting her down in my notes, as either a public player, or a singer, or, perhaps, both'. Travelling alone (in itself regarded as highly suspicious), she repeatedly engaged the writer in conversation, and all without anything approaching a formal introduction! Her final display of wickedness, when the party had retired to a Koblenz hotel for the night, was to place the numbered key of her room on the communal dining table, where our hero could not fail to notice it. 'This adventurer, who had set out upon an expedition to find some dupe, more especially, if she could, some English dupe, upon whom she could fix herself for a while, and from whose pockets she might extract as much money as she could.' Quin, of course, was more than able to take care of himself – indeed, one suspects that he quite enjoyed the threatening situation, which anyway constituted good 'copy'. The tale is included as a warning to other less worldly-wise and naïve Englishmen who might subsequently cruise down the Moselle. Warming to his theme, he next recalls a recent disagreeable

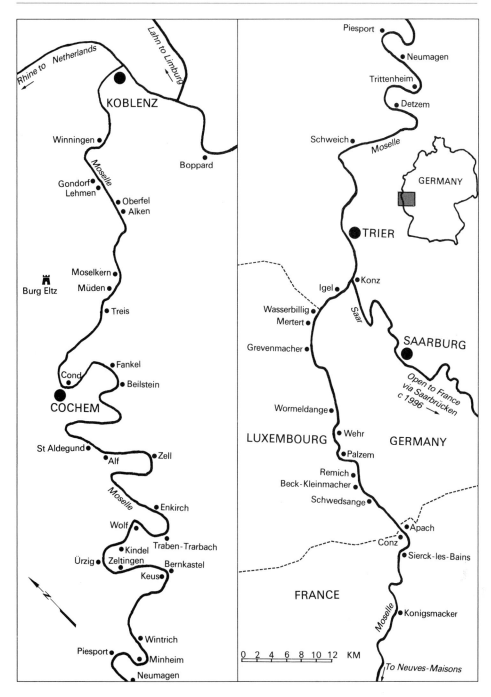

The course of the Moselle, from the Rhine and past Luxembourg to France.

encounter aboard the diligence on the road between Namur and Dinant:

> A man, not ill-dressed ... told us that he was an officer in the police, and produced a very handsome tortoise-shell snuff-box from which he requested us to take snuff. This we declined. He then called our attention to a painting upon the external side of the lid of the box. The painting represented a group of figures at cards, and was certainly very beautifully executed. As he conceived that he had thus made some way with us, he said that there was on the inside of the lid another painting much better executed even than the one we had seen, and instantly turned it up and placed before us a scene of the most disgusting description. Desiring him to shut his box instantly, I told him plainly that he was an agent of Satan, and that if he did not quit the *coupé*, at the next stage, I should denounce him to the conducteur. I must admit that he appeared utterly dismayed at the suddenness of my attack:– 'You are quite right, Sir,' he said; 'I am indeed what you have described me.'

These events took place more than 150 years ago, so one can only make guesses as to the precise nature of the picture that so shocked Quin.

For a long while, the only cultivated crops on each side of the waterway had been vines, which had been planted, pruned and hoed with a Prussian thoroughness that made French vineyards appear positively untidy. Tractors trundled between the serried ranks, dispensing poison spray. Where the terrain was too steep or rocky, this task was undertaken by workers wearing tanks on their backs. Some of the larger, more prosperous concerns employed low-flying helicopters: several times we were fearful that they might score a direct hit on the smart little British ship plodding slowly upstream. Each parcel of land bore the name of its owner in large white-painted lettering, while elsewhere were elaborate, rectangular, stone sundials set in the cliff-faces.

Negotiating an acute bend at K75, we passed the roofless ruins of Stuben Abbey and soon joined a 1500-tonne barge and nine other cruisers in the St Aldegund Lock. A considerable wait here prompted me to chat to a German pleasure boatman. He assumed from our undefaced blue ensign that we were Australian. I explained that Britain was a country where you are forbidden to fly the national flag on your boat. Instead, we have a choice of red, blue and, in very special circumstances, white ensigns. 'How much easier it is for you Germans,' I commented. 'Not in my case,' he replied. 'My boat was built in England, but I keep her in the Netherlands and so use a Dutch ensign with a German courtesy flag!'

The town of Alf (K82) marks the start of a huge 12 km loop, whose neck is barely 500 m wide. Had this been a French navigation such as the Rhône, a short bypass canal or tunnel would almost certainly have been excavated here. Alf's great attribute is a section of convenient, central, deepwater quay where we paused (without charge) for a walk ashore and coffee. Zell (K87) made an excellent overnight stop, after we had consulted the tripping boat operators as to where we could lie on a wall with bollards, close to the pedestrian bridge. Soon after, two cruisers had followed our example, proving that if you are seeking solitude, inland waterways are not necessarily the best place to find it. Here, Schwarze Katz ('Black Cat') wine is enthusiastically promoted. Feline souvenirs fill shop windows and one fierce stone specimen is at the centre of a 1936 decorative fountain.

Knowing that the present navigation works were only a quarter of a century old, it came as a surprise to read in Octavius Rooke's *The Life of the Moselle* of 1858 that a considerable freight business flourished on the unlocked river in the middle of the nineteenth century:

> Boat building is carried on at nearly every village, and the smoke from the accompanying fire wreathes among the walnut trees. ... The ribs of the great flat-bottomed boats look like the skeletons of some curious animal. ... These boats, when finished, are used for all sorts of purposes. The want of good roads, and the fact of the stream being less rapid than that of the Rhine, as

Moorings three-abreast, upstream of Trier Lock.

well as the absence of steam-tugs, makes the Moselle more lively with barges and small boats, especially the latter; though, of course, there being only three or four steamers on the whole distance between Trèves [Trier] and Coblenz, the absence of those puffing drawbacks to tranquil enjoyment renders the Moselle more quiet on the whole.

The larger barges carry iron, earthenware, charcoal, bark, wine, and general cargoes; while the smaller ones are filled with market produce of all sorts going to be sold in the larger towns, and numbers of these small boats are kept in each village for the residents to cross to their farms or vineyards on the opposite bank. There are also ferry-boats, large enough for carts and oxen, or horses, at nearly every cluster of houses.

Strong flows in the reach leading to Enkirch Lock (K103) had placed *Avonbay* trailing well behind a convoy of barges and high-speed pleasure boats. Fortunately, the keeper held the gates for several minutes, allowing us a chance to catch up. A little downstream of the twin towns of Traben and Trarbach (K107) we took on diesel and water from a charming Dutch girl, who ran the family-owned bunkering station. As we might have expected, she spoke excellent English – as did the majority of shopkeepers, restaurateurs and lock staff we encountered. Equally, our German was now showing mild signs of improvement with the acquisition of new vocabulary. Proper grammar would wait until the course of lessons that preceded our voyage to Berlin, but the mixture of nouns and gestures was working surprisingly well.

Trarbach was one of several towns (including Zell, Zeltingen and Bernkastel) seriously damaged by fire in the autumn of 1856. Rooke was staying on the opposite bank and provides a graphic account of the disaster:

As may easily be imagined, from the fact of the very old houses, all built of wood, being crushed into narrow streets and enclosed within walls, the flames spread rapidly; so fast, indeed, they came on, that the poor people flying were forced to throw down the goods they were trying to save and run for their lives. The church, being on an eminence a little out of the town, was thought quite secure, and in it were stored the effects from the neighbouring houses until it was filled from roof-tree to floor. The night now set in dark as pitch; still the fire crept on, reaching its red forked tongue over the narrow streets, in spite of the water which was freely supplied from the river; at last the church caught, and the flames, bursting from windows and roof, consumed all the goods that were stored, and destroyed the old building itself.

The sight was superb; the whole space, enclosed by the hills in which the town lay, surged in great waves of fire: in this molten sea great monsters appeared to be moving, whose shapes seemed writhing with pain as those of the devils in hell.

A crazed arsonist was blamed for this destruction and the other fires in the neighbourhood. Trarbach was duly rebuilt, but 20 years later merited the

OPPOSITE *Die Pfalz Castle, in the Rhine Gorge at Kaub.*

OPPOSITE *On the Neckar in Heidelberg.* ABOVE *Hungarian musicians perform in a Cologne street.* BELOW *An old-time paddle steamer on the Rhine at Andernach.*

ABOVE *Heading upstream through the Rhine Gorge at the Loreley Rock.*
LEFT *The Russian church by the Lahn at Bad Ems.* BELOW *Courtyard at Stolzenfels Castle, junction of the Rhine and Lahn.* OPPOSITE *Moselle vineyards by a dramatic reach of the river at Minheim.*

ABOVE *Ochsenfurt's celebrated* Rathaus *clock.* BELOW *Baroque finery on the Bonn* Rathaus.

ABOVE *Decorative house number in Neumagen, River Moselle.* BELOW *Bavarian inn sign, near the River Main.*

oechsner bier

ABOVE *A Berching balcony decorated for the opening of the Rhine–Main–Danube Canal.* BELOW *East German holiday home on the banks of the Dahme, near Berlin.*

ABOVE *Rare (and elegant) street advertising in Genthin, Elbe–Havel Canal.* BELOW *Heraldic device at Spandau Citadel.*

description of 'a dull new town'. Time has mellowed the nineteenth-century Scottish baronial architecture of Traben-Trarbach, now a pair of resort towns thick with hotels and where the roadbridge is approached via an elaborate stone gateway.

Wolf, Kindel and Ürzig – where a private stage is reserved for the use of boating clients of the Moselschild Hotel – brought us to the river's most famous wine town, Bernkastel (K129). Although a kilometre upstream of the centre, a large harbour provides splendid moorings. So *Avonbay* rested here for 24 hours, allowing us ample opportunity to visit the streets of crooked half-timbered houses and indulge in a frenzy of souvenir hunting. June has good reason to remember her tour, partly because it was here that we discovered a massive painted sculpture made of cast concrete and depicting a team of horses pulling a cart laden with wine barrels. Not without difficulty, this was conveyed home, where it now occupies a suitably spotlit space on the kitchen wall. Struggling under the weight of this trophy, we started to return to the boat, carefully picking our way through debris that littered the cobbled street; a major sewer replacement exercise was in operation. When a workman lost control of the bucket he was lowering into a water-filled excavation, poor June was drenched from head to foot with a shower of filthy mud. As we negotiated for the taxi to take us back to *Avonbay*, the rest of us stood around her protectively, afraid that our contaminated companion might be considered an unfit passenger.

Just as we had replenished the boat's cellar in Champagne, Alsace, Burgundy, on the Lahn and in Languedoc, now seemed an appropriate time to acquire several cases of Mosel-Saar-Ruwer. A few steps from our mooring, several producers were advertising their wares. We approached the firm of Hoffman-Mahsem and, after a brief sampling session, stacked our shopping trolley with a very drinkable 1983 Kardinalsberg. The finely engraved label depicted a collection of jolly bearded characters enjoying the pleasures of alcohol. In the days before excessive wine consumption was considered in any way harmful, the 'Bernkasteler Doktor', as one product is still known, became famous for its health-giving qualities.

Minheim (K144) deserves a mention for its landing stage, bearing the legend 'Welcome to moor'. Sadly, we had no reason to use this rare facility. Beyond the bridge is the Loreley Rock, a rather more impressive and intact example than its better-known namesake in the Rhine Gorge. Soon afterwards, one of the very few British boats we have met on the Moselle bore down on us at high speed. She was a large and gleaming white motor cruiser named *Francis Holly*. We exchanged enthusiastic waves and hoots.

The next sizeable town after Piesport is Neumagen (K153), where we hovered in the evening light wondering if we dared make fast to a private landing stage. To our great surprise, the proprietor of the adjacent café

OPPOSITE *Aschaffenburg's Johannisburg Palace and the River Main.*

beckoned, unlocked the gate, and announced that we could stay until a passenger boat arrived at 11 am the next morning. In gratitude, we patronised his bar before investigating the village. During the nineteenth century, an amazing hoard of Roman stone carvings was unearthed from the third-century fortifications. This included 13 intact tombstones, various altars, and the famous Neumagen wine ship. Designed as a monument to a barge builder and wine-transporter, this galley-like vessel is loaded with barrels and a row of near life-size oarsmen. Sadly for the village, the original is in the Trier Landesmuseum, although an authentic replica stands near the church.

Early next morning I was woken by an insistent tapping outside my cabin window. Half expecting to see an irate German trying to expel us from the mooring, I was instead greeted by a hungry swan. When he had established that *Avonbay* was occupied and prepared to serve breakfast, he signalled to 'Frau Schwan' and her cygnets who glided up for a generous helping of *Landbrot*.

Preparations for a wine festival were under way at Trittenheim (K156), one of dozens along the river that take place from August until well into the autumn. Shortly before Detzem Lock, the hotel ship *Europa* subjected *Avonbay* to the worst inland buffeting she has ever experienced: for several minutes the river was considerably rougher than anything we were to encounter on the hectic lower Rhine. Water poured off our foredeck and we pondered on the different standards of navigational behaviour in Germany and England. I lost the contents of my wine glass. Another tiny cruiser was all but capsized by the furious wash. We screamed angrily at the maniac in charge, fully aware that this would not have the slightest effect. Only with the greatest difficulty could it be believed that the skipper held inland waterways quali-fications, resulting from a number of years of full-time study! Detzem village (K166) takes its name from the site of the tenth Roman distance marker on the highway out of Trier, just as Quint, 16 km upstream, was the fifth.

We were eagerly anticipating a prolonged tour of Trier, Germany's oldest city, which had celebrated the 2000th anniversary of its foundation in 1984. Gradually, surroundings began to become urbanised, with a large commercial harbour at K184. One of our charts marked a possible mooring in a backwater at the head of an island within a short walk of all the leading attractions. Several jetties were clearly reserved for tripping vessels. We considered anchoring, but gave up the attempt after five minutes of stirring thick mud just outside the navigation channel. It is quite disgraceful that such an important city, with more Roman relics than anywhere else in northern Europe, should utterly ignore the requirements of passing cruisers. If the city authorities are determined to do nothing, then surely private enterprise could be encouraged to undertake the necessary dredging and install some pontoons. Such an investment would certainly be profitable, and attract dozens of passing pleasure cruisers throughout the summer. The situation remained unchanged when we returned in 1990. Deeply disappointed, we passed through the arches of the Alte Römerbrücke, whose red sandstone foundations really are of Roman origin. In medieval times, three defensive towers protected this important road crossing, while the city itself was ringed by fortified walls. Once there must have been a commercial quay, for a pair of magnificent roofed cranes stand on the river bank. Each is fitted with twin jibs and a conical roof and the whole of the upper part of the structure was designed to revolve, so facilitating the transfer of cargoes between barges and carts. The older example was built in 1413, while its neighbour is an eighteenth-century replica.

On the port side, 500 m beyond Trier Lock, a converted naval vessel named *Uranus* appeared to offer overnight moorings. We breasted up to two other cruisers and found ourselves part of a strange, slightly seedy, drinking establishment. The owner, however, was quite affable, charging a reasonable 10DM and assuring us that, 'Here you will be safe, provided the wind does not increase.' With an open weir not far downstream, I made a point of

Replica Roman wine ship in Neumagen.

checking the warps of the other craft to which we were attached.

Trier was well beyond walking distance, so we ordered a taxi in the morning and devoted a full day to the city sights. These included the second-century Porta Nigra, a massive gateway hidden within the church of St Simeon from the eleventh to the nineteenth century; the impressive Roman Palace (*Basilika*), built of thin red bricks; an amphitheatre, said to be the tenth most important in the Roman Empire, holding 30 000 spectators; and the formal gardens of the eighteenth-century Elector's Palace. Our taste of culture ended with a visit to the original Roman wine ship, discovered at Neumagen, and now attractively displayed in the Landesmuseum. We bought a scaled-down replica in stone that now resides, with brass plaque, on an alcove shelf in the Humphries' downstairs loo. Then followed a good lunch, with some serious shopping around the *Hauptmarkt*. In spite of the earlier difficulties, Trier more than repaid the effort we put into its discovery. A taxi deposited us, and our food supplies, back at the boat.

Normally, it is possible to distinguish between inland waterways that never advanced beyond the planning stage, those that were built but fell derelict, and others that are still open. Here, fragments of evidence exist to suggest that portions of a canal were excavated to link Trier with Cologne. Octavius Rooke describes the legend as follows:

> For more than a hundred years the people of Cologne had been endeavouring to raise a cathedral that should eclipse all others. The master-builder was busy making measurements for the arch of the great door, when one of his apprentices jeeringly said the building would never be finished, but would ever remain in fragments. Thereupon the master waxed wroth and dismissed the apprentice, who departed, saying: 'Woe to thee, O my master! Never shall thy work be finished; sooner shall I complete a canal from here to Trier, than shalt thou place a tower upon thy cathedral.'
>
> Years passed on, and the cathedral was rapidly approaching to completion, when the master saw a huge worm creep from the ground. This was the fiend, by whose assistance the apprentice had made a canal from Trier to Cologne: the apprentice appeared to the astonished master and said, 'Lo, my canal is complete, while thy church is yet a fragment!' and water flowed from the canal, on which a duck came swimming from Trier.
>
> The water rose and encompassed the master, who thus perished, and his cathedral is still unfinished; but the wicked apprentice fared still worse, for the great worm strangled him, and he is doomed evermore to haunt the cathedral, measuring the uncompleted works. The canal thus formed was used to send wine from Trier to Cologne, without the trouble of putting it into casks.

Enough truth exists in this tale to support the theory that some form of wine pipeline was once at least proposed.

Several hours of peaceful cruising remained as we left Trier in the evening, starting with a broad reach, ideal for dinghy sailing and extending almost to the junction with the River Saar at Konz. Present estimates predict that the large-capacity Saar Navigation will be completed to Saarbrücken and thence to the French Canal des Houillières de la Sarre by 1996. When we visited, the main portion of the 85 km route, with six locks 190 m × 12 m, was open to shipping, carrying coal supplies down to the Rhine. For much of the distance there are spectacular wooded surroundings with several acute bends that demand one-way working. Of all Germany's most beautiful waterways, the Saar is among a small number that *Avonbay* has yet to visit. We decided to postpone a cruise until it was possible to reach the Canal de la Marne au Rhin, at the far end.

Wasserbillig (K206) marked entry to Luxembourg, whose 42 km of riverbank is the frontier with Germany. From here onwards, we flew a pair of courtesy flags from appropriate sides of the mast, a situation so unlikely that it receives no mention in any of the published works on flag etiquette. With a startling lack of ingenuity, the Luxembourg ensign is virtually identical to

Ornate city square fountain in Trier.

that of the Netherlands, except that the lowest horizontal stripe is a slightly paler shade of blue. A much prettier maritime alternative uses a red lion rampant on a blue and white background. Direct contact with Germany had come to an end. Although we scanned the bank for a Customs post, none could be found, and so Luxembourg has no official record of our visit. Quite rightly, this little country, some years in advance of relaxation of trade barriers throughout the European Community, had better ways of spending public funds than to bother bone fide pleasure boatmen. Several months earlier, however, we had come through this border crossing by car. Most travellers were being waved on without stopping. But noting our British registration plates, the officer in charge detained us briefly, so that his young trainees could be given some practical instruction on the content of British passports.

Work was started long ago on a waterway intended to follow the course of the Sûre from Wasserbillig, ascend into the Ardennes, and finally reach the Belgian Meuse near Liège. It was never completed.

Now, having no other navigation routes, Luxembourg makes maximum use of its single bank of the Moselle. Mertert commercial harbour (K208.5) is home to the nation's tiny merchant fleet, handling more than 1 million tonnes of freight annually, while all along the starboard side are facilities catering for pleasure craft. No objections were raised to our appropriating a length of commercial quayside for the night some distance below Grevenmacher Lock (K212), although the Flemish-speaking skipper of Luxembourg's passenger-carrying flagship *Princess Marie-Astrid* suggested that we might be more comfortable on the downstream end of the wall. Shops ashore gladly accepted any of the local currencies we offered, while the people appeared equally happy to speak German, French or Flemish. Years ahead of their larger neighbours, life had become an admirable advertisement for the benefits of a united Europe, with no hint of national identity getting in the way of profitable trading. It was all rather refreshing.

Commercial and pleasure traffic had decreased substantially. I seriously wondered if the vast expense of making a 2000-tonne capacity waterway to beyond Nancy had been justified, as the majority of barges were 300-tonne *péniches*. None wished to accompany us through Grevenmacher or Palzem Locks (K230), so we paid a 9DM toll at each, soon afterwards arriving on a central quay in the flourishing resort town of Remich (K233). Shops of all kinds displayed a remarkable range of alcohol and tobacco products at what appeared to be duty-free prices. Diesel fuel, when purchased on a subsequent visit to the country's sole marina in Schwebsange (K337.5), was also markedly cheaper than in Germany or France. In some ways it already felt as if we had crossed the French border. Although riverbank and streets were not maintained with the same careful precision as in Germany, there was a welcome atmosphere of freedom. At last we could moor nearly anywhere we chose without being accosted by officials whose conversations started with '*Es ist verboten* ...'

Although less well-known than the vineyards of the German Moselle, Luxembourg's wine-making industry is nevertheless considerable. On the waterside at K222 we had passed the Caves Co-operatives des Vignerons de Wormeldange, housed in an elegant 1931 building reminiscent of the Art Deco cinema style. Also renowned for the quality of its wines, Bech-Kleinmacher (K235) boasts a fascinating wine and folklore museum, with recreated house interiors that depict domestic life throughout the centuries. The best day of the year to visit Schwedsange is 1 September, for since 1953 its village fountain has flowed with wine on that day.

The frontiers of Germany, Luxembourg and France meet for an instant a few metres downstream of Apach Lock (K242). As at Basle, on the German/Swiss/French border, this would be a suitable moment for a boat to fly all three flags at once. In our case, the lock's light signal showed green, so we lost no time in entering the great chamber. Exactly a year earlier, *Avonbay* had cruised into Germany for the first of five memorable voyages during 1986 and 1987. Now, in the months ahead, we would explore the Belgian Meuse and pass through the waterways of France to the Mediterranean coast. We could never then have guessed that a reunified Germany would quite soon be tempting *Avonbay* into unknown waters beyond the Elbe and the mythical lakeland of Mecklenburg.

5 Eastwards to the Elbe

KANALBAUTEN.   Dortmund-Emskanal.
                          (Das Hebewerk von Henrichenburg).

LIEBIG'S FLEISCH-EXTRACT.

*Henrichenburg Boat Lift on an early 20th century
advertising card.*

The credit for *Avonbay*'s 1991 exploration of former East Germany lies squarely with novelist C S Forester. Through the summer of 1929 he diligently mailed reports to *The Motor Boat*, describing the progress of his outboard-powered dinghy from Hamburg to Berlin. Only when he reached the capital did he learn of a magical series of waterways to the north – the Mecklenburg Lakes – and his descriptions of those mouth-watering navigations had for two decades made me long to go there. A book, *The Annie Marble in Germany*, followed soon after. This is peppered with numerous tiny monochrome photographs, often featuring little more than expanses of water and sky. But his elegantly written text vividly brings to life a lost world, rather like a long-vanished Norfolk Broads but on a much greater scale. Forester was firmly of the opinion that his was the first British ensign to fly in these waters. Clearly, he never discovered another, now equally rare, cruise account, *Our Wherry in Wendish Lands. From Friesland Through The Mecklenburg Lakes to Bohemia*, by H M Doughty. This really was a pioneering voyage, completed in 1891 and 1892, and features the travels of a Norfolk sailing wherry.

Forester's photographs and Doughty's daughters' line drawings were a tempting bait, especially when I discovered that all these waterways remained fully operational. But this seemed to be a dream that would never be realised.

East Germany was tight in the iron grip of Russian communist rule, an area forbidden to all western pleasure craft. Limited access to the country was possible by train or car, but private boats were another matter. Then I heard of a scheme whereby craft based in the capitalistic 'island' of West Berlin were able to cruise to the Baltic under escort of accredited East German freight barges. With 114 km of navigable water in West Berlin, the idea of making this journey in the reverse direction seemed worthy of investigation. The official reply arrived with typical German humour: 'Why do you wish to come to the city when everyone else is trying to get out?'

Certainly the trip could be made, though. We would be under tow from the border between the two divisions of Germany, with the use of our engines banned except when passing through locks; and an armed guard would ensure that we behaved in a manner acceptable to the DDR (presumably this implied rigorous restrictions on photography). The cost of the exercise would be considerable and, done like this, it didn't sound like fun. The final drawback was that only two adults were permitted to accompany our boat; short of drawing lots, we could never have devised an acceptable method of so reducing our normal crew. Instead, we contented ourselves with a long weekend on Berlin waterways, as guests of our diplomatic friends Sir Michael and Lady Henrietta Burton. Fascinating though this experience was, it only served to increase my frustration at being unable to explore all those unknown canals, rivers and lakes beyond the watchtowers, prohibition signs and barbed wire. That was in May 1989.

Events in eastern Europe then began to move with an unimagined rapidity. Mikhail Gorbachev's far-reaching reforms were to bring about the destruction of the Berlin Wall six months later on 9 November. Thereafter, the timetable of change was relentless: 1 December, the communist government of the DDR collapsed; western pleasure craft were permitted to enter the east from 1 April 1990; currency unification followed on 1 July; Germany was declared a single nation once more on 3 October. *Avonbay* penetrated the old Iron Curtain on 12 June 1991, the first British pleasure boat to reach eastern territory on her own keel since the 1930s.

Throughout the previous winter, I had accumulated a massive file of correspondence, pestering all known sources of German waterways expertise. Doughty and Forester turned out to be reliable and trustworthy guide books, in spite of their great age. One evening, while moored in the Mecklenburg Lakes, I discovered the extraordinary fact that exactly a century earlier *to the very day*, Doughty had spent the night aboard *Gipsy* at the same anchorage! At first, I despaired of ever locating vital route maps. Reborn east Germany had yet to learn western habits of efficient letter writing, and telephone connections seemed non-existent. Finally, at great expense, a set of four elegant hardback chart books arrived in England, covering in minute detail most of what we planned to see. These were later augmented by several equally useful publications, rushed through the press in answer to a considerable demand from west German pleasure boaters.

Half a term of school German lessons, long ago, while just adequate for our previous cruises in the west, seemed barely enough to equip me for everyday situations in a country where little English would be spoken and Russian had for more than 40 years been the second language. June and I therefore booked a course of 12 hourly sessions with the German teacher from a local public school. Largely ignoring correct grammar, we compiled a list of useful nautical phrases, including 'How soon can you mend the engine?' 'What time does the lock open?' and 'We have something on the propeller. Can you please find a diver?' In the event, provided we maintained a firm control on topics covered, we were usually able to make ourselves understood and much of the time we could follow the gist of the answers received.

Additional insurance cover for the boat was sought from our broker. That the policy now bore a clause permitting us to navigate 'not east of 16° east' indicated that the company had spent time poring over an atlas. Thinking that help might be difficult to obtain in the event of problems, we devised a

Our invaluable guides to east German waterways, dating from 1892 and 1930.

plan of self-sufficiency: extra fuel supplies in jerry cans, portable drinking-water containers, copious supplies of tinned meat and purchase of a worn Leyland 1.5 marine engine to be used for spares. Later, these precautions were proved totally unnecessary – but we were pioneers in a frugal land, and it wasn't worth taking any chances!

Meanwhile, British press and television seemed bent on carrying out a hatchet-job on east Germany. Stories of escalating prices, growing unemployment, decay, gloom and pollution all contrived to destroy remaining vestiges of enthusiasm for the adventure among *Avonbay*'s co-owners. The Elbe, an integral part of our planned route, was allegedly the most contaminated stream in Europe. Quite apart from certain sources claiming that it was too shallow for our boat, we had visions of chemical action destroying our steel hull within days. Fifty years of neglect suggested that the canals could be rubbish-filled with barely workable locks. Worst of all, our much-loved vessel might be the target of neo-Nazi thugs. Hoping that all these fears would turn out to be groundless, I avoided, where possible, discussing them with June and John. Several times they both appeared to be dangerously near to pulling the plug on the whole exercise.

Avonbay had wintered in Burgundy. Stage One of our four-part 1991 voyage involved an Easter cruise from St Jean-de-Losne to the Canal de la Marne au Rhin at Hesse in Alsace. Before we started out, a well-meaning German-Swiss friend made a six-hour return journey by car from Basle to provide us with the latest information on east Germany. His knowledge was prodigious, judging from the wealth of detail contained in his recently published 546-page guide book to waterways of the former DDR. As we talked in German, I was relieved to realise that language would not be the worst of our difficulties. But to my dismay, his constant references to food shortages and *kriminal* people very nearly resulted in June cancelling the entire project! Fortunately, Charles Gérard, the German-born proprietor of our H$_2$O marina, came to my help: '*Avonbay* is a beautiful boat, but not a gin palace,' he declared. 'You will not attract unwanted attention.' Luckily, we all chose to believe him.

Stage Two of the cruise saw us leaving Strasbourg Docks astern on 3 June. Our route lay over 467 km of the Rhine before reaching the Rhein–Herne Canal at Duisburg-Ruhrort. With only two locks to negotiate, the downstream marathon was completed in a mere three days. Delays here for sightseeing trips ashore were not part of our plan. On board with me were marine surveyor and engineer Jim Macdonald and his wife Mig, both very experienced inland boaters. For once, all worries concerning the mechanical health of the ship were removed from my shoulders.

During my last visit to Ruhrort, the excellent local waterways museum was closed: and little had been gleaned by squinting through the windows. Before leaving the Rhine to head eastwards across the heart of Germany, we now tied up by a fuel jetty in the Eisenbahn Hafen and spent an enjoyable morning looking at a range of models, artefacts and wonderfully powerful

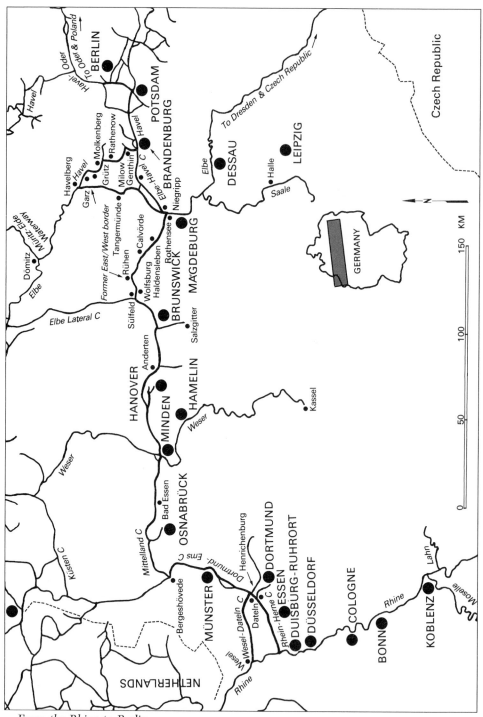

From the Rhine to Berlin.

paintings of massed steam tugs, illustrating the long history of this, the biggest inland port in Europe.

Everything that lay ahead was 'new' water, always an exciting prospect, although in this case we had slight reservations about the scenic attractions of the Rhein–Herne Canal, which carved through the heart of Germany's famous Ruhr steelworks district. I expected industrial squalor quite the equal of Belgium's dreadful Charleroi iron foundries, whose clouds of chemical-laden smoke and blazing chimneys we were to brave the following autumn. Roger Pilkington, writing in *Small Boat Through Germany* (1963), found 'inky water' on the Rhein-Herne and noted 'from the sky a continual fall of sticky blackish-brown treacly droplets of tarry ooze'. A glance at the map shows this to be perhaps the most heavily populated region of Germany, where one industrial town merges into the next without a break. But seen from the canal, its damning reputation is no longer deserved. Some parts now have the air of a well-tended water park – a magnet for anglers and dog walkers.

First, it was necessary to pass through the docks, seemingly endless basins branching off the main line. Free from the constraints of the fast-flowing Rhine, there was now ample time to look around and absorb the atmosphere of a flourishing inland waterways environment. Numerous large barges edged past the wharves; modern cranes, bearing individual names like 'Hans', 'Urlich' and 'Kurt', were heaving loads of coal, scrap and chemicals. Amid this hectic activity, our little boat was neither out of place nor felt threatened, provided we nipped smartly into locks when requested over our VHF by the lock keepers. Six locks are spread through 47 km to a junction with the Dortmund–Ems Canal.

Traffic has reached saturation point and continues to grow. Generally, there would be a small space for us at the back of the chambers. As on other German routes, commercial craft and passenger boats invariably take precedence over private cruisers. With typical efficiency, each bridge is numbered and carries a distance plate accurate to the nearest metre. We were on the outside steering position, passing under bridge 325 at K13.035. At this very moment an express thundered over the open girders. I looked up and was hit full in the face by a shower of liquid. Thus I realised that use of German train facilities is *verboten* only when they are standing in stations.

Doubtless, we would be forbidden to spend our first night moored to a quay among a clutch of barges on the main line. Pleasure craft are generally expected to congregate in marinas or at least on quaysides set apart for their exclusive use. This time, though, no inquisitive police launch was to disturb us in our shallow cutting, bright with drifts of purple lupins. Major enlarge-ment works were in progress when we reached Wanne-Eikel Locks at 9.30 am. Already six barges were waiting to work through, and with only one chamber functioning a prolonged delay was inevitable. The guide book quoted a locking length of 163 m. As most barges were exactly 80 m long (dimensions are conveniently painted on their sides), the most elementary calculations made us realise that we might be here for a very long time indeed. The morning was passed watching newly arrived pairs working uphill, while we attended to various domestic chores which included sorting out many years' accumulation of nuts, bolts, washers and screws into labelled tins. Eventually, unable to tolerate the delay, we joined a deputation from two local cruisers and sought out the keeper. His depressing advice was that we had no alternative but to remain patient until a 50 m barge presented itself. Finally, a suitable combination edged forward. We followed them in, having waited six hours.

Further on, there was more heavy construction in progress, where another lock was being rebuilt and a basin excavated. Here we were expected to negotiate a form of slalom course through half submerged heaps of gravel: easy for us, but rather less so for the constant succession of barges in each direction. In canal terms, this is a modern waterway, opened as recently as 1914 and thus creating a vital link through the Ruhr between the Rhine and the Dortmund–Ems Canal of 1899, which we were about to join.

Quite soon, *Avonbay* reached a compulsory stop, for at Henrichenburg Junction there is so much of navigational interest that it was unthinkable not to spend a couple of hours exploring ashore. This point, where the Dortmund–Ems swings south-eastwards towards its Dortmund terminus, is marked by a sudden change in levels. To build a 14.5 m-deep conventional lock would have been wasteful of precious water supplies, so between 1894 and 1899 the remarkable Henrichenburg *Schiffshebewerk* was constructed, following the recently successful operation of similar boat lifts at Anderton in Cheshire, St Omer in northern France and on Belgium's Canal du Centre. Within a year, the equally remarkable Foxton inclined plane would go into service on the Grand Junction Canal in Leicestershire. The turn of the century certainly saw some extraordinary advances in canal technology. This example at Henrichenburg – for all its Meccano-like lattice of steel girders – boasts a proud and distinctive Germanic character. Massive tapering columns of carefully hewn stone are topped with huge gilded orbs, which in turn sprout lightning conductors. Fitted with a single caisson for 950-tonne capacity barges, it worked on a float principle: five floats rose or fell into deep wells, as water was added or taken away by electric pumps. Screws at each corner, also electrically driven, maintained a level on the caisson and controlled its smooth travel.

Traffic was soon to outstrip the lift's capacity, so a shaft lock shared duties from 1917, equipped with economiser side-ponds, five on each edge of the unusually deep chamber. Demand for still larger barges caused both lift and shaft lock to be superseded in 1962 by a new vertical lift. This also operates on floats, although this time they were reduced to two. The latest development is a further deep lock, completed in 1989 with a 4200-tonne capacity and working alongside the 1962 *Hebewerk*. So, within the space of a few hundred metres, there are four methods of moving boats between the two levels, illustrating the progress of canal engineering over a 90-year period.

In spite of remaining operational until just 30 years earlier, the original

ABOVE *The lower level of the Henrichenburg Boat Lift, photographed soon after its completion in 1899.*

RIGHT *Its modern replacement, dating from 1962.*

lift looks as if it has been derelict for considerably longer: mature trees choke the dry bed of the approach cut at its upper entrance. Fortunately, after a period of indecision, its future is now secured as a unique example of late nineteenth-century industrial archaeology. Even if it never again carries boats, at least the structure is well maintained. In the lower basin we found a slightly sad collection of historic steam tugs and other waterway craft, the nucleus of a planned canal museum. Additionally, two yacht clubs have moorings here, where *Avonbay* was to be left in safe keeping for several weeks at the end of our summer cruise.

As we watched barges and pleasure boats work through the modern lift and the latest deep lock, a coachload of young adults descended. They clutched clipboards, and began to dash through the site making notes. Several fired questions at me (in German) relating to construction dates and other more technical matters. Presumably, we had been overwhelmed by some form of canal-based treasure hunt. It was gratifying that unfamiliarity with language and local history did not prevent us from being of some assistance. If there was a prize, I would have been justified in claiming it.

Scenery along the Dortmund–Ems was pleasant rather than spectacular, with well-wooded banks and occasional evidence of small towns. Berlin and the east were proving to act as a powerful magnet, so there was little incentive to linger. A 64 km level pound extended to Münster and, like us, all northbound traffic seemed intent on reaching the first lock before its noon closing time the next day, Sunday. Often we sailed past side arms, showing where the length of the original canal had been reduced. These frequently provide overnight shelter at yacht clubs – very necessary in view of commercial traffic running for most hours out of the twenty-four. In addition to regular tripping boats and cruisers, barges of up to 2000-tonnes' capacity appeared at ten-minute intervals; these caused us minimal disturbance as the channel is uniformly deep. Freighters included Czech, Polish and east German vessels – the 'DDR' on their sterns crudely altered to a plain 'D' signifying their allegiance to a newly unified Germany. Coal and scrap metal appeared to be the most popular cargoes: carriage of scrap gradually became synonymous in our thoughts with commercial barges from the east. Massive quantities are shifted in all directions, leading you to the conclusion that the nation is indulging in a great orgy of destruction. The barges from the east were invariably utilitarian craft, with mean and ugly wheelhouses, and lacking the gleaming paint and sleek lines of their western counterparts. One obvious comparison was between Trabants and Mercedes.

Mig and Jim are both adventurous devotees of shore food, believing this to be the best way of getting to know the people through whose land we are passing. Or, put another way, they see little point in slaving in a hot galley when someone else can be paid to slave in the hot kitchen of a restaurant. The only flaw in this arrangement can be a determination to keep cruising until late into the evening in the expectation that an agreeable eating house will materialise. That night we were lucky: a short distance up an old arm at K36, Lüdinghausen, we spotted the Gasthaus Peters Scheune, an extensive establishment prepared to serve gargantuan portions of food to a very large number of people. Outside, on a welcoming jetty, lay a pretty little green-painted German cruiser oddly named *Old Bottle*. (How often do those in search of 'chic' foreign names for their boat – or house – stray into the totally banal! This example was nearly as dreadful as *Chez Nous*.) Our meal completed, six jolly characters from *Old Bottle* joined us at our table and, being 'knowledgeable' boaters, began dispensing advice: 'So you are travelling to Berlin? Should take you little more than three days from here. Four at the most!' As it was plain that their cruising was not likely to extend further than the next canalside bar and they later admitted as much, the information needed to be taken with a large pinch of *Salz*. Even without wasting time, Berlin still lay another eight days away.

Saturday night moored outside a German 'pub' is not really to be recommended. Long after we had gone to bed, there was much merry activity as Mercedes and BMWs roared off into the darkness. Then a passenger boat returned to moor immediately beyond my cabin. Amplified community singing provided free entertainment until after 2 am. One much-repeated number was a German version of 'Roll Out the Barrel'. Eventually, all became reasonably quiet. My next log book entry reads: 'Jim jumping around at 4.00 am to stop swan tapping with beak on *Avonbay*.' Despite this disturbed night, we were up and off by 8.30 the next morning.

Three duplicated locks in Münster were reached by 11.45 am. Each displayed a red light and my immediate thought was that we would be unable to move any further until the next morning. Luckily, two barges were noted moving into the farthest chamber; we reversed rapidly from a mooring on the other side of the canal and joined them seconds before the gates began to close. One was a very friendly Dutchman, once more confirming that all British boaters can expect to be treated with utmost courtesy by anyone from the Netherlands. Especially in Germany, where the Second World War remains more than just a distant memory. He was fascinated by our destination, not yet having been to east Germany himself: 'But my Mummy and Daddy went there by car several weeks ago!' he informed us in excellent English. So anxious were we to pass this lock that we ignored a tempting bunker station shortly beforehand. The tanks had not been filled since leaving France, a considerable distance back. I produced the dip-stick and discovered that the level was worryingly low. Two jerry cans were poured in. With luck, we should now be able to reach the next fuelling point, 35 km on at Bergeshövede, junction with the Mittelland Canal. Somehow none of us was very interested in visiting Münster, the cathedral city which is capital of Westphalia; I felt better about this decision on reading that it had been largely destroyed during the last war.

Fuel problems seemed to be solved as we approached the wide expanses of Bergeshövede Junction, for here was not one but two diesel suppliers and an extensive barge chandlery. A quick investigation showed that both closed on

Sunday afternoons. Rather than waste time by waiting until the morning, we made a potentially rash decision to continue in the alarming knowledge that the next prospect of fuel would be in Minden, exactly 100 km down a lockfree level of the Mittelland Canal. The rest of that afternoon and the morning that followed, *Avonbay* somehow discovered unexpected reserves in her tanks; never before had the engines been allowed to so nearly run dry.

It is possible to admire the Mittelland Canal as a triumph of twentieth-century engineering, sweeping imperiously through the heartland of Germany. Cuttings alternate with embankments and aqueducts, while almost all towns lie well inland from the banks. This journey could never be described as exciting. Of the six crew members involved, I was the only person who had to endure a double dose of this far from thrilling waterway when *Avonbay* returned towards the Rhine at the end of that summer. With rather less interest to be found than on London's Paddington Arm (perhaps my least favoured British waterway), we whiled away the time with mental word games, including compiling alphabetical listings of car makes, birds, German Christian names and finally, as the weather deteriorated, songs whose lyrics contain references to rain. We stopped for the night in a basin at K48, but exploration by bicycle failed to reveal any shop, restaurant or hamlet within a wide area.

Once more under way, nothing was allowed to divert us from the quest for diesel. When we returned here in August, the mood was more conducive to sightseeing. We moored at K61 to seek out a charming little town of timbered houses called Bad Essen. Although a little suburbanised in recent years, at its heart was an intact collection of farm buildings, drinking houses and church, clustered around a shady cobbled square. Visitors have long been drawn here by the curative properties of the water.

Minden was reached by mid-morning. Although approaching their last gasp, the engines had gallantly kept running and were rewarded with a prodigious 530 litres (117 gallons) of *Gasöl*, at the considerable cost of 625.52DM. Commercial traffic increased as we neared a junction with the River Weser, flowing to the North Sea via Bremerhaven and coming southwards from Kassel, Münden and Hamelin. Some weeks later, we considered diverting up the Weser to at least Hamelin. But the local yacht club's harbourmaster was emphatic that our 1.3 m draught was half a metre too great. River levels were low, the current quite fierce, and I had no desire to listen to our propellers polishing their blades on loose gravel.

'The River Weser, deep and wide
'Washes its walls on the southern side.'

Clearly, Robert Browning had never tried to bring a boat up to the city of the Pied Piper, for 'deep and wide' the Weser is not! I had already digested Roger Pilkington's comments on his 1961 journey:

> Had we realised earlier that the Weser was such a fast-flowing river that the powerful steamers took two days for the trip from Hamelin to Münden but returned in one day, I very much doubt if we would ever have set out to visit

it, however keen the *Commodore* might have been to try her skill against such a flow. We certainly would not have undertaken the voyage if we had been told beforehand that for the entire 162 miles of its course there would be a relatively narrow dredged channel not marked with a single spar or beacon, and that outside this fairway the depth of water was such that we could have kept our knees dry when paddling.

Dr Pilkington's *Commodore* gallantly reached Kassel; but *Avonbay* had no wish to emulate such an achievement which might easily have ended with a serious stranding. German waterway authorities could hardly be relied upon to provide a flush of water by opening the sluices of the distant Eder Dam. It would be much safer to explore Rat Catcher Town by car! The days are long gone when I would consider dragging my boat through the navigational equivalent of a damp meadow.

Minden demanded a tour of inspection. On our port side, a large basin beyond a wooded island leads to the *Schachtschleuse* ('shaft lock'), dropping boats 12.7 m down to the river. Although the public are invited to view this

Minden Aqueduct, carrying the Mittelland Canal over the Weser. The section shown here was rebuilt after wartime destruction.

operation, performed in a classic example of early twentieth-century Prussian architecture, we were unable to master the slot machines providing access and resorted instead to vaulting over a low gate. Continuing its eastward course, the Mittelland Canal now strides over the Weser on an aqueduct of eight reinforced concrete arches, totalling 375 m in length. Its channel is unusually wide at 24 m, enabling a fairly aggressive passenger vessel to overtake shortly after we had entered the trough and reduced speed to admire the view. One sizeable portion of the structure was bombed during the Second World War and was rebuilt several years later.

Already the Mittelland, completed to Hanover by 1916 and extended to the Elbe by 1938, had been enlarged in width. Now, in 1991, further widening was in progress, requiring renewal of every bridge, and felling trees all along one side and excavating a bigger channel. Our lasting impression was of commercial freight levels undreamed of in Britain and rarely to be seen even in France. Germany certainly values its canal network.

The prospect of an evening's entertainment ashore materialised at K117 where a large restaurant lurked in a wooded clearing. Equipped with a rugged landing stage to hold boats off the sloping bank of rough boulders, we pulled in to book a table for 7.30 pm. It took just one 1350-tonne barge banging *Avonbay* against the hard bottom to make me insist that we continued cruising, thus abandoning what promised to be an enjoyable dinner. We had moved barely 300 m when a moored workboat came into sight. It was deserted and made an excellent jetty, so our dinner appointment materialised after all. Safe overnight moorings can be a real problem on German canals like this, although study of the chart will often identify a yacht club off the main line. We were passing through the Mittelland as a means of reaching other, infinitely more glamorous and exciting, areas; it was difficult to understand how local boating enthusiasts could base their craft permanently on such a dull navigation. Surely, all club members cannot regard their cruisers as immobile weekend hideaways? Yet there is little scenic encouragement to mount an afternoon's excursion on a featureless waterway like this.

At 7 am the next morning the crew of 'our' workboat noisily arrived and were well tucked into a substantial breakfast as I glanced in their cabin to wish them '*guten Morgen*'. This was not a memorable day in terms of weather or scenery, but at least we moved 100 km nearer the east. Mig and I took to the bikes at Anderten Lock in search of seriously needed galley replenishments. Unaware that all the necessary shops were in nearby Anderten village, we cycled far in the opposite direction, arriving breathless at the cheapest, nastiest and least useful of any supermarket ever discovered in Germany – east or west! This disaster was later rectified by discovery of both a butcher's and a cake shop. We ate well on board, having made fast to vertical piling at K217, beyond the branch leading to Salzgitter.

Given a good enough reason and time to adjust to the idea, I can manage well enough without a night's sleep. But if I go to bed at midnight, expecting to remain undisturbed until 7 am, only to be aroused by an insistent beating on the cabinside at 5.45 am, I suffer from excessive grumpiness. Friends know this and wisely leave me to slumber until the appointed waking hour. On this occasion, the thumping was so loud, prolonged and business-like that I feared impending disaster. I pulled on my bath-robe and blearily staggered to the saloon to discover a water policeman standing on the towpath. 'It is *verboten* to moor here!' he said. As the canal was wide and offered a clear view in each direction for several kilometres, such uncivil, unsociable and unnecessary information did not go down well. But it was too early to launch into a German explanation that the three of us possessed canal cruising experience totalling almost a century, and which ought to ensure our selecting a mooring that didn't place us in danger or obstruct other vessels. 'There is a *Sportboot* mooring beyond the next bridge,' suggested our tiresome guardian of correct behaviour. Too angry to be other than perfectly polite, I began to release our warps. At least this very early start would almost certainly enable us to reach east Germany by evening, a very exciting prospect and the culmination of many months of planning.

The improbability of the eventual fall of communist Germany is illustrated dramatically at K233.5. To port, a huge new waterway, the Elbe Lateral Canal, swings northwards for 115 km, close to the old border, and provides a totally west German link with the Elbe upstream of Hamburg. Conceived as a reliable alternative to the often uncertain navigation of east Germany's Elbe, the Lateral Canal drops 23 m through an economiser lock at Uelzen and makes a final mighty descent of 38 m at the great Sharnebeck Vertical Lift. We, however, would be staying on the Mittelland, and soon arrived at Sülfeld, last of just three locks in a total distance of 320 km.

Falling to the lower level with a Czech barge and a pretty little pleasure boat converted from an old tug, we suddenly noticed that she was registered in Dresden. It was our first encounter with a cruiser from the east. Her name, *Zukunft* ('Future') had become prophetic for the elderly couple on board, at last able to explore a part of their country denied to them for 50 years. In the reach beyond, a long train of scrap-filled east German barges, close-coupled with iron cables, was like a museum exhibit: the sort of vessels that disappeared from the west decades ago. Massive wooden rudders were controlled by great iron steering wheels, mounted parallel to the open decks. This is agreeable enough for their helmsmen in the summer months but extremely unpleasant when winter temperatures plummet below freezing and the Elbe is awash with ice floes.

Motoring history was made at the vast Volkswagen factory by the canal in Wolfsburg, for here was born the world's best-selling 'Beetle'. Even though he never learned to drive, Adolph Hitler offered personal interest and backing and is pictured at a foundation-stone laying ceremony in my copy of the souvenir album published in 1938 to mark completion of the eastern section of the waterway to the Elbe.

Just short of the old border, *Avonbay*'s port engine started to fade, picked up briefly, and then died on us altogether. Something similar had happened several days before, but seemed to have been sorted by 'bleeding' the fuel system. I agreed with Jim that a permanent cure was now called for, so we tied to a long, deserted quay and began to attack the injectors and fuel pump. Components were spread on rags all over the saloon carpet, while Jim struggled to free reluctant bolts in the open engine compartment. Although it was black oil and not blood, the scene reminded me of urgent surgical treatment in a hospital operating theatre. Two or three hours of hard work seemed likely. Without paying too much attention, I saw a green *Wasserpolizei* car pause on the opposite bank. It then drove off at speed and within five minutes had arrived outside our wheelhouse doors. Several of the five young officers spoke annoyingly good English: 'You must not tie here. It is reserved for laden tanker barges! Have you not seen the sign?' There was indeed a mystical symbol mounted on a post right alongside. I explained our difficulties. In fact, with much of one engine spread out for inspection, the problem was rather obvious. As we had not seen a tanker barge all day, let alone a laden one, while 500 m of identical mooring remained unoccupied, such zealous insistence on regulations seemed quite unnecessary.

This was our second helping of police obstruction in one day. I assured them that we would leave just as soon as possible. Unacceptable! 'It is *verboten* to remain here!' Next, as captain, I was asked to produce my Overseas Helmsman's Certificate. With oily fingers, I pulled it from the appropriate file, to be sternly warned that it expired in 14 days (I carried a replacement). They then claimed that our navigation lights did not conform to Mittelland Canal requirements, for 'port, starboard and masthead must be in line, beam to beam, and all mounted at the same height above water!' We greeted this news with disbelief; Jim is, after all, one of Europe's leading inland waterway craft surveyors, and *Avonbay* complies with the most stringent of maritime regulations. Anyway, it was broad daylight. Long after, when there had been time for mature reflection, we realised that this particular *Polizei* posse must have been former east German border guards, uneasily settling into a rather new kind of job. Suffering considerable inconvenience, we shifted *Avonbay* on her remaining starboard engine to a recognised pleasure boat basin, out of sight round the next bend. Jim's mechanical efforts were a complete success: that particular fault has yet to occur again.

Suddenly, we were there! Boarded-up Customs buildings, a deserted café and, further east, a bridge hole artificially narrowed with yellow-painted steel piles, allowing only one barge to pass through at a time. Could this dereliction really have occurred in less than two years?

On the far side, remains of security fencing extended for several hundred metres along each bank, rather like a giant rat trap. Broken searchlights swung from their concrete standards. We could appreciate the hopelessness of swimming to freedom amid a hail of President Honnecker's bullets. *Avonbay* had penetrated the Iron Curtain!

6 Elbe and Havel

A powerful Elbe steam tug, dating from the early 1920s.

At first, there were no obvious differences between east and west as we cruised along the remainder of the Mittelland Canal from the former Rühen frontier. The waterway was in good order: deep and with well-maintained banks. Few signs of human activity were evident in woodland so recently alive with armed guards. We passed a series of small waterside towns: Calvörde, Bülstringen and Haldensleben. There were moored barges, a collection of noisy children intent on drowning their capsizing canoeing instructor, and several stationary police launches painted in a dejected battleship grey. No one paid the slightest attention to the first British private pleasure cruiser to enter old DDR territory by water in over half a century. Later when we tried to engage people in conversation, many displayed an extraordinary lack of curiosity, remaining perfectly polite but tight-lipped. For too long they had lived in fear of the 85 000 full-time staff of the *Staatssicherheit* (state security organisation) which had relied on up to half a million paid informers. If you knew that you could not trust your next-door neighbour or cousin, there was every reason to remain cautious of foreigners from the west who suddenly appeared in a gleaming vessel with the attributes of a superior *Polizeiboot*, and flying an official-looking blue ensign. Only when circumstances permitted an in-depth discussion did the bolder citizens allow themselves to talk freely. Yet even here, their chief concerns centred on life in Germany. Few questions were ever posed about conditions in Great Britain.

By 8.30 pm we were moored above the Rothensee Vertical Lift, which would lower us next day to the mighty River Elbe. Going ashore to explore our first 'eastern' town, we found a cobbled street of fading, paint-peeled houses, where most of the shops had long ago ceased trading. There were few cars, a total absence of advertising hoardings, and the sole telephone kiosk had been vandalised.

In the morning, outside our windows we saw a gang of mechanics engaged in exchanging the engine of a workboat for a rebuilt six-cylinder model. As the newly painted machinery was craned on board, Jim and I examined it for some form of manufacturer's name plate. But this example was totally anonymous. We soon realised that in a country so recently lacking choice or competition, there was little point in creating different brand names. It was a similar situation with the utilitarian and identical outboard motors that powered many elderly private cruisers. After several years on the waiting list, prospective clients would be informed: 'You want an outboard? This is it!' If the technology of the 1950s had produced a workable machine, why waste research and design skills in the 1980s by updating it? For this same reason, the streets of New Delhi are filled with new 1954-model Morris Oxford saloon cars.

Whereas the Henrichenburg Boat Lift of 1899 is designed in the Imperial Prussian Gothic style, Rothensee, opened 39 years later, owes something to Art Deco cinema architecture. Smartly painted in green and cream, it functions on very similar principles, with a water-filled 1000-tonne capacity caisson rising or falling on a pair of columns floating in 55 m-deep wells. Giant electrically driven screws at each corner of the tank maintain stability as 5400 tonnes of water and steelwork travel an average change of levels of 16 m. The keeper asked me to complete a questionnaire, detailing name, craft dimensions and destination so we could be included in statistics recording up to 80 boat passages each day.

But for the outbreak of the Second World War, there would have been two further engineering marvels in the vicinity of Rothensee. Work was started on a nearby high-level aqueduct, taking the Mittelland Canal over Elbe shipping and through a second vertical lift to lower the navigation on the far, Brandenburg, shore. At 900 m, this bridge of water would have been the world's longest navigation aqueduct. We saw its weedy approach canal, heading eastwards at Rothensee, and from river level, the concrete arches intended to lead to the water-filled viaduct over the Elbe.

Since 1938 all barge traffic bound for Berlin has had no alternative but to enter the river immediately downstream of Magdeburg city and run with the stream for 10 km to join the Elbe–Havel Canal at Niegripp. This part of the journey had been a cause of great anxiety for months. Throughout its 700 km course from the Czech border to the estuary below Hamburg, the Elbe runs free of locks or weirs. For more than half of every year, barges are only able to navigate when lightly laden. A new passenger ship that had recently gone into service between Hamburg and Dresden was specially constructed with an unusually shallow draught and water-jet propulsion rather than more vulnerable propellers. Several summers of low rainfall had enhanced the

Elbe's unenviable reputation; 1990 photographs published in the German boating magazines had shown yacht club moorings around Lauenburg reduced to a sea of dry mud! What chances for *Avonbay* with her 1.3 m draught? To have come so far only to be defeated by 10 km of shallow river would be sickening. Correspondence with several local pleasure boating clubs had prompted us to have a go.

The original plan had been to ascend 334 km of the Elbe to Czechoslovakia, visit Prague on the Vltava (Moldau) and return to Berlin for the winter. The Elbe's uppermost reaches in Bohemia offer spectacular scenery, we would be adding another 'new' country to the growing list of nations visited by *Avonbay* (preparations reached the point where I purchased a Czech courtesy flag), and in Dresden would be found one of Europe's greatest concentrations of passenger craft still driven by steam. But then a growing number of minuses began to accumulate on the 'Shall we? Shan't we?' equation. River speeds reportedly reached 6 knots in places, while for much of the journey surroundings in the flat landscape would be very bleak. Attempts to extract navigational information and charts from the Czech authorities were a total failure until I finally contacted our Ambassador in Prague. His rapid reply enclosed a two-page letter – in Czech, together with an apology that the

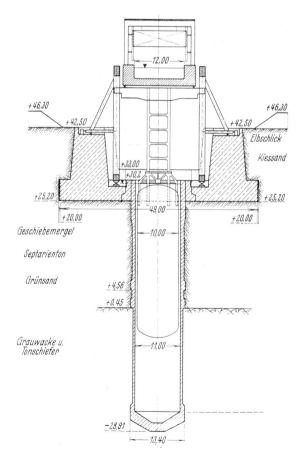

Cross-section of the Rothensee Boat Lift, from a drawing published in 1938. The water-filled barge caisson (top) is surmounted by guillotine gates. Hidden below ground is a pair of 55m-deep wells, containing floats on which the tank rises or falls, as water is pumped in or out.

Embassy had no access to translation services! The £50 decoding fee paid in London revealed that these Czech waters lacked pleasure boat refuelling facilities; private craft movement through Prague was limited to a short period each day; berths for the exclusive use of foreign visitors existed in the Prague-Smichov port; and that facilities 'may be extended during 1991, depending on the interest shown'.

One correspondent, describing the glories of Dresden, commented: 'Use of brown lignite coal produces quite disgusting pollution on the valley floors. The waterways lurk in the gloom at the bottom of all this; take a gas mask!' Not then knowing that such scare stories are largely apocryphal, we sadly deleted the delights of Prague from our itinerary. It was a consolation some months later to hear that by August maximum draught in the upper river had fallen to 0.9 m, so we might easily have become trapped.

Emerging from the cut below the Rothensee Lift entailed stemming a strong flow until a train of Polish barges had cleared the canal exit. With few buoys marking any channel in a broad expanse of water, we stared nervously at the echo-sounder, which showed a depth under the boat of between 0.6 m and 1.5 m. Confidence grew as *Avonbay* overhauled a Czech pushtow of coal barges. I chose not to consider what problems we might face if water levels had dropped when we came back ten weeks later.

Traffic lights at Niegripp guard Lock were red. The crew of a German pleasure boat relayed the information that a temporary stoppage had closed a lock farther up the line: 'As you are travelling to Berlin, you must instead go down the Elbe to Havelberg!' We studied the chart, calculating that such a change in plan would involve a further 79 nail-biting kilometres. Nothing so far had been over-alarming on the river; there remained sufficient time in our schedule to make this long diversion; best of all, I had been told that the lower River Havel was an outstandingly attractive waterway. Anyway, we appeared to have no choice. Apart from one moment when the depth coincided rather convincingly with our draught, we enjoyed a mainly trouble-free day. Interest was maintained by numerous sandy bays among the willows, occasional horse-drawn carts loaded with new-mown hay, and red-brick towns built well above the flood plain. It was all very much as described in C S Forester's *The Annie Marble in Germany* of 1930. Contented anglers and children swimming made us doubt that the Elbe really was the most polluted river in Europe.

Stopping for sightseeing depended on finding suitable deepwater moorings, and the possibilities were few. So, at K388, when the red-brick walls and turrets of Tangermünde appeared to port with a vertical harbour wall marked on our chart by an anchor symbol, we immediately decided to go ashore. Quite by chance, we had chosen one of the finest towns in east Germany, boasting the most intact encircling wall in the whole country. Scrambling through ancient fortifications, we arrived in a small park to be confronted by a statue of Kaiser Karl IV. He set up court here in 1373–8, when the town was briefly capital of the Holy Roman Empire.

Smoky two-stroke Trabants spluttered through cobbled streets where scores of carved and painted half-timbered houses were already benefiting from restoration after their long years of neglect. We replenished our galley stores, finding a good choice of fresh meat and vegetables in little 'western'-style supermarkets and on stalls outside the impressive fifteenth-century *Rathaus*. Prices were sometimes remarkable: 20 Pfennigs (8p) for a large bag of salt crystals. Trade with the west was represented by jars of new potatoes bottled in Maidenhead. Good-quality electrical goods filled other shops, presumably at prices within the reach of townsfolk. It was difficult not to imagine that this was an English provincial town of the 1940s, especially when we saw a horsecart filled with loose brown coal which was poured in a heap on to the pavement before being shovelled into the cellar of a private house.

Moving on, we encountered a curious form of captive car ferry near the pleasure craft harbour in Arneburg. Attached to a series of dinghies strung in line down the centre of the stream, it appeared to work as a slow-moving pendulum while the river flow pushed it from one shore to the other. As the ferry was tethered to starboard and still loading passengers, we passed to port of its line of boats. Suddenly, the skipper launched into mid-river, crossed our bows, and effectively trapped our exit with his cable. *Avonbay* braked hard in the powerful current, turned, surged upstream for several hundred metres and turned again, before we were clear of this inconsiderate vessel. We gathered on deck to yell Anglo-Saxon oaths and received a cheerful wave in return! It crossed my mind to suggest that he didn't know his arse from his Elbe, until I realised that this insult might lose a little in translation.

1938 design for a Mittelland Canal aqueduct over the Elbe at Rothensee. More than half a century after World War II brought construction to a halt, plans were announced in 1993 to improve navigation between the Mittelland and Berlin by completing the structure.

That incident apart, the waterway provided unexpectedly easy downstream navigation. Matters might have been very different at the end of the summer with reduced water levels; and under most conditions a long upriver journey would be tedious unless given greater reserves of power than *Avonbay* has available.

We turned off at K423, entered the mouth of the Havel, and lay for the night below the first lock. Our 'jetty' was a curious barge fitted with green-painted bungalow complete with TV aerial, stove pipe and living accommodation for canal maintenance staff. These craft are widely used in east Germany, enabling the workers to stay on site instead of returning home at the end of a day's labouring at lock stoppage or bank protection.

The Havel is a real gem. Rising in the province of Mecklenburg, it runs in a broad loop through Berlin, then westwards to the Elbe, where it has attained a width barely that of the Thames at Windsor. By late August I had navigated much of its considerable length. One unusual characteristic is that in this flat landscape it periodically broadens into huge lakes, often several kilometres across. Ideal for motor cruising or sailing, the Havel was just the kind of route I had hoped to discover in east Germany. Well buoyed, the lake sections nevertheless demand navigational skills rarely needed on inland waterways.

Avonbay worked through a massive lock and passed a marina filled with private boats. That these exist at all was the greatest surprise of the voyage. Traditionally built wooden cruisers, cabined sailing boats, canoes (often with sails or tiny outboards, angled in the manner of our long-vanished Atco boat impellers), restored steam tugs and folding motorised dinghies were often of pre-war origin. But by no means all: private ownership of boats and charming

Decorative brickwork in the town defences at Tangermünde.

waterside weekend cottages had obviously continued through 45 years of communist rule. For the lucky or intelligent East German citizen, life hadn't been at all bad – *and* they used to enjoy full employment!

To sail past Havelberg without stopping was a serious mistake, but it was difficult to launch into a shore excursion only half an hour after setting off from an overnight mooring. Doubtless there would be many similar little red-brick towns to discover. A huge network of waterways awaited our exploration, and time was already limited. Nevertheless, I regret not visiting the impressive twelfth-century St Marien's cathedral, towering over a sea of rooftops on the island where the core of the town is situated. Circumnavigation is possible by smaller motor cruisers.

The little willow-fringed river twisted through water meadows carpeted with drifts of wild flowers, its banks ablaze with yellow irises. Somehow, it was a very English landscape, not unlike the Great Ouse, set under broad East Anglian skies. Not much chance of meeting barges up here, we thought, just seconds before a 1500-tonne pushtow appeared round the next bend.

Frequent and well-signposted junctions with lesser streams would have provided days of dinghy investigation. A dozen alternatives were ignored in as many kilometres, when, in the village of Molkenberg, the word *Kahnschleuse* and a lock symbol on the chart prompted a detour along the parallel Gülper Havel. *Kahn*, according to the dictionary, was 'boat' or 'barge'. Did *Avonbay* qualify as either? It seemed not, for we grounded firmly a short way into the river mouth. We lowered the anchor and took to our inflatable. In this context, *Kahn* turned out to be a small punt or rowing boat. At the first corner, there was indeed a lock – a toy-sized DIY structure manually worked with single gates at each end of a chamber barely 12 m long and about 1.8 m wide. The summer was just sufficiently advanced to risk taking a swim in the agreeably clear water; inevitably, I then turned my attention to scrubbing the boat's hull. Lunch included a fat bunch of asparagus, purchased from the keeper at Garz Lock. Such examples of private enterprise were still rare. We approved of his produce, and were more than happy to pay him 6DM, a price that included several fresh hens' eggs. Easterners have something of a reputation for lack of initiative – even laziness – in the eyes of their western cousins. Where possible, we tried to reward all attempts to make an honest Pfennig. If service was sometimes slow or disinterested in bars and restaurants, we tried to remember that until recently there was little incentive to work any harder than was strictly necessary. Opportunities abound for the eastern entrepreneur: if they are not careful, others will capitalise on these possibilities, leaving the locals in menial jobs. While cruising in June, we repeatedly tried to eat out at waterside restaurants, often in the most idyllic situations, only to discover them closed for business. By August there was much more activity, but it just isn't realistic to run such an enterprise for an eight-week season!

Once more cruising up the main river, villages of market gardens, chimney stacks decorated with storks' nests, and small collections of pleasure craft, brought us through Grütz Lock and into the outskirts of Rathenow. Here, a series of channels suggested a diversion off the through route and into the town centre. This resulted in sightings of a refuse cart drawn by two horses in the fume-filled main shopping street – and a firmly closed *Stadtschleuse* ('town lock'). Careful study and translation of the chart should have told me that this backwater only provides access to the next reach of the Havel in July and August. A town in any European country appears in a fascinatingly different light when viewed from its backdoor waterways. Rathenow was no exception, for we gained a considerable insight into some extremely dilapidated housing. Some inhabited buildings were already in a state of partial collapse: for the only time during our cruise, I sensed angry resentment on the faces of these dejected residents as we slowly cruised past. Probably our little world seemed altogether more agreeable than their immediate surroundings.

Avonbay backtracked, worked through a large *Hauptschleuse* ('main lock'), and completed a circuit of the town by approaching the upstream side of the *Stadtschleuse*. We now found ourselves in a much more affluent and pleasant district. Our passage was noted with interest and pleasure by people waving from their waterside gardens. Rarely would so large a vessel as *Avonbay* have ventured up this backwater which was normally frequented by canoes, rowing boats and open launches. That a brass band was giving a concert from the roof of the church tower was perhaps coincidental, although we pretended that the performance had been staged to mark our arrival.

One stunning river reach followed another. To do justice to the Lower Havel, a fortnight would hardly be enough – not to forget equal periods of time for exploring Greater Berlin, the Spree and Dahme, the Upper Havel and then several months in the Mecklenburg Lakes. An entire long summer would serve as a mere introduction to all these delights.

On seeing a riverside eating house in Milow and aware that little close contact had yet been made with the locals, we prepared to come alongside a small wooden jetty. The proprietor ran across his lawn to assist. By this time, *Avonbay* had settled on a gravel bed well offshore, so we devised a complicated system of anchors, lines and gangplank to prevent propeller damage, should a barge come sweeping past. Our first east German hostelry appeared to be boat club, bar and restaurant.

Intense interest was aroused by the trio who had arrived in a blue and white ship from England. Our host told us that he had only lately set up in business, renting the premises from the local council. He was both jolly and kind, spoke no English, and without delay provided us with a young man as interpreter. Helmut seemed quite content to join us at a table, where we plied him with a succession of drinks. He was very forthcoming, which was precisely what we wanted. He asked endless questions about the purpose of our voyage, the value of our boat, and then the (anticipated) enquiry as to how much money we earned. Bemused by his country's changed situation, he was obviously concerned for its future. 'I work in a polyester production factory,' he told us. 'To compete with western companies like BASF, employees have already been reduced from 6000 to 2000 and they say this is still not enough.'

Unsure if he was a labourer or a qualified scientist, we asked: 'Are you a chemist?' He looked startled and answered: 'Neither left nor right, but we don't talk about communism any more!' Sensing that this linguistic misunderstanding could lead into deep water, I changed the subject. We dined remarkably well on soup and a substantial meat dish. Including liberal drinks for the four of us, the bill amounted to a derisory 25DM – about one-third of the cost in west Berlin.

Days had passed since I had telephoned England, and by now there were several reasons why I needed to speak to my office. Street kiosks were clearly incapable of international connections, so I tried the little post office in Pritzerbe. Almost certainly no one had *ever* tried to ring Britain from there. After several abortive attempts by the elderly counter clerk, I began dialling for myself. Eventually I got through to a voice apparently speaking Russian, but that was the limit of my success. Neither surprise nor regret could be detected on the features of Frau Telecom. No further efforts were wasted on the east German phone system for it appeared that connections between east and west Berlin were regarded as little short of miraculous. For the time being, *Avonbay* would have to remain incommunicado.

Until now, the Havel had behaved like most normal rivers. After Pritzerbe we were to begin an association with lakes large and small, each with their

Horse-power at work hauling a refuse cart, Rathenow.

own distinct character. Those on main through routes, while rarely busy with other boats except within the confines of Berlin, generally featured a scattering of craft. But when we chose to stray into a sheltered bay or turn up a 'dead-end' arm, an expanse of water would open up that was frequently ours alone to enjoy. Soon I was to lose count of the number of these wonderful meres over which *Avonbay* travelled. Later calculations showed that my east German voyages included nearly a hundred. Perhaps three times as many remain for discovery on another visit. The scope for leisure development is so immense that it is nearly impossible to imagine that the magic can ever be spoiled. Certainly steps will have to be taken to prevent the most crass commercialism, although I think it unlikely that the lakes of east Germany will ever degenerate into a Norfolk Broads.

First came an unnamed 17 km expanse of water dotted with fish farms in floating cages. This in turn led to the wider Plauer See, where periodic compass checks were useful to confirm our position. A turn to starboard would have found us in the Elbe–Havel Canal and the route we had expected to be cruising several days before. We overtook a passenger-carrying steam tug, pouring clouds of black smoke from an exceptionally tall funnel, and made for the lake's north-east corner and the Silo Canal which skirts one side of the city of Brandenburg. A notice at its entrance seemed to say that this waterway was reserved for commercial traffic, a fact that was confirmed by the crew of a west Berlin motor cruiser, so we headed south and found ourselves once more in a portion of the Havel that looked just like a river again. All pleasure boats were directed to a small lock built in Brandenburg's

Low headroom beneath the guillotine gate of Brandenburg's pleasure boat lock.

former moat. Guillotine gates lifted just sufficiently for us to pass, and ahead was a splendid waterside tower, part of the ancient fortifications. Torrential rain fell, and much amplified pop music issued from a funfair in a tree-shaded park.

A brief inspection showed that Brandenburg had reached a state of advanced neglect. Narrow streets of potentially beautiful houses were in ruins, with doors and windows hanging drunkenly on their hinges and clumps of grass colonising roofs and guttering. A good third were open to the elements and wore banners across their carved stone doorways bearing the enigmatic legend: *Bis bald, alte Haus* ('See you soon, old house'), indicating some form of municipal rescue operation. The most flourishing part of town is built in deathly 1950s concrete. Poor historic Brandenburg! I was unaware at the time that the communists had built East Germany's largest steel works here, hence the hideous and soulless blocks of apartments for the workers. It is claimed that an annual 9000 tonnes of heavy metal dust pours into the atmosphere and, when it rains, a film of black, greasy grime descends from the sky. To be truthful, this unappealing picture remained hidden from us. It merely seemed that the once proud Prussian city had fallen on hard times.

Near our temporary mooring was a deserted little boatyard, a veritable treasure store of rusting vintage marine engines, ancient canoes and little wooden carts on cast-iron wheels. All of them were potential museum exhibits, although it seemed that no one appreciated their value.

That evening, we continued for about 12 km up the Havel, where pleasure craft activity increased considerably as the river widened to form lakes and alternative channels wriggled in and out of each bank. With no suitable mooring on *terra firma* evident, we dropped anchor for the night in a corner of the Trebelsee (lake), 200 m offshore. There was every prospect of arriving in Berlin the next day, so *Avonbay*'s decks and superstructure were carefully scrubbed and nameplates, horn and searchlight treated to a generous dose of Brasso. Berliners had seen few British cruisers for a long while: we intended to sparkle for our arrival.

By early morning a fresh wind had sprung up. Still half asleep, I parted the curtain over my bunk and saw that we had moved a considerable distance in the night: the remains of a dead tree lying in shallow water were now worryingly close. A quick check on the echo-sounder confirmed that we had nearly been driven aground. Rapid work on the anchor winch soon found us mobile again and following the Sacrow Canal towards the city of Potsdam. Here we refuelled and watered at a bunker station operated by the east German Weisse Flotte passenger boat company. To our great amusement, the skipper of one large vessel ran astern at high speed to collide with his own jetty. Our own, fortunately rare, navigational mishaps paled into complete insignificance. Just 13 days out from Strasbourg, *Avonbay* had achieved what had so recently seemed to be the impossible. We were now ready to explore Berlin.

7 Berlin

Water and Electricity join forces in a strange illustration from the 1906 album produced to mark the opening of Berlin's Teltow Canal. Hydro-electric plants were an important feature of the enterprise.

Noon on a hot, sunny Sunday in mid-June. Here we were, in the most affluent, gilded, self-confident city of Europe. The Havel had expanded into a vast lake, the Wannsee: 13 km of forest-fringed watery expanse. Barge-tows chugged purposefully up a central channel, and all around it seemed as if the entire population was afloat in passenger boats, sailing cruisers, rowing eights, canoes and hideously ostentatious fast motor cruisers. While the city's western sector had remained an island of capitalism in a sea of bleak communism, its 114 km of navigations were thronged with no fewer than 55 000 pleasure craft, considerably more than twice the number registered on the Upper Thames. That day, most of them appeared to be in use. It was hardly surprising that tempers were reaching breaking point as large sailing boats impudently tacked across our bows while we weaved an erratic course in the almost hopeless effort to avoid them. With some relief, we pulled into the jetties of a yacht club at Kladow and went ashore in search of drinks and a telephone.

My first visit, just over two years earlier, was under very different circumstances. June, John and I, never expecting to come here in our own boat, were guests of Sir Michael and Lady Henrietta Burton for a long weekend's tour of the waterways. Under the title of British Minister, Michael was the UK's leading civilian in Berlin, a form of Ambassador, who shared a sort of peace-keeping role with the British Army, headed by Major General Sir Robert Corbett. West Berlin, divided after the Second World War into

British, American and French sectors, had continued for 40 years to accept this curious 'occupation' force, established as a deterrent to the Russians. West Berlin had risen in spectacular style from the ashes of 1945, as was evident from the lavish lobster barbecue party to which we were invited one evening. Our host, a leading film producer, held court at his waterside mansion where guests included tennis champion Steffi Graf and several government ministers.

We worked hard to absorb as many sights as possible: André Previn conducting the Berlin Symphony; the Europa Shopping Centre and the luxury-filled Kaufhaus des Westens department store; a collection of antique gas street lamps that twinkled attractively in the dusk at the Tiergarten; Brandenburg Gate, symbol of the Divided City; and Frederick the Great's Charlottenburg Palace. There was an excursion into East Germany by ambassadorial mini-bus, for which we carried special British Military Government passes. They were issued with strict instructions that they should be shown to border guards at Checkpoint Charlie, while keeping the vehicle's windows tightly closed. Many of the Prussian capital's finest buildings, monuments and museums were situated in the Russian sector, where we walked through unexpectedly pleasant streets near the Nikolai-Kirche and then discovered unbelievable decay and desolation several blocks away. East German guards goose-stepped at the Tomb of the Unknown Soldier near the once-fashionable Unter den Linden. Somewhere on the River Spree, we watched a tug negotiate a lock, never suspecting that *Avonbay* would pass through two years later.

The highlight and chief purpose of our visit was a tour of West Berlin's rivers, lakes and canals, for which General Corbett's smart motor cruiser *Sea Horse* was placed at our disposal, complete with the Burtons' butler and a uniformed army crew. A framed portrait on board showed that Queen Elizabeth the Queen Mother had been an earlier passenger. *Sea Horse*'s skipper experienced some difficulty in threading his way through the maze of city navigations: not surprisingly, for we canal enthusiasts wished to see commercial docks and less salubrious byways not normally on the itinerary of visiting dignitaries. When it was our turn to explore in *Avonbay*, I found similar problems in interpreting the chart and to this day I have a slightly sketchy mental picture of Berlin's watery geography.

A fantasy castle, rising from the trees of *Pfaueninsel* ('Peacock Island'), was built in the late eighteenth century as a romantic retreat for Frederick William II and his mistress, Countess Lichtenau. This was shortly followed by the Byzantine-style Heilandskirche at Sacrow. This technically remained in West Berlin, but thanks to the snaking line of the Wall it was approachable only by boat. Some 24 km of the 161 km Berlin Wall rose from the banks of navigations. Then came the steel girders of Glienicker Bridge, a famous crossing point, decorated with Russian flags and a familiar spy-exchange location of many cinema epics. Beyond, warning signs in English and German showed where the border lay across the centre of a lake. *Sea Horse* attracted

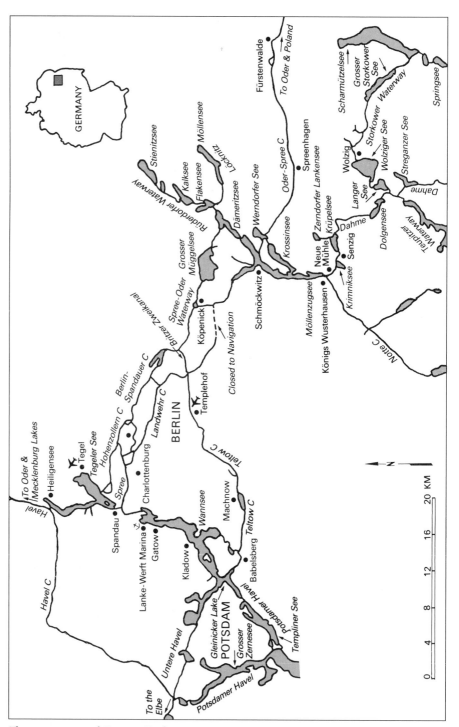

The waterways of Greater Berlin.

the hostile attention of a grey patrol launch that hovered on the other side of the line. It was clear that our diplomatic immunity would not be much use against these armed guards, had we strayed into 'enemy' territory.

Throbbing with affluence, with West Berliners at play on the water, relaxing on the Wannsee's huge artificial 'beach' (the largest in Europe) or strolling in the gardens of sumptuous lakeside houses, the city seemed oddly claustrophobic. It appeared that residents rarely made trips through East Germany to the west and then only in sealed trains or via the neutral autobahn corridor. Even the aircraft that brought us in was compelled to fly across the DDR at exactly 3048 m (10 000 ft) – the normal cruising height of airliners when regulations were formulated in the 1940s.

West Berlin put on a brave face but could never ignore its siege-like situation or the frightening consequences of an escalation of the Cold War.

Before leaving, we made a final visit to the banks of the Spree, close to the Reichstag parliament building. A sadly pathetic row of wooden crosses served as memorials to several dozen East Germans, shot while attempting to swim to freedom across the narrow river that divided the two nations. Some refugees had actually been hauled into patrol boats, unable to drag themselves to safety up the sheer quayside. We suggested to Michael that the West Berlin authorities should install steel ladders at this point and so save lives. To our delight, a photograph in *The Daily Telegraph* some weeks later showed that our idea had been implemented.

While movement of pleasure craft between East and West was strictly forbidden, there was a constant exchange of barge cargoes – those from the DDR presumably manned by carefully screened and monitored crews. Among inland ports in Germany, the Westhafen was second only to Duisburg-Ruhrort. A major consignment was the transport of scrap metal to the East for processing and subsequent re-sale to the West.

Navigable waterways in Berlin date back to the mid-sixteenth century when the first pound lock was constructed on the Spree, downstream of the Mühlendamm. Thereafter, gradual development was to provide links to the Oder in the east and the Elbe, westwards. By the mid-eighteenth century the city was at the centre of a waterway 'cross', with barge transportation facilities to Russia. But the Golden Age of canal building in Berlin was to come after the middle of the nineteenth century. Important new routes included the Berlin–Spandau Canal of 1859 and the 38 km-long Teltow Canal, opened in 1905, running from the Lower Havel to the Spree near Köpenick. Problems in operating the waterways of West Berlin were not as great as might be supposed during the years of division, although various improvements that would have greatly assisted traffic generated in the western sector were never carried out by the east sector. Surprisingly, Berlin's worst bottleneck, the single chamber at Spandau Lock, confidently expected to be duplicated as long ago as 1970, remains to this day.

Fleets of sizeable passenger craft operate throughout the system, enabling extensive exploration to be made without your own boat. Without doubt, the most popular vessel is *Moby Dick*, built in the form of a massive, motorised silver whale. Its approach is signalled by a gaping 'mouth', into which the forward saloon's windows have been inserted. The rear deck terminates in a large curving tail. If five craft are waiting for customers at a Berlin jetty, *Moby Dick* will always be full to capacity, while the others remain half empty! Careful study of timetables would make long cruises possible, even into the more isolated Mecklenburg Lakes. Since German reunification, a number of hire-cruiser firms have also been established; unlike most waterways of the former Federal Republic, clients do not require navigational qualifications (see Appendix 1).

The plan was now to investigate as much of the network of waterways within Greater Berlin as possible, including an extensive system outside the city limits. This Dahme Waterstrasse, with its chain of lakes, looked tempting on the chart even if there was considerable doubt that we could pass under certain low bridges. Clearly, the overcrowded, albeit extremely beautiful, Wannsee was not a suitable place for peaceful cruising on a Sunday afternoon. Halfway up the great lake, a turn was made into the Grosse Wannsee, at the southern end of which 4 km of Prinz-Friedrich-Leopold Canal would take us to the Teltow Canal. This link, although not markedly narrow, appeared to work on a one-way system, with craft travelling in our direction having right of entry during the first 20 minutes of each hour. While pondering whether we should start or not, a large cruiser flying the American stars and stripes called out that we could proceed.

Immaculate lawns, sizeable thatched houses and elegant craft on garden moorings all pointed to this area being a prime residential district. It had come as a considerable surprise to discover just how much of Berlin comprised parkland, woods and water.

On joining the Teltow Canal, we began our passage along the southern boundary of the city. While pleasant, this was a decidedly commercial transport route and (to our relief) almost deserted by pleasure seekers. Consulting the chart, we found that a substantial distance lay in former eastern territory, including Klein-Machnow Lock and a little lake just beyond. The old border then ran along the waterway's starboard bank for a time, before we returned entirely to the west for the last 13 km. We invented a fascinating game, testing each other as to exactly where the border had been drawn. Affluence or dereliction of buildings were useful clues; most remnants of the Berlin Wall itself had already vanished, leaving a wide swathe of No Man's Land through which scores of family groups, pushing prams or walking dogs, were taking a defiant Sunday stroll, exercising rights where they so recently risked being shot. The barbed wire had all been removed, but concrete floodlight standards and watchtowers are likely to remain for a while. One ugly structure was now converted into an informal restaurant. What could the Russian soldiers, still based in this area, now be thinking? An important benefit of the Wall was that it had stifled any form of development for nearly three decades, creating a valuable wildlife habitat –

much of which will be retained as a linear nature reserve.

During the years of division, the canal had been closed at the eastern enclave of Machnow Locks. We approached the triplicated chambers, where top and bottom sets of guillotine gates were covered by lofty barn-like structures, dating from the line's completion in 1905. All was suspiciously quiet, so we moored in order to find a keeper. He was young, remarkably pleasant, spoke better English than I spoke German, and asked if we realised that the locks were officially closed on Sunday afternoons. 'But I can let you through,' he added. 'It's all the same to me!' The concept of 'It's more than my job's worth' seemed quite unknown. We repaid his helpful attitude with a suitable financial reward.

Over the years, a handful of encounters with some especially exciting working boats will long remain in my memory: seeing a riotously decorated pair of Blue Line narrow boats work north up the Grand Union at Uxbridge, one sunny evening in the summer of 1966; meeting the very last horsedrawn *berrichon* barge at Le Guétin aqueduct on France's Canal latéral à la Loire two years later; and then there was a magnificent two-masted square rigger which appeared like a phantom in the heat haze of the Baltic islands off the Mem entrance to the Göta Canal in the early summer of 1984. Now, we overhauled a deeply laden motorised sand barge, 40 m × 4.6 m, sidedecks awash. Ticking along, with the slow beat of a large, archaic semi-diesel engine, she was obviously very ancient and would elsewhere have been consigned to the breaker's yard long before. Her superstructure shone in immaculate dark brown and cream paint, while the pipe-smoking skipper, standing at a wheel on the open stern deck, was the very picture of contentment. That freight traffic thrives on these routes is one of the leading attractions.

Some 3 km of Britzer Zweigkanal brought us to the Spree–Oder Wasserstrasse, leading due east to the Polish border at Fürstenberg. Very wide and at first lined with old-fashioned dumb barges fitted with giant tiller-steered wooden rudders, this was to be the start of a long period back in the east. A concrete grandstand (perhaps the setting for the 1936 Berlin Olympic rowing events?), yacht and barge building yards, innumerable sailing clubs and riverside restaurants all indicated that pre-war prosperity had somehow remained intact. Several times we stopped to investigate eating establishments, including one with a man-sized wine jug perched on the end of its jetty. Some of the larger concerns had dozens of tables arranged on pleasant lawns. Not one of them was open for business on this Sunday evening in mid-summer: why this should have been so remains a complete mystery.

Coming into Köpenick, a small fleet of substantial naval cruisers was moored at the Berlin Yacht Werft. We decided now to head south, leaving the rest of the Spree until later. The new waterway was identified as the River Dahme; it gradually widened to become lost in a broad, elongated lake called the Langersee. This was utterly charming, packed with (moored) boats and densely wooded. Somewhere near Karolinenhof, we found a tree-covered island that appeared perfect for the night's mooring. Provided no other boats arrive after you have made fast, an island can seem just like a private kingdom. I have always sought out rivery islands, from my earliest explorations of the Upper Thames as a 14-year-old when motorised camping dinghy *Chérie* often colonised the islands in Cliveden Reach, upstream of Maidenhead. Another equally romantic but quite different island mooring was to be found 30 years later: a tamarisk-covered sand bar in the lonely Camargue reaches of the Petit Rhône. Sadly, on this occasion, we grounded while still a boat's length offshore, so instead we hooked on to a sailing club jetty on the Zeuthener See section of the Dahme Wasserstrasse. That night, a magnificent deep-red sunset made me think that tomorrow would bring the heatwave that had so far eluded us. In reality, it turned out to be our gloomiest and most rain-filled day to date!

Even the weather, though, could not conceal the charms of our route. After a junction in Königs Wusterhausen, we left all commercial traffic behind and entered a world that was more remote, with lower bridges, shallower channels and much smaller locks, generally 41 m × 5.3 m. With her air draught of about 3.2 m and a water draught of 1.3 m, *Avonbay* remained easily within the limits: had we attempted to explore every available backwater, we would have discovered that some bridges offered a clearance of only 1.2 m and the Upper Spree towards Lübbenau is just 1 m deep in places. Given more time, I could easily have been persuaded to leave *Avonbay* in the safe keeping of a boatyard and continue with dinghy and outboard into a watery maze extending southwards to Cottbus. Known as the Spree-wald, this is a land of water lilies, overhead arches of alders, and picturesque little wooden drawbridges. All is within an easy three-days cruising from central Berlin.

Neue Mühle ('New Mill') Lock was typical of a number we were to use on the smaller east German waterways, now almost exclusively reserved for pleasure craft. With the exception of just one, all were electrically worked by friendly keepers and were invariably ready for use within moments of our arrival. The lower approach to this example was spanned by a sizeable bascule bridge. After we had risen to the upper level, we moored to a deserted landing stage, close to a long row of well-maintained varnished sailing dinghies. As a quick alternative to the lock, small craft could be hauled up a twin-track railway, equipped with little wheeled cradles.

Unexpectedly high standards of canal maintenance included use of bundles of larch poles, arranged horizontally against timber uprights for bank protection. Plastic sheeting on top, covered with a layer of turf, produced an environmentally sensitive finish. Using these low-cost materials, available in bulk in the immediate area, struck us as an excellent idea.

Now came a whole series of lakes, interconnected by winding river sections where small holiday houses usually had a boat at the end of their gardens. How could all this have so recently been the polluted, repressive, grey land of communism? Such properties in England would have been highly sought after, with prices to match. And so the Krimnicksee was followed by the Krüpelsee, Dolgensee, Langersee and extensive Wolzigersee, each well buoyed but sometimes providing much confusion as we searched the wooded shores for an exit into the next portion of linking canal. Diamond-shaped leading marks were frequently obscured in beds of tall reeds, but with 3 m of water generally under our keel, minor navigational errors were unlikely to endanger *Avonbay*.

We reached the western end of the Storkower Canal in torrential rain. Somehow it seemed pointless to continue under these conditions, so we tied to a passenger boat jetty on the edge of Wolzig village, put on waterproof suits, and explored the puddle-filled streets. At one newly opened supermarket the proprietor laid on a guided tour of his shelves, patently unaware that such a friendly service to customers would be unthinkable in western food stores. Our arrival was clearly noted with great excitement! The latter part of the afternoon was usefully filled with routine engine maintenance, including giving the hard-worked Leylands their first oil change since leaving France.

A small restaurant/café, Zum Grüne Baum, was open for business. Over our dinner of asparagus soup, and the nearly obligatory pork steaks and ice cream, our 35-year-old hostess, shyly speaking in hesitant English, was discussing her daughters' education. The 16-year-old learned Russian as her first foreign language, whereas her sister of 11 was soon to begin English, with French as an optional extra. It appeared that east German schools were awash with unemployable Russian teachers.

Now, with only three days remaining before our departure for England, we retraced our route up the Dahme, to enter 'new' water once more in the Grosser Zug and Krossinsee. These Berlin explorations seemed confusingly complicated at the time, but merely served as very elementary practice for infinitely more taxing chart work, which was required some weeks later in Mecklenburg.

Jim was seated outside, banned from the wheelhouse by Mig and me on the grounds that it would be selfish not to share his concertina practice with the local population. Initially, we assumed that the elderly man frantically waving a white handkerchief from his waterfront garden was expressing musical approval. But when he began to shout (in an amicable manner), we reversed, came alongside, and then introduced ourselves. With tear-filled eyes, our friend explained that he had never expected to see an English boat in Berlin. As a boy in the late 1920s, he had once stayed with a London family; in spite of all that subsequently happened, he retained a deep love for the British. It was an emotional encounter.

Heading westwards again for a brief spell on the Spree–Oder Wasserstrasse, much reduced speed was necessary as we approached the stern of a heavily laden pushtow piled high with brown lignite. Once more, the waterway widened; we turned north-east into the Seddinsee and then west again along the Muggelspree, which was lined with astonishingly affluent houses in an area known as Neu Venedig ('New Venice'). In the tree-shaded grounds of one house, we noticed with amusement the conical thatched roof built to protect an elaborate barbecue. Admittedly, there was a spark arrester halfway up the central chimney, but this form of construction did seem to constitute a serious fire risk.

Very choppy conditions on the 4 km Grosser Muggelsee made us realise that windy weather demanded respect in such wide waters. Spray crashed on to the deck, so much so that at times we briefly lost sight in the waves of the police launch that was following our course.

Familiar waters through Köpenick took us as far as a major checkpoint at the former border. Pleasure boats were directed into one of a series of channels formed by wooden dolphins. Obviously this was where searching questions had once been asked of barge crews. We had intended to continue via the Berlin–Spandau Ship Canal; signs, however, directed *Sportboot* traffic into the Landwehr Canal and through Oberschleuse Lock. This route appeared to be taking us into the west Berlin city centre, although precisely where we would end up became mainly guesswork. I had wanted to cruise directly past the great Reichstag building, but somehow we never discovered a permitted method of achieving this.

A securing pin in *Avonbay*'s gear controls snapped by the junction of the Landwehr and Neuköllner Canals. With the choice of tying up either in the former east or west sectors, we chose the banks of a small public park in the west. Here Jim clamped the boat's vice on the back of a cast-iron seat, and crafted a replacement pin from a rod of stainless steel. Intended only as a temporary repair, it was to last intact until we were on the Dutch Maas the following autumn. In our secluded corner of the park, filled with uninhibited sunbathers and strollers enjoying a warm afternoon, we were somewhat astonished at the amorous activities of a group of young people. Their antics would only have been possible in Paris, long after dusk had cast a discrete shadow over the quays of the Seine. But this was in broad daylight, albeit shielded from the gaze of passers-by – if not from those aboard an inconsiderately moored pleasure boat! One young lady, presumably in the interests of preventing her dress from being marked by the damp grass, removed it altogether and suspended it neatly from a convenient branch. How very practical the Germans are!

Once more under way, the tree-lined urban waterway ahead, extensively rebuilt towards the end of the nineteenth century, featured a succession of decorative bridges in carved stone and iron, solidly constructed mansions sprouting turrets and balconies, and a number of rather dubious characters who had gravitated to the water's edge for an evening's serious consumption of alcohol. Overnight moorings would need to be chosen with some care, for this is a part of the Berlin network where pleasure craft facilities are scarce. A bosky reach passing through the zoo seemed to offer possibilities. When, to our surprise, the Unterschleuse (lock) opened to admit a passenger vessel containing several dozen noisy gentlemen, a five-piece band and an enthusiastic belly dancer, *Avonbay*, intrigued, followed them in. We were more than a little annoyed to be charged 25DM for 'after hours' use of the lock!

Uncertain of how safe we would be from the attentions of uninvited guests on this mid-summer evening, we found perfect security well offshore in the Charlottenburger Verbindungs Canal. Bow and stern lines were fixed to a widely spaced pair of steel piles, doubtless intended for the use of freight barges. Undisturbed sleep was thus assured, for no one but a determined swimmer could reach us here. Stupidly, our old friends the west German *Wasserpolizei* had not been included in these calculations. Late dinner arrived on the saloon table at 11 pm, neatly coinciding with instructions from a

Brandenburg Gate, once symbol of divided Berlin, seen here in an engraving made in 1878.

police launch to move on without delay! We now knew better than to ask why mooring was *verboten*. Ordered to go alongside a (silted and thoroughly unsuitable) quay opposite, we tied to a pair of tree stumps only to be awoken at 7.30 am by the deafening whine of a chain saw. A gang of workmen were attempting to extract our 'bollards', with *Avonbay*'s lines still attached!

The morning passed quickly, as we each adopted the roles of ship's carpenter, painter and cleaner. Our chosen harbour, where the boat would now rest for seven weeks, was reputedly a very high-class concern: we British had standards to maintain. A final lock at Charlottenburg, 6 km of the Spree to Spandau, and a short run down the Havel to the upper Wannsee, saw the completion of a circuit that had enabled us to explore the majority of waterways in Greater Berlin. Not yet an expert, I was nevertheless starting to become familiar with this wonderful watery labyrinth.

Months earlier, our friends the British Minister and Herr Norman Halfar, Director of west Berlin Water Transport, had both suggested the Marina Lanke-Werft as a safe haven until August. Our reception was most cordial, with negotiations conducted in English. In this agreeable residential suburb of Gatow, we were an easy bus ride from the shops and city centre. But I did wonder how 1000DM could be justified for the planned 50-day stay. I now know that boatyards in the east provide similar facilities at a much reduced cost. Yet Lanke-Werft's several hundred berths were full with (presumably satisfied) clients' boats. So full, in fact, that we were directed to a very vulnerable jetty directly alongside the approach to a boating club next door; considerable skill would be needed if cruisers were to come off the lake under full sail and avoid damaging us. The marina suggested we left our British ensign flying, perhaps to intimidate anyone so ill-advised as to complain about our presence; the UK remains very popular with most west Berliners. This would have contravened all rules of flag etiquette and anyway could have subjected our new and expensive flag to unnecessary weathering. When we returned, *Avonbay* had been removed to a less contentious mooring.

After a final day of Berlin sightseeing ashore, we set off by taxi, trains and then taxi again to recover my car from near Strasbourg. This gruelling exercise, much of it at slow speed along decayed railway tracks, lasted 13 hours, compared with the 13 days by water. East Germany had far exceeded expectations, but even more enchanting cruising was yet to come.

Spandau is famous three times over: it has the largest and most complete fortress in Europe; its prison held Rudolph Hess, as sole resident until his death in 1987; and Spandau's lock is a notorious bottleneck.

When *Avonbay* arrived in this north-east corner of Berlin, we were jubilant that we had just refilled two French gas cylinders and one Dutch one at a nearby Shell bunkering station. This meant that we could avoid buying the expensive German bottles. Our empties were placed on a sturdy weighing machine, hoses connected from a tank, and quick calculations made regarding the quantity of butane purchased. In all our European voyages, we had never before encountered this system.

Two days earlier, on 9 August, Henrietta Burton had generously collected June, Evelyn and me at Tegel Airport in the British ambassadorial Jaguar. Three and a half hours after leaving Heathrow we were on board our cruiser, bringing us to the startling conclusion that you could easily fly to Berlin for a weekend's boating and be back at work in England the following Monday morning!

First, there was the question of finding galley supplies, which were eventually taxied from a supermarket several kilometres away in the Heerstrasse. Next we travelled into the city to give Evie her first taste of Berlin: the Brandenburg Gate, shops along the Ku'damm, and the head of Nefertiti in the Ägyptisches Museum.

A schedule of 12 days had been set aside for a cruise northwards to explore as much as possible of the famed Mecklenburg Lakes, before coming back to Berlin where John would join us for the first leg of the long voyage back to the Rhine.

So, on a hot Sunday afternoon, we presented ourselves at Spandau Lock. Several Czech, Polish and German inland ships were waiting to pass the shallow 67 m × 10 m chamber – as were two passenger vessels, half-a-dozen little cruisers, and a swarm of rowing fours and canoes. It was useless to envy the ease with which portable craft were quickly hauled up to the upper level on a miniature railway. Priority traffic – barges and passenger carriers – continually jumped the queue, generally leaving space at the back of the lock for newly arrived cruisers. But there was never enough room for *Avonbay*'s 11 m. We watched three lockfuls disappear; eventually, when the keeper seemed to wave us in, we charged forward, only to be greeted by a deafening chorus of '*Nein, nein, nein!*' Yet another tripping boat took our place as we retreated ignominiously and were at last admitted on the fifth working. Ahead, the river broadened into a busy lake, the Spandauer Havel. Our chart showed how the old east/west border had lain up the centre of the waterway. This was readily confirmed by numerous boat club moorings to starboard (in former West Berlin), while the other side was deserted woodland with an occasional derelict factory. It had lately been designated a nature reserve.

Now on the Havel–Oder Wasserstrasse, at Hennigsdorf came the only bad case of antiquated and polluting industry that we were to encounter throughout our east German travels. Chimneys belching smoke created a thick fog at water level, and numerous barges filled with scrap metal were being unloaded by cranes from which disc-shaped electro-magnets were slung.

Had it been a little later in the evening, we might have stopped at the Lehnitzsee, a long and broad lake that is fringed by boat clubs and some promising-looking restaurants. A lock loomed up at Lehnitz. According to the chart, we would only be allowed to pass in the company of a commercial vessel. This seemed improbable at such a time on a Sunday. VHF radio communication had yet to reach east German locks; I walked ashore to speak in person to the keeper, but was frustrated by an impenetrable, locked gate.

Suddenly, the guillotine rose to release a single barge and before we had time to move into the chamber, it fell once more, only to lift within a few minutes. The lights changed to green, so *Avonbay*, along with a small, open launch, rapidly entered and rose to the upper level. There, we discovered the reason for our being worked through. No fewer than four barges carrying coal and gravel were approaching, destination Berlin.

The lady keeper spoke to us over her loud speaker, but I was unable to follow a single word! From her viewpoint, our British flag was invisible; even if she had seen it, I doubt if the blue ensign would have signified our nationality. There were occasions when it was distinctly disadvantageous to be treated just like a German pleasure boat. This was the moment when I hunted through the flag locker for our pilot-jack, a virtually obsolete white square with union flag at its centre. From then on, this attractive device fluttered on our bows, instantly identifying our country of origin. No more did disembodied loud speakers address us in rapid German – indeed, on rare occasions we were even spoken to in English. On the Thames, irate lock keepers have greeted this flag with a sarcastic 'Got the Queen on board, then?', oblivious of the fact that British flag etiquette allows it to be flown under two specific circumstances: if dressed over all (as we would be for the Grand Opening of the Rhine–Main–Danube Canal in Bavaria), or alternatively when signalling 'I am seeking an English-speaking pilot'. We chose to use our pilot-jack with this latter purpose in mind. More than a year later, Geoff Bradshaw, Chairman of the Dutch Barge Association, supplied me with written evidence from the Flag Institute and the Ministry of Defence, both agreeing that use of this flag is quite appropriate as a means of identifying the nationality of a British vessel when travelling on European inland waterways.

Sandy banks, pine forests and an ever-present possibility of meeting wild boar brought us to a junction with the Upper Havel Navigation, where steel dolphins provided a secure stopping place for the night. An important decision had now to be made. To continue down the Havel–Oder offered the prospect of running to the border with Poland, so adding another country to the seven already visited by *Avonbay*, but, equally exciting, 38 km of level water would bring us to the great Niederfinow boat lift of 1934. With its 85 m × 12 m caisson, rising a mighty 36 m, such a diversion would have taken little more than a long day. At that time, though, I hardly appreciated the significance of the structure, having researched our route into Mecklenburg with rather greater care. With 2434 km of inland waterways in east Germany, in excess of 120 locks and two vertical lifts, we had to be selective. Niederfinow awaits discovery another year.

8 *Mecklenburg Wonderland*

Rheinsberg Schloss, with Doughty's wherry Gipsy.

Now that a decision had been made to forsake commercial barge routes and take to waterways used solely for pleasure, we were prepared for a sharp deterioration in maintenance standards. Quite possibly, no boat as deep-draughted as *Avonbay* had penetrated the Obere–Havel Wasserstrasse for several decades. A succession of distinct navigations comprise this line, beginning with the short Malzer Canal. Soon we reached Liebenwalde Lock, a smart, electrified structure, $51.3\,m \times 10.5\,m$, open to traffic between 6 am and 8 pm (7 am to 6 pm at weekends). There was no question of us waiting until the keeper had discovered some obscure reason for not working us through. The gates opened instantly, admitting both us and a smart little cabined sloop with a pale, varnished hull. As she was flying no ensign, we assumed her to be from east Germany: generally, it was only residents of the onetime FRG that displayed any national allegiance.

Early in the morning, on a bright and sunny day in mid-summer, we decided to tie up for a shore excursion in the little town of Liebenwalde. Our first attempt to stop by a bridge was frustrated by an inability to gain access to the main road. Outlying farm buildings soon gave way to a grassy square by a large cream-painted church (locked) and an elegant brick *Rathaus* with wooden portico. Several shops and the premises of various craftsmen shyly displayed small boards, indicating the trade that was carried on there. But

not a single advertisement hoarding, neon sign, parking meter or any hint
of 1991 spoiled the cobbled streets. Most buildings didn't seem to have seen
fresh paint in a long while, although one sparkled in a newly applied blue
and white colour scheme; outside, the owner's smart Mercedes contrasted
strongly with a handful of Trabants and Wartburgs. It was clear that
westerners had begun to move in. At the time of reunification, a sizeable
family house in the east could be purchased for just one month's salary in
the west. Within easy commuting distance of Berlin, Liebenwalde was ripe
for gentrification.

Maintenance workers using modern equipment were dredging along the
next reach. Our confidence grew as we found that it was possible to come
alongside the banks virtually anywhere we chose. This little-known route
was in much better order than many heavily used canals in England!

Although flanked on each side by clusters of flooded clay pits and a number
of brickworks chimneys, the next town, Zehdenick, was extremely attractive,
with a terrace of well-decorated houses overlooking the broad millpond by a
lock. Frau lock keeper fussed around us in a thoroughly chatty fashion,
telling me at high speed where we might obtain water, shopping and fuel. I
interrupted with *Ja* or *Danke* where appropriate, gradually and inevitably
revealing that I was a foreigner. 'And where have you come from?' she
asked, getting really excited when I told her. 'You are the first boat from
England to pass through my lock!' she cried. I suggested that, most likely,
ours was the first vessel to arrive from the UK since the 1930s. This was
discounted with a dismissive 'But I was then a very small child!'

Over the mouth of the Klienitz, a narrow channel containing several
cruisers, was an unusually elegant cast-iron towpath bridge, rising to a
considerable height at its centre: it would not have been out of place in the
grounds of a nineteenth-century stately home.

Life seemed nearly perfect as we cruised slowly through a landscape filled
with wild flowers and water birds until suddenly a minor disaster struck
soon after a junction with the Wentow Canal. A fan belt had parted on the
port engine, necessitating removal of another from the water pump in order
to replace it. Jim (or any competent mechanic) would have solved matters
within 20 minutes. I struggled for $2\frac{1}{2}$ hours, but soon forgot my frustration
when everything finally seemed to be functioning normally. Both Doughty
and Forester in their accounts of this area had enthused over a town called
Templin, surrounded by walls and fortified gateways. We required no further
recommendation to make an eastwards detour along the Templiner Canal.
Admittedly, it might be risky to rely too heavily on two guide books of which
the most recent was 61 years old, but there was only one way of finding out
how much had changed.

No sooner had we left the main route between Berlin and Müritz than it
became obvious that few craft venture along this cul de sac. Thick patches
of white and yellow water lilies were close to invading a narrow strip of
clear water down the centre of the channel. Until we later met several small

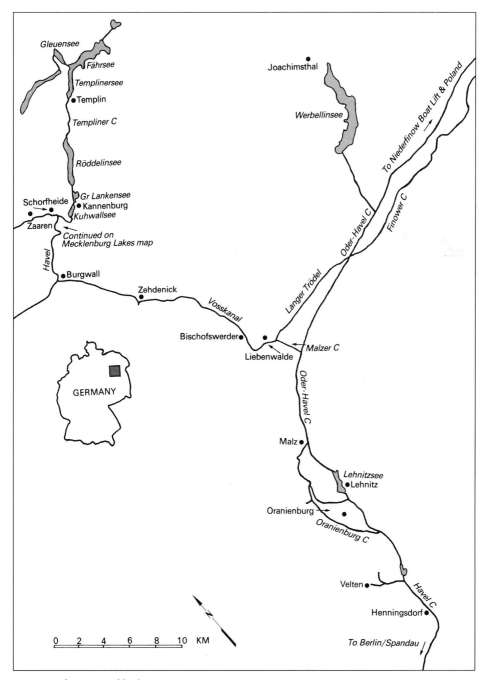

From Berlin to Mecklenburg.

cruisers, it was by no means certain that the line was still navigable. Dangerously decayed trestle bridges of rough logs only just provided sufficient beam and headroom. Often the echo-sounder revealed that *Avonbay* was virtually in contact with the bottom. Running cautiously ahead, we saw a small lake – the Grosser Kuwallsee. But barring our exit from the canal was a floating bridge over which a steady succession of army lorries was passing. A dozen very young soldiers gathered to witness our arrival and, without a word, attacked the central section with spanners, pushing it to one side. This took considerable effort, so we offered them a quarter-bottle of whisky in our fishing net. They smiled wanly, still saying little; had my German been so very incomprehensible?

Beyond the lake a narrow cut opened up, curving round to the gates of the very rustic Kannenburg Lock. We learned from a plate on the lower wing wall that it had been rebuilt in 1909; probably, very few modifications had been carried out since. It was now late, so we tied to a grassy towpath and began to prepare dinner. Soon an elderly man arrived, followed by his stout wife. She wrestled with the manually worked paddles and the sloping-sided chamber started to empty. I insisted that we were happy to wait until morning. After all, the 8 pm closing time had passed three-quarters of an hour earlier. 'It really is no trouble,' they replied. 'There is a much better mooring just beyond and a restaurant in Röddelin.' With difficulty, I eventually persuaded them that we actually would *prefer* to wait until the next day. Only in the morning did I realise that they lived elsewhere and had made two journeys by car to see us off their patch. We chatted briefly and they mentioned a nearby group of Russian conscripts: no wonder I had achieved little conversational success with the lads on the floating bridge! These forests on the borders of Brandenburg and Mecklenburg appeared to be littered with Russian ammunition dumps. United Germany was insisting that the 270 000-strong 'occupying' force will stay until all explosive reminders of the Cold War had been removed. Now we clearly understood why many military vehicles bearing red stars had been seen rumbling through the countryside. For as long as the troops remained in Germany, they would be fed and housed; neither of these things is guaranteed when they return to the Confederation of Independent States by 1994.

Long after dark, a knock on the cabinside preceded a request from several Russians for 'Benzin'. With just a few words of English, these boys aroused our sympathy, but we were none the less grateful that *Avonbay* carries no petrol! In the morning a group of them watched us lock through, their eyes filled with wonder at the sight of a boat from England. I photographed one of them and he requested permission to take a picture of our blue ensign. We were quite as much an object of curiosity to them as they were to us. The encounter was as extraordinary as coming across a Russian pleasure boat on the Grand Union. Glowing with satisfaction at our small efforts towards international understanding, we glided off into the tree-fringed expanses of the unbuoyed 21 m-deep Röddlinsee.

In this remote backwoods country, a number of sailing cruisers lay at anchor in sheltered bays. The new freedom of east Germany offers many possibilities to the capitalistic entrepreneur, but I would strongly advise against investment in the swimwear business – most of our boating companions were totally naked. Combine quiet waters with sunshine, and many Germans cannot resist baring all. *Freikörperkultur* ('free body culture') has long been normal in a country where nudism should not be confused with sex. At first, it was difficult not to reach for the binoculars; but as one warm day followed another 'FKK' somehow became an integral part of the lakeland scene. English reserve even started to disappear aboard *Avonbay*. One evening, midway through dinner in our saloon, a family tumbled out of their car, removed their clothes, and plunged into the water – all within a few feet of our windows. By this stage we were so blasé that it was scarcely worthy of comment. In fact, it was mainly the Germans who were responsible for the cult of nudism, now widespread along much of the French coastline.

If there had once been a leading mark at the far end of our lake, it had disappeared long ago. The small-scale chart offered only the vaguest hint as to where the Templiner Canal might be found. Eventually a narrow inlet offered some prospect of forward progress, reminding us vividly of our narrow boat voyage up the then moribund Caldon Canal in Staffordshire in 1969. Several times, the keel touched bottom, while a black slick of rotting vegetation lay in our wake. Carefully, we slipped past kitchen gardens and red-brick medieval walls, punctuated by fortified gateways. Seen from the boat, little of Templin had changed since the comments recorded by Doughty and Forester. Disappointingly, the town lock was out of service, although I have used far more decayed structures than this in the British Isles. Six tempting lakes beyond were thus outside our reach. Making a circuit of the walls on foot, we found several streets of old timber houses, prettily enhanced with carved and painted beams. One five-storey gabled gateway remained almost exactly as in Doughty's 1891 drawing. Food shopping, while short of western standards, was perfectly adequate. Perhaps we should have been more adventurous in selecting sausages from the dozens of kinds on offer. A lasting impression, however, was the lack of civic pride which allowed so many characterless concrete buildings to appear during the years following the Second World War. Back in the west, this architectural treasure would have been a tourist-filled showplace, equal to Miltenberg on the Main. When restoration comes (as surely it must), I pray that the cobbled streets are not replaced by tarmac, or the narrow arches torn down in the interests of improved traffic flow.

By our mooring, a ten-year-old boy expertly lowered a square net into the millstream, repeatedly pulling up handfuls of minute, sparkling fish. These were unceremoniously tipped on to the ground to be eaten by a white cat. We struck up a brief conversation, but *Avonbay*, England or other possible topics were obviously of lesser interest than fishing for cat food.

By 7 pm *Avonbay* was back on the Havel once again. Here, the broad river soon reached Schorfeheide Lock, a beautiful spot in water meadows with a backdrop of dense pine woods. Unaccountably, the helpful and otherwise agreeable keeper declined to let us pass through, even though official closing time was an hour off. Meanwhile, two lockfuls of craft were worked down in the opposite direction. A group of campers came to chat, saying that they were here from east Berlin for a week's fishing holiday.

Next day began misty, with delicate spiders' webs hanging on the boat's rails. This was a turf-sided lock, very much like those that were once a common feature of the Wey and Kennet in England. Vertical wooden piles inside the chamber made for an easy ascent, as we unwound our hose to replenish water tanks. In spite of having a variety of fittings, none could be found to match the overwide spout of the tap. Rarely do boats take on more than a few litres: we needed in excess of 200. This took 20 minutes, all the while holding the end of the hose – under pressure – in firm contact with the tap.

A delightful section now opened up, very sinuous and passing through sandy heathland. Deepest countryside was devoid of any buildings except for lock cottages at Zaaren and Regow, until we came to a village at Bredereiche Lock. Here was the first of many rows of timber-built boat 'garages' we were to pass, designed to protect craft from the harsh winter.

We knew that a huge cluster of lakes would be ours to enjoy, as we neared the border with the province of Mecklenburg. *Avonbay* had travelled far to meander through this astonishing area, easily the most complicated series of navigations anywhere in Europe. Growing familiarity with our east German *Wasserwander Atlas* reduced the likelihood of making too many serious navigational mistakes. Bankside finger posts sometimes showed the way to the next town. But as the chart's north pointer was frequently aimed at the bottom of a page and the link between one sheet and the next could only be found by matching up microscopic letters printed in red, there was regular scope for onboard disagreement.

A chain of lakes connected with the large Stolpsee eventually reached to the town of Lychen. We considered making a diversion and then agreed to remain on the main line. At least, ample 'new' water would remain for another year. Never before had *Avonbay* encountered another pleasure boat flying the distinct Czech ensign: we exchanged enthusiastic waves with this tiny cruiser, both realising that such a meeting would have been unthinkable two years before. Here also, an equally small dayboat was in the service of the *Wasserpolizei*. Unlike their over-zealous colleagues in the west, these officials expressed little interest in us. They maintained a refreshingly low profile – in stark contrast to their recent activities.

Unpretentious motor cruisers that might have featured in reports published by *The Motor Boat* in pre-war years lurked in the basements of thatched holiday homes, built on wooden piles. It all recalled a long-lost Norfolk Broads of more than half a century ago, but on a far more extensive scale. *Avonbay* had penetrated a veritable pleasure boating time-warp.

C S Forester was so delighted with these lakes, sincerely (but wrongly) believing that he was the first Englishman ever to travel them by boat, that he embarked on a frenzy of exploration. At the end of three weeks he claimed to have 'sailed every sea displayed on the map of Mecklenburg'. He and his wife Kathleen nevertheless found time, respectively, for writing (the manuscript of *The Annie Marble in Germany* was begun here with fountain pen and notepad) and knitting. After their long period afloat, I detect that they were

A Templin town gate, seen by Doughty a century before we arrived.

so enjoying themselves that proper record keeping became neglected. This part of the *Annie Marble* odyssey occupies a mere 38 pages out of a total of 317. While we were to spend far less time here than Forester and perhaps visited only one-third of the available lakes in Mecklenburg, I like to believe that the present account is a little more detailed and useful to those who will follow us. Some months after our return to England, I calculated that *Avonbay* had visited a grand total of 96 east German lakes, the majority of which were cruised twice.

By navigating the length of the Stolpsee, a short portion of the Havel and passing through two smaller lakes, Schwedtsee and Baalensee, we reached the sizeable town of Fürstenberg, surrounded on three sides by water. To describe it as a tourist town gives a quite false impression, for everything in Mecklenburg is decidedly low key. But there is a small boatyard, canoes for hire, and (from 1993) the French company Locaboat Plaisance have offered *Pénichette* self-drive cruisers, marketed in Britain by Andrew Brock Travel Ltd. Passenger craft continue to operate as they have for many years, for there was a weathered sign on a building in the main street dating from the early part of the century announcing *Dampfer nach Rheinsberg* ('Steamers to Rheinsberg'). Drinking-water is laid on above and below the lock, with a fuel point just beyond. As we waited for a tripping boat to emerge, before ourselves entering the chamber surrounded by a flotilla of four-man canoes, an air of surrealism coloured the proceedings. Give Evie a good book and somewhere comfortable for some serious sunbathing and she is utterly contented. Conventional tourist attractions hold little interest; she's a willing and competent boater and the only person I have ever heard of who can lie asleep on deck while her boat makes an ascent of the unique and mighty Ronquières inclined plane, south of Brussels. So when she suddenly cried: 'Look, there's a camel!' I did not instantly turn round to check this startling observation. Instead, I gently reminded her that we were in east Germany, not the Middle East. 'And another one!' she shouted with growing excitement. Sure enough, two ships of the desert were ambling over the Fürstenburg Lock roadbridge, followed by an irate convoy of Russian army vehicles! Presumably, a circus had arrived in town. How appropriate, we thought, when shortly afterwards we were standing outside the house of nineteenth-century Egyptologist Heinrich Schliemann.

Fürstenburg is not best known as a boating resort: its greater claim to fame is the nearby Ravensbrück concentration camp on the far shore of the Schwedtsee. Now a memorial and museum, the camp opened in May 1939 and held up to 70 000 women and children at a time. This was one place that none of us especially wished to visit.

So we moved onwards through the Rüblinsee to find a further reach of the Havel with a lock near Steinförde. Here the owner of a *Minimarkt* had attached an advertisement board to the stonework of a bridge – unremarkable in the west, but very enterprising in these waters. That afternoon, a catalogue of lakes followed, each as lovely as the last: Menow, Ziern, Ellbogen, Pällitz,

Viltz, Mössen and Zotzen. By this time, the through waterway had changed its name to Müritz–Havel Wasserstrasse: I had completed my discovery of the Havel all the way from its confluence with the far-off Elbe and through Berlin. Several further hours on the river's topmost reaches might have been possible, before it finally petered out near the hamlet of Krienke. Such a detour would have included the awesomely named Woblitzsee, surely the most wave-tossed lake of them all! Further shallow locks occurred in Strasen, Canow and Diemitz. These we shared with a Hamburg-registered motor

Ancient steam tug encountered on the Upper Havel.

cruiser named *Störpsel*. Amazingly, the family on board had been befriended by *Avonbay*'s builder, Joe Parfitt, during their holiday on the Canal du Nivernais in 1990. They required little encouragement to buy autographed copies of my two French canal books, resulting in a welcome addition of cash to the purser's funds! To be earning money while lazing in this beautiful area was highly satisfying.

Page 11 of the *Wasserwander Atlas Teil Mecklenburger Gewässer* emphasises what an extraordinary region we had reached. This patch of countryside, approximately 25 km × 13 km, contains no fewer than 33 individual, inter-connected lakes. As time passed, it became difficult to recall which had been the most beautiful, although one in particular will always be remembered with affection. Being a Doughty recommendation and barely lying off our chosen course, the Mirowersee was approached up an artificial channel that must have been navigated by boats over several centuries. Thatched boathouses increased in number, announcing our arrival at the little town of Mirow. Through a narrow road bridge, an exquisite prospect opened up on the far side of the lake: a row of ten or twelve holiday cottages, each with wooden verandahs directly fronting the water. Sharply pitched roofs of reed thatch extended nearly to the surface of the lake. We named these delightful buildings 'Wendish houses', after the ancient people who first invaded the surrounding marshes 900 years ago. The Wends were a fierce race of Slav hunters, whose leader Prince Niklot was killed in a skirmish with Christian Henry the Lion. That was back in the twelfth century when this area must have been a reasonably desolate spot, especially in the winter. Our own Queen Victoria's grandmother, Queen Charlotte, Princess of Mecklenburg, was descended both from Niklot and Henry, meaning that the present monarch of Britain is in part Wendish. The people we met every day, whether in the guise of lock keepers, bakers or professional fishermen, were doubtless Wends, every one of them. Not many generations earlier, they would have been wild folk, trapping deer and boar in the forests, living in rudimentary huts of thatch and timber, and generally resenting the Saxon ruling families – many of them were to colonise England.

Henry Doughty writes of another local tribe, members of which I felt we were less likely to encounter. These are the *Lutchen*, a German variant of the Little Folk, leprechauns or goblins. Dwelling underground or perhaps in caves formed by the tangled roots of trees at the water's edge, they characteristically have enlarged heads, stand about the height of one-year-old children, wear red clothes and (quite understandably) are afraid of dogs. I rather liked the sound of them, although didn't fancy my chances if accosted by a sizeable crowd. For some strange reason, June developed a deep dislike of the *Lutchen*, an attitude possibly a result of her Danish ancestry. Denmark, after all, is not far from the land of the Trolls, probably the most disagreeable collection of under-sized creatures you are likely to find anywhere.

Avonbay pushed her nose into the moat of the Mirow *Schloss* for the night, one of the finest moorings we had ever used. Admittedly, she was somewhat overlarge for the tiny creek, but none of the small boats returning from their day's sailing complained as they edged past us. Here people are almost naïvely agreeable. This refreshingly relaxed attitude reminded me of English canals in the early 1960s, when all boaters could be regarded as instant friends. Leading from the quayside, a grass-grown lane passed a strange half-timbered turret (the town fire station) and the ruined outbuildings of a school whose boundary wall was smothered in purple balsam.

We sat on deck as dusk fell, watching a blood-red sun float gently into the placid waters of the lake. A young couple arrived under sail in their elderly but obviously cared-for dinghy, lit an oil lamp beneath the awning, and jumped overboard for a final swim. Then, with the arrival of night, a deep silence descended on the Mirowersee.

Early next morning, the skipper of a passenger launch politely asked if *Avonbay* could move so that he might load copious crates of beer on board. We readily agreed and breasted up with a three-generation family, holidaying on their pretty little converted tugboat. Inside, the unmatching scraps of carpet and roughly finished fittings told of a boat that had been equipped at minimal cost to provide maximum pleasure. Our new friends kindly offered to take June and me on a shopping expedition, fearful that we couldn't possibly cope in a foreign town. This we tactfully avoided, but when it was time to leave some small token of thanks seemed appropriate. With a skill that surprised me (but I did have sympathetic listeners), I was able to say in German: 'Here, *mein Herr* and *meine Frau*, is a small bottle of whisky for you; for the children, a bar of *Shokolade*; and for your *Hund* a dog biscuit!' June had discovered this last item at the bottom of her handbag, but it is far too complicated to explain how it had found its way to Germany. Suffice it to say that east German mongrels seem unfamiliar with Bonios!

Nearby was an impressive gatehouse of the onetime *Schloss* of the Grand Duke of Mecklenburg-Strelitz. Designed in 1760 as a medium-sized Baroque structure, and now divided into seedy apartments, the lakeside house retained just a hint of its former grandeur, while in the overgrown grounds the vault of a brick church contained the remains of many Mecklenburg princes.

Mirow offered several useful shops, but we could find only one design of postcard, showing the lack of awareness of the considerable tourist potential. By a crossroads was a Russian army memorial with a score of tombstones, each bearing a red star. In the main street an ancient harrow, drawn by a pair of chestnut farm horses, clattered over the cobbles. Life is set for change, but it will be a long time before Mirow catches up with the late twentieth century.

Forester's route to Mirow from the great sea of Müritz had taken him due south, through the Bolter Canal and a succession of small lakes. Not long after his 1929 visit, a new link was built: the Mirower Canal, all part of the navigational improvements once intended to increase commercial capacity from the Elbe down the Elde–Müritz Wasserstrasse. We met no freight barges whatsoever, whereas in 1855 some 260 sailing *Kahns* regularly traded on

Mecklenburg's waterways. Some traffic lasted at least until 1929, including rafts of timber laboriously poled through lake, river and canal to Berlin. Working single-handed, a raftsman would meet up with others at towns like Fürstenberg; from then onwards, they could share the back-breaking toil. Deep water, of course, had to be avoided, working round three sides of a lake instead of taking the shorter line across the centre. Three raft journeys a season were generally possible, before ice put a stop to traffic for that year.

Avonbay suffered an unexplained delay waiting for the Mirower Canal's only lock, a time usefully spent as I swam under the stern to remove debris from one propeller. The canal, while pleasant enough, was not uppermost in our thoughts: at its far end, we were to join the largest inland sea in the whole of Germany. Müritz extends over $117\,km^2$, with a length of $27\,km$ and a width across the centre of $13\,km$. Not since cruising off the French Mediterranean coast two years before had our little boat enjoyed such a vast expanse of water. The small-scale chart was barely adequate but, with fine visibility, navigation was not too difficult, working up the middle and to starboard of a succession of green buoys. Two potential anchorages are passed: Röbel, on an inlet in the south-west corner and once renowned as a centre for raising geese, and Sietow, roughly halfway up the western shore. Much of the eastern side is designated a nature reserve, with boats prohibited from approaching too close to the side. Depth is variable, changing very quickly from $18\,m$ to as little as $1.9\,m$ at the very centre. While we crossed, there was no shortage of company from other cruisers, passenger craft and especially sailing boats, many of which travel from Berlin in the summer.

Homing in on a prominent *Schloss* at Klink (now accompanied by a state-run form of holiday village, with long, sandy beach), we arrived at a narrows (beach and public moorings) and so reached the smaller Binnen-Müritz, on which Waren is situated. *Avonbay* is a good little seaboat, operated by somewhat reluctant mariners. Given the choice of sea or canal and river, we generally prefer to stay inland. Negotiation of Müritz, comparable with a Dover–Calais crossing, provided a degree of pleasurable satisfaction. But this pride was slightly dented when we met a wide-beam 'narrow boat', with exposed tiller steering, heading out of Waren, destination Mirow. This was one of a small fleet of Dutch hire cruisers, run by Friesland Boating and lately established as the first charter company in east Germany. They reported a highly successful initial season, with few problems resulting from their slightly unusual choice of craft. Our Swiss boating friend Freddy Solèr was an early client. He told us that his only difficulty on Müritz was caused by water entering a keyhole as waves crashed over the open forward cockpit! Clearly, like all large lakes, Müritz must be treated with respect. Some advance anxiety had been generated by C. S. Forester's alarming comments. Seven people had been drowned here in 1928, while his own crossing seems to have come worryingly close to disaster as the wind increased and waves threatened to swamp the outboard. But *Annie Marble* was a very small, flat-bottomed, open punt, just $4.5\,m$ long.

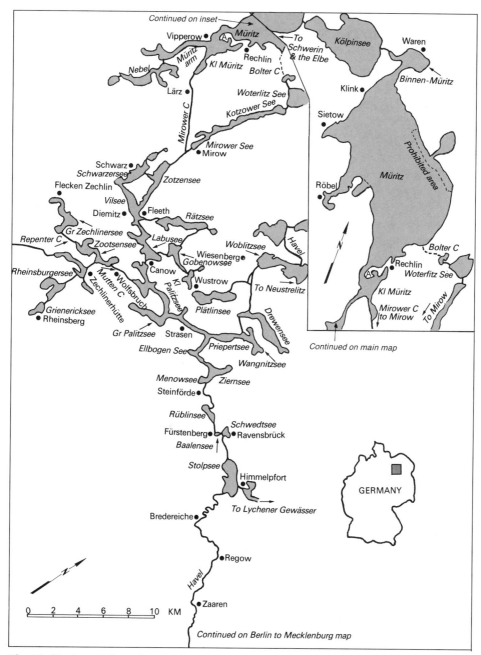

Continued on inset

Vipperow •   Müritz   To Schwerin & the Elbe   Kölpinsee   Waren •

Nebel   Müritz arm   Rechlin   Binnen-Müritz

Kl Müritz   Bolter C

Lärz •   Woterlitz See   Klink •

Kotzower See   Sietow •

Mirower C

Mirower See   Müritz

Schwarz •   • Mirow   Röbel •   Bolter C

Schwarzersee   Zotzensee   Rechlin

Flecken Zechlin •   Woterfitz See

Vilsee   Fleeth   Rätzsee   Kl Müritz

Diemitz •

Gr Zechlinersee   Labusee   Woblitzsee   Havel   Mirower C to Mirow   To Mirow

Repenter C   Zootsensee   Wiesenberg   Continued on main map

Rheinsburgersee   Canow   Gobenowsee

Mutten C   Wolfsbruch   Kl Palitzsee   Wustrow   To Neustrelitz

Zechlinerhütte   Plätlinsee

Grienericksee   Drewensee

• Rheinsberg

Gr Palitzsee   Strasen   Priepertsee

Ellbogen See   Wangnitzsee

Menowsee   Ziernsee

Steinförde •

Rüblinsee

Fürstenberg •   Schwedtsee   GERMANY

Baalensee   • Ravensbrück

Stolpsee

• Himmelpfort

Bredereiche •   To Lychener Gewässer

• Regow

Havel

0   2   4   6   8   10   KM   • Zaaren

Continued on Berlin to Mecklenburg map

The Mecklenburg Lakes, almost certainly the most complicated network of inland waterways to be found in Europe. Shown here in simplified form.

All signs of land were obscured in a haze for much of our return voyage; nevertheless, we were pleased to find that Müritz was well within our capabilities. June was congratulating me on the accuracy of my navigation skills as we approached the narrows off Rechlin and the southern exit, when – Crash! We had run hard aground on a gravel bed. By sounding all round the ship with a pole, little water depth could be found anywhere – even astern. Careful use of the engines eventually put us back on course between a pair of buoys, one of which I swear had not been there half-an-hour before.

At least *Avonbay* was not the first boat to experience minor problems. Doughty's wherry *Gipsy* became stranded on a shoal outside the harbour mouth at Waren and had to be winched off. Almost inexcusably, we made the same mistake, although following in the wake of a passenger cruiser with a presumed greater draught. This came after an abortive attempt to tie on the inside of a steamer jetty, extending from the town's waterfront. Five minutes of listening to our hull thumping on the hard sandy bottom convinced me there must be a safer place to lie. And so there was, once we had discovered the correct approach into the rectangular harbour. Here, we stayed overnight on 15 August, dining ashore in celebration of a safe arrival at the northernmost point of our east German travels.

We liked Waren enormously, probably more than any other town discovered in Mecklenburg. Dominated by the rusty red towers of two fourteenth-century churches standing on a hilly peninsula, it has long been a waterside

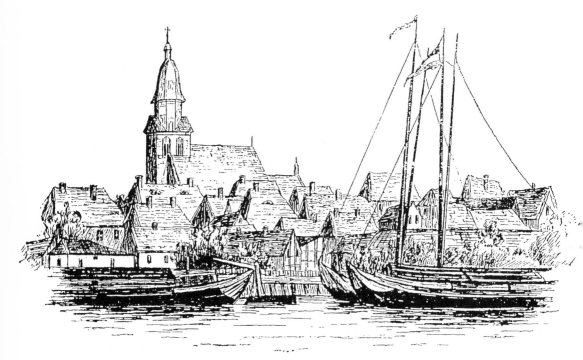

The harbour in Waren, seen a century earlier by Doughty.

resort. There's a bright and cheerful pedestrianised area around the *Rathaus*, a sizeable and flourishing fish-dock and well-landscaped promenades along the shore of Binnen-Müritz. Although our chosen restaurant was packed with customers, the meal, promptly served at a table on lawns overlooking the lake, was excellent: quite up to the standards expected of French provincial hotels. Including wine and coffee, the three of us were charged a very reasonable 96DM (then about £32).

Fronting the harbour was a group of magnificent but very derelict brick warehouses which would have been demolished long ago in the west. Alternatively, assuming they had somehow survived, they would now be ripe for conversion to offices or waterfront apartments. I would be so pleased to find them restored on my next visit. Of all the decayed structures noted in Mecklenburg, their design and location offered the greatest potential to a sympathetic developer.

In 1991 further westward progress was prevented by an inoperative lifting bridge in Malchow, between the Plauer and Fleesen lakes. Even if we had been able to pass this obstacle, entry to the Elbe at Dömitz was frustrated by a lock rebuilding programme. Both points were reopened to navigation in 1992. One day, our return to Mecklenburg will be through this route, with an obligatory diversion via the Störkanal to visit the Schwerinersee and its fairy tale palace, rising from a lake in a nineteenth-century pastiche of the Renaissance style. Such an approach avoids the tedium of the endless Mittelland Canal, but does include some rather trickier cruising in the Elbe estuary, downstream of Hamburg.

It was time to start on the homeward run to Berlin, again picking our way through all those superb lakes. Once more, *Avonbay* would be sidetracked by *Our Wherry in Wendish Lands*: this time, leaving the Müritz–Havel Wasserstrasse near Canow and heading south for several hours to a terminus at Rheinsberg. Back on the fiendishly complicated page 11 of our *Wasserwander Atlas*, we returned to the timeless world of sailing canoes, unsophisticated boating, camp fires burning on beaches of fine sand, and family groups concentrating on acquiring all-over suntans. One 'new' lock appeared on the Hüttenkanal at Wolfsbruch. Needing to go ashore to seek the keeper, we tied to some kind of water intake sluice and were fascinated to read a sign prohibiting just that, printed in German and Russian! Did the communists seriously expect that Russian would replace the native language? Certainly, few Muscovites were ever likely to arrive by boat in this forgotten backwater. Some rather pleasant middle-aged holiday-makers from Dortmund, discovering the east in hired canoes, stopped to talk to us, astounded to meet a British boat.

Not long after the lock we made our only serious chart-reading blunder of the trip, mistakenly straying into the Zootzensee and grounding badly under a canal bridge. Boats with our generous draught must have been rare, for we touched bottom again several times in the cut leading to the Rheinsbergersee, only just carving a channel through the silt by hogging the centre of the cut and once causing a much larger tripping vessel to pull hard into the bank (without any ill effects).

With special authorisation, canoes can navigate beyond Rheinsberg along the twisting course of the River Rhin, eventually reaching the Upper Havel at Oranienburg. But for us it was the end of the line. We tied first to a broken-down wharf and then moved up the Grienerick lake to anchor facing the twin pepper pot towers of *Schloss* Rheinsberg, once home of young Frederick the Great. That evening, we enjoyed a Mozart concert free of charge, performed on the castle lawns. Seated in our comfortable saloon, we felt vastly superior to the ticket holders on their wooden chairs!

Rising from a water-filled moat, Rheinsberg was built in its present form in 1739. Rococo interiors, a well-manicured park of clipped beech avenues, classical statues and specimen palm trees in wooden tubs are all on public view, although the building is now a sanatorium for diabetics. An open-air theatre, a grotto folly and weedless gravel walks recall the castle's original magnificence. But gone are the intricate eighteenth-century *parterres* as depicted in an engraving of 1773, reproduced in a locally purchased guide book. Frederick used to enjoy relaxing in a gondola or sailing in his gilded barque on the lake where we now lay.

In the small town, Königstrasse ('King's Street') – the original name was still visible in faded paint – had been altered to Karl Marx Strasse, but was

Rheinsberg Schloss. Compare with the 1891 view on page 109.

doubtless now in line for another change. Several inmates of an old people's home were deposited in wheelchairs on a windswept and sunless pavement: there must have been a long waiting list for new admissions.

Some months after our visit, it came as quite a shock to read that in Rheinsberg is located the DDR's first nuclear reactor, Soviet-designed and dangerously generating electricity since 1966. With the lessons of Chernobyl still ringing in their ears, the authorities were now carrying out a winding-down operation. Total safe removal is, of course, another matter.

Within two days *Avonbay* was back in Berlin, returning down the Havel. Re-entry to the former west sector was notable for a sour episode that was both strange and inexplicable. In urgent need of stamps for our accumulated postcards, we pulled into a boatyard jetty in the flourishing suburb of Haselhorst. A gentleman on a neighbouring cruiser confirmed that there was a post office within 400 m. I was walking through a gate on to the road when an elderly and most aggressive man in the boatyard shouted (in German): 'You cannot leave your boat there!' He glared as I patiently explained that we needed to stop for just ten minutes. He insisted that we moved on immediately. Perhaps he hated the British; if true, this was the sole example of Anglophobia we have ever knowingly encountered in Germany. Perhaps he hated visiting boats – illogical for one in his line of business, but just possible. While we prepared to leave, our embarrassed neighbour helped to untie the lines, saying: 'I am *so* sorry.'

After more than a week in the welcoming east, we had been quite unprepared for this reception – but it was nothing compared with the news that greeted us the other side of Spandau Lock.

9 Return to the West

Sailing Kahns *on the Plauer See (from Doughty).*

We could easily have continued down the Havel, to spend the night in 'our' Lanke-Werft marina at the top of the Wannsee. But, needing food supplies next morning, it seemed a better idea to stay close to the convenient shops of Spandau. Two unoccupied pleasure boats lay beneath a wall near the mouth of the River Spree; we joined them, fairly confident that the *Wasserpolizei* would not present us with a 'parking ticket' at midnight.

A sea-going motor sailer called *September Song* appeared, and noting they were flying a Red Ensign I motioned to them to pull in alongside. Later I learned of several other British craft in east Germany at this time, none of which had arrived in advance of *Avonbay*; but this was the first we had seen.

'Have you heard the news?' they asked. 'Gorbachev has been deposed in a Soviet coup!' That night, Europe was in turmoil. It seemed quite possible that revolution would erupt throughout the continent. And here were we, sitting on our boat in Berlin of all places! As we listened to regular news bulletins on the BBC World Service, prospects for continued political stability appeared to grow bleaker by the hour. At this stage the whereabouts of Gorbachev were unknown. It wasn't even certain that he was still alive. Mikhail Gorbachev – whose *perestroika* had brought about the downfall of communism, given freedom to the states of eastern Europe, and been the

OPPOSITE *Schloss Prunn overlooks the new Rhine–Main–Danube Canal, where it passes through the Altmühl Valley.*

ABOVE *This was our idyllic mooring, overlooking one of the Mecklenburg Lakes at Mirow. 'Wendish' houses on the far shore.* LEFT *A similar view as evening advances at the Mirower See.* BELOW *Magnificent but sadly decayed warehouses by the harbour in Waren, northern side of Mecklenburg's huge Müritz lake.*

FACING PAGE, TOP *The most prolific craft on the Mecklenburg Lakes are canoes, frequently equipped with sailing gear or tiny antiquated outboards. Note the diamond marker, indicating entry to a canal, providing a link with the next lake in the chain.* FACING PAGE, BOTTOM *Avonbay in the Rothensee Boat Lift, which connects the Mittelland Canal with the River Elbe near Magdeburg.*

ABOVE *Early morning on the Dortmund–Ems Canal at Lüdinghausen, where an old arm of the waterway provides peaceful overnight moorings.* BELOW *Frederick the Great's Sans Souci Palace at Potsdam. The terraces are planted with vines.* OPPOSITE *June filming in former East Berlin, where many of the city's most historic buildings are located.*

Grand Opening of the Rhine–Main–Danube Canal, September 1992. TOP Arrival of Regina Danubia in Berching. ABOVE Medal showing Ludwig's Canal and the new waterway. LEFT The Canal's 'wavy' bridge at Essing, seen on a postage stamp. BELOW Fire hoses during the summit level opening ceremony (photo Hugh Potter).

ABOVE *A laden freight vessel descends the Main near Miltenberg, on the fringes of the Odenwald forest.* BELOW *Wertheim's medieval castle overlooks the middle reaches of the River Main. Throughout the waterway, there are numerous passenger craft.*

dominant factor in enabling us to undertake our pioneering cruise. At least we were now in some kind of safety in west Berlin, but just how safe was that, surrounded by 270 000 Russian troops stationed on east German soil? The world was soon to learn of the outcome of Gorbachev's reinstatement after a worrying few days; and then of his final removal from high office.

Judy and Jonathan Wiesner had just arrived in *September Song* after a voyage from the Baltic. They seemed totally unperturbed at the momentous news, calmly announcing that they were now bound, by water, for St Petersburg by way of Poland. While wishing them luck, we resolved to stay well clear of Russian territory until the political climate had stabilised. In the morning the news stands were screaming anxious headlines, best summed up by the front page of *Bild*: '*Gorbi gestürzt. Mein Gott, was nun?*' ('Gorbi overthrown. My God, what now?')

Nothing could be achieved by worrying, though, and we had plenty of important cruising to finish. John flew in from London and we entertained Henrietta and Michael to dinner at the very pleasant Blau und Rot restaurant overlooking the lake, next door to our marina mooring. Although the Burtons' diplomatic post had begun in Berlin some years before, only this summer had they been able to explore widely in the east. Henrietta bubbled with enthusiasm as she described once-inaccessible sights: thus encouraged, we decided on a route back towards the Elbe which would allow us half a day investigating the royal residential city of Potsdam.

First, it was necessary to locate a reasonably central mooring. All likely quaysides being occupied by tripping craft, we sought permission to use a maintenance depot by the fuel pumps of the state-controlled Weisse Flotte passenger boat company, not far from the Glienicker Bridge.

Potsdam is known to have existed in the late tenth century; it was to remain an ordinary and insignificant town until chosen as a hunting base for the Great Elector, Frederick William, towards the end of the 1600s. A palace and associated buildings, barracks for military personnel, a Dutch quarter for immigrants from the Low Countries, three new churches and numerous additional houses saw the population increase from 1500 in 1713 to 11 708 by 1740. Triumphal gateways provided entry through an encircling wall. The most significant structure is Sanssouci Palace, built to the design of Frederick the Great from 1745. Intended to rival Versailles, it stands in extensive landscaped parkland, a masterpiece of German rococo. Steep terraces planted with vines cascade towards a monumental fountain, surrounded by assorted examples of classical statuary.

We walked through the elegant town, came to the Nauener Gate – a confection of Strawberry Hill gothic – and eventually reached Sanssouci Park. No hint of neglect here: complicated beds of summer annuals, pains-

OPPOSITE, TOP *We cruise past the watergate at the Franconian wine-producing town of Frickenhausen, River Main.* BELOW *1916 steam tug* Gredo *leads* Avonbay *down the Danube as dusk gathers upstream of Regensburg.*

takingly raked gravel paths, and clipped hedges that would have pleased Frederick the Great. The only incongruous element was provided by a gang of dejected women in headscarves, cutting a lawn with hand scythes. Cheap labour had yet to be replaced by mechanisation. Two days would barely be long enough to discover all of Potsdam's treasures, ranging from later palaces to summer houses, an *Orangerie* and a Chinese Teahouse. By the time the Kaiser was deposed in 1918, it had long been the leading showground for German architecture. Churchill (soon to be replaced by Attlee), Truman and Stalin met at the Cecilienhof *Schloss* in 1945 to determine the future of post-war Germany, with consequences not universally deemed satisfactory.

We eventually found a taxi to take us back to the boat. Our driver seemed unfamiliar with the area, and we didn't have a map. By a combination of guesswork and intuition, though, we located our floating home.

Mapping out a route through the Potsdamer Havel provided the prospect of more unexplored cruising water and a sense of achievement in that I should soon have travelled on virtually all the waterways of Greater Berlin.

Avonbay slid past Potsdam's Nikolai Church, a curious amalgam of London landmarks: St Paul's Cathedral dome, mounted on a portion of King's Cross Station! Even stranger was the multi-coloured minaret of an 1841 steam engine house, built in the form of a mosque to provide power for Sanssouci's fountains. Our last east German lakes lay ahead: a succession of pleasing meres, not unlike those in Mecklenburg but more sophisticated and thronged with commercial pushtows and large white passenger craft. I could have stayed here for months, threading a way into hidden bays; absorbing in detail each town and village; discovering further navigable circuits. By the time we left east Germany, calculations showed that *Avonbay* had travelled about 1100 km, including return runs. With more than 2400 km of canal, river and lake available in the former DDR, as much as two-thirds of the network remained to be discovered another year.

The Templiner, Schwielow and Zern See led us back to the Lower Havel and Brandenburg, via waterways familiar from the June cruise. This time, we selected a more direct way west, taking 58 km of the Elbe–Havel Canal between the Plauer See and the mighty Elbe. For such a large and fairly recent waterway, this turned out to be unexpectedly agreeable: enough commercial traffic to provide interest, no delays at the three big locks, and several interesting small towns. First lock was Wusterwitz. We entered behind a pair of cargo boats, selecting convenient bollards on the right. Following us was an oversized, very ugly gin palace, inexpertly handled by a husband and wife. Needless to add, they came from the west and behaved as if this was their introduction to locking procedure. With starboard fenders already lowered, they asked, none too politely, if we would move forward. As this would have left us with nothing to make fast on, I refused. There was ample space on the opposite wall; I was even prepared to have them lie alongside us. Herr Gin-Palast issued a stream of angry expletives (not covered in our 12 hours of language instruction), reduced his wife to tears, and glared at us for the next ten minutes from his perfectly acceptable position on the other side of the chamber. When I come to power, I shall pass laws to prevent spoiled adults being in charge of over-priced motor cruisers! As might have been anticipated, he raced past us at the first opportunity, burning as much fuel in five minutes as we should use over the next hour.

With its convenient pleasure boat quay, Genthin offered the chance of a quick tour ashore. John and I cycled into the centre, but found few shops were open on this Saturday afternoon. A clean, tidy but slightly characterless little town, its chief object of interest was a kerbside 'grandfather' clock of pure 1930s Art Deco design. The tall cast-iron base bore a painted glass advertisement for Persil washing powder ('*Persil für alles Wäsche*') complete with a long-skirted satisfied customer in freshly laundered sunhat.

That night we tied to a group of rusty dumb barges in the cut after Niegripp Lock. Elbe water levels must have been low, for both lock gates were wide open instead of controlling a normal rise and fall quoted at between 1.5 m and 5 m.

Shortly after dawn several massive and unladen canal ships slipped past in the mist, to head downriver towards Hamburg. While assured by the keeper that sufficient water remained to see us through 10 km of river to Rothensee and the Mittelland Canal, an element of doubt lingered. To have to winter here would be far from convenient. Luckily, good progress against the stream and no immediate danger of hitting the bottom found us past the potentially tricky section. On the far side of the vertical lift, a west Berlin barge captain talked as we filled our water tanks. On learning of our draught, he shook his head in disbelief that we had not grounded. Loaded with his present freight, he required 1.7 m in the Elbe, and fully expected to plough his way through silt and gravel.

For five and a half days of endless sunshine, we made the best of a featureless Mittelland Canal, diverting for several hours to the outskirts of Hanover up a branch line and spending one night at a peaceful yacht club on the Osnabrück Arm. Then down the Dortmund–Ems Canal, where we hoped to arrange moorings until the autumn. The Yachtclub Hebewerk Henrichenburg turned out to be an inspired choice, and *Avonbay* squeezed between a pair of piles at the entrance to a vacant berth in the shadow of the old boat lift. Hanspeter Jünkers, accountant and honorary harbourmaster, calculated a very reasonable charge and proudly showed us his own boat, one that now seemed to serve more as a weekend cottage than a cruiser. Built in 1944 as a police launch, she had been 'captured' by the British at the end of the war, then converted by the Bishop of Emden into a tiny floating chapel for the boatpeople. Known as *St Nikolai*, a subsequent private owner abbreviated this to *Niko*, shortened still further to *Nik* when she passed to our Henrichenburg friend. Frau and Herr Jünkers joined us for dinner in the garden of a suburban restaurant that evening. We felt reassured that *Avonbay* was to be left in safe hands.

My only concern was the powerful surge created by 1500-tonne barges.

If one passed on average every ten minutes throughout a 16-hour working day for the 42 days that we planned to be absent, our mooring lines would come under strain rather more than 4000 times! I took the precaution of doubling up on all warps. When we returned in October, a single one had been replaced by caring club members.

Not then suspecting that the Rhine–Main–Danube Canal would at long last be declared open to boats in September of the next year (an eagerly awaited event that we were determined to attend), *Avonbay* was to be laid up for the winter at the Bruxelles Royal Yacht Club. More convenient starting places could have been selected for the 1992 cruise into Bavaria! Our autumnal voyage to Belgium involved dropping down the Rhine into the Netherlands, up the Maas (Meuse) and northwards through the Canal de Charleroi à Bruxelles. We started through the 'unknown' waters of the Wesel–Dateln Canal. Commercial traffic, represented by 1500-tonne barges, reigns supreme.

At each of the six duplicated locks, with towering guillotine gates, groups of these monster cargo carriers edged forward with bursts of exhaust coughing as their air-start engines briefly stopped and started again to engage reverse. Dispensing with clutches and gearboxes, the system appears to be more reliable than might be expected. None the less, there were many moments where silenced leviathans seemed to be drifting uncomfortably close to us. As we emerged from the fifth chamber at Hünxe, we counted 20 of them slewed across the channel, all looking as if they were intent on mowing us down while we nipped smartly through a series of ever-diminishing gaps.

Our final German lock released *Avonbay* into the fast-flowing Rhine. We would be in Dutch waters by lunchtime.

10 *Main*

German canoeists portage round a lock, from a 1925 boating guide.

News that the Rhine–Main–Danube Canal would finally be opened in September 1992 came while *Avonbay* was hibernating at the Bruxelles Royal Yacht Club in Belgium. In four stages, we would cruise up the badly flooded French Sambre to Reims; take the Canal de la Marne au Rhin to Strasbourg; hurtle down the Rhine to Mainz; and there join the wriggling River Main, running in a vaguely easterly direction for 384 km to Bamberg.

This magnificent navigation, bordered by the Odenwald, Spessart and Rhön forests and finally the famed vineyards of Franconia, was used with difficulty by 200-tonne barges well over a century ago. Frequent summer droughts made it one of the least reliable inland waterways in Germany, a factor that prevented Ludwig's Canal ever becoming a commercial success in carrying the line forward to the Danube. Improvements started with construction of five locks between the Rhine and Frankfurt in the 1880s together with the introduction of a fleet of eight Royal Bavarian chain tugs. These were in service to Aschaffenburg by 1886, Miltenberg by 1892, and eventually over the entire route to Bamberg – provided water depths were sufficient.

In 1913 plans emerged for a new, large-capacity Rhine–Main–Danube Canal. This envisaged further Main improvements upstream to Ochsenfurt, where 262 km of channel would be created to make a connection with the River Isar, downstream of Munich. There were also to be branches serving the cities of Nuremberg and Augsburg. The chief feature was a 19 km tunnel; had this materialised, it would easily have been the world's longest underground navigation. Alone, its estimated cost was 63 million marks, while total expense of the whole enterprise was put at 188 million marks. Like so many grandiose canal schemes, it was never to leave the drawing board.

A 1921 proposal for the Rhine–Main–Danube Canal selected a route very similar to that eventually finished, and utilising the Main to Bamberg. Construction started almost immediately, with 1500-tonne capacity locks from Mainz to Aschaffenburg being ready by 1925 with other major works on the upper Main and Danube in service by the end of the decade. Some of these earlier structures, such as the sloping-sided lock at Krotzenburg, were later considered inadequate, requiring rebuilding many years later as European inland ships carried greater payloads. After a break during the Second World War, work on the Main was effectively completed by 1962. Thirty-four locks, each at least 300 m in length, now provide year-round navigation.

This was to be our third exploration of the river. Knowledge of towns offering safe and central moorings greatly enhanced our enjoyment of the area, as did a spell of very hot weather, lasting the nine days we had allocated for the journey. Apart from occasional violent thunderstorms, temperatures on board regularly reached 31° C (88° F). Most days, we would anchor briefly in the mid-afternoon for a swim – but not in the Main's lower reaches, where effluent from Frankfurt produces water even more polluted than that of the Rhine. This time the crew consisted of June, Evie and me, and John joined us a little later at Aschaffenburg.

Four of the early locks are duplicated, side by side, making for rapid progress in spite of constant barge activity. Further upriver, single chambers are equipped with intermediate sets of gates. White light signals are used to inform skippers as to whether all or part of the pen is to be used. Not appreciating the purpose of this system, we were several times requested by loudspeaker to advance up the chamber until finally the truth dawned. Another potential embarrassment concerns the self-operated, automatic *Sportboots* locks, provided as alternatives for small pleasure craft. Reference to the chart book showed that at 2.5 m wide, the majority are considerably narrower than *Avonbay*. Several on the lower part of the waterway exactly matched our beam of 3.5 m. The keeper at Krotzenburg directed us to a newly completed little lock, not yet included in the guide. Fractionally wider than the others, it suited *Avonbay* perfectly, once a young couple emerging in their dayboat had explained the push-button controls. Bearing in mind they were complete strangers, their direct approach to conversation was startling: 'You have a fine boat!' 'Thank you,' I replied. 'What did it cost?' I supplied an acceptable figure, believable without verging on the extravagant. 'You must be very wealthy,' came the response. 'What is your work?'

To begin with, the Main is not especially attractive. An Opel car factory, fuel depots and the vast Hoechst chemical works do little to enhance the first 30 km. Then comes Frankfurt, a vibrant city that feels much more like a capital than the little town of Bonn. *Avonbay* spent the winter of 1986–7 here, in the century-old Westhafen, a mooring that is both central and secure. Sportbootwerft Speck charged 800DM for six months, a bargain that we failed to appreciate until asked for much greater sums on other German waterways later. Careful winterisation of engines and the domestic water system ensured that the boat came to no harm during our six months' absence. For much of January and February the Westhafen was frozen solid. Fortunately, friends in the city made periodic checks and sent occasional postcards, intended to be reassuring. One read: 'Yesterday, *another* of your neighbours sank. *Avonbay* seems OK!' The weeks couldn't pass quickly enough until it was time to return for our Easter cruise.

Large cities are not particularly to our taste, but Frankfurt is one that we

A reliable method of measuring Avonbay's *beam: working through the pleasure craft lock at Krotzenburg, River Main.*

have come to know better than most, arriving in Germany via its impressive international airport and once unwittingly selecting a hotel near the main station, surrounded by a den of iniquity second only to Hamburg's Reeperbahn red-light district. Moorings for private boats can generally be found along the landscaped Mainkai promenade, between the Alte Brücke and Eiserner Steg bridges (K35.5), close to the cathedral and charming Römerberg market square. It is simply a matter of finding somewhere to tie, clear of the frankly aggressive passenger craft. On one occasion police launches interrogated us twice as we approached the city centre; we detected an unwelcome nervousness, for on shore the streets were filled with police cars. Within minutes of making fast at the quayside, the crew of another police boat homed in. 'Today,' they said emphatically, 'stopping in the city is *verboten*!' They explained that delegates of an international anti-terrorism

Aboard the floating chandlery/provisioning vessel at Offenbach.

conference were shortly to arrive by motorcade from the airport. The tension on their faces reminded me of the time I stopped my car outside the Elysée Palace in Paris to ask directions of a *gendarme* at the very instant President Mitterand was being driven through the gates in a black Citroën. Arrival of the same French president in Frankfurt was expected at any moment. We were forcefully pushed off into the Main, forbidden to go shopping for food.

But for that episode in 1986, we might never have discovered one of a dying breed of provision barges, lying below Offenbach Lock (K38). Run from a cavernous vessel, stocking huge reels of cable and rope, drums of oil and other nautical necessities, it was owned by an elderly Dutch couple. Alongside, a smaller mobile shop and fuelling barge provided us with baskets of meat, vegetables, fruit and wine. Best of all, we exchanged an empty *French* gas bottle for an identical full one and I bought a genuine bargeman's cap, decorated with a sombre but distinctive pattern of appliqué leaves. As we neared the end of our business, the barge's VHF crackled into life and, with no thought other than the prospect of further trade, the floating shopkeeper let go his lines and accosted a freighter in mid-river – *Avonbay* still secured alongside.

Six years later, a sad change had taken place. The old couple had aged considerably and could walk only with difficulty. Their food stock was so depleted that it was difficult to select anything that we actually required. Most modern inland ships now carry a car on deck, enabling the captain's wife to visit land-based supermarkets and so fill her deep freeze with supplies that will last several weeks. Our old friends at Offenbach were in an unenviable situation, no longer able to run their business – for which there was a much reduced demand – efficiently. They would be fortunate to find anyone willing to take it off their hands.

The success of an inland cruise often depends in part on the interesting people encountered en route. One evening was spent with 70-year-old Ernst Hanselmann, a retired Mercedes service agent, whose sailing cruiser *Optimist IV* was now bound for the Black Sea, crewed by a miniature dappled dachshund. What first impressed us about him was the authoritative manner in which he removed a group of surly anglers from the quayside at Bürgel (K43.6), beyond Offenbach, so we could lie alongside for the night. Definitely the kind of German to cultivate as an ally! The evening progressed as British gin and tonics were replaced by Ernst's fine Franconian wines. It was several hours later that this unassuming gentleman revealed that his recent cruising experience extended as far as Sweden, Finland, St Petersburg and all corners of the Mediterranean. As a parting gift, he gave us a Royal Bavarian flag and this elegant device of blue and white lozenges henceforth flew from our crosstrees in company with the Germany courtesy flag. Surprisingly, Ernst failed to materialise at the great canal opening in September; perhaps he could not face the prospect of all those people, and so delayed his arrival on the Danube for a few days.

Sometimes chambers of disused locks remain as convenient little yacht

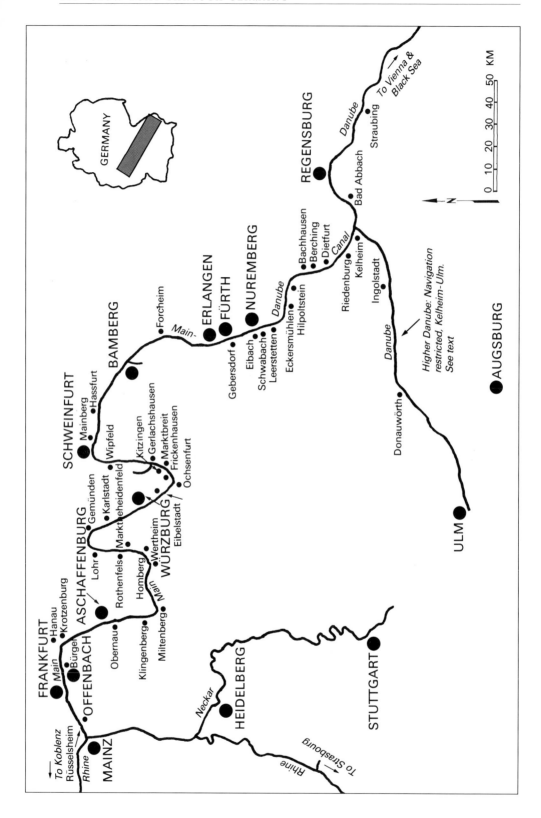

harbours. There was one opposite Rumpenheim (K47), with others at Grosskrotzenburg (K67) and up a side arm in Aschaffenburg. More than 170 towns and villages directly front the river as it drunkenly swings through all points of the compass. The best of them comprise clusters of gingerbread houses of intricate half-timbering, with shops and hotels advertising their wares on elaborate wrought-iron painted signs. In the time available, we could visit only a small proportion of the total; as on the Neckar, shore excursions are dictated by availability of moorings.

All the way between Frankfurt and Aschaffenburg, a well-surfaced water-side track with carved finger-post direction signs is heavily used by cyclists – who are, for the most part, slightly overweight and riding sturdy machines. Looking at the map, we found at Hanau (K57) that we were crossing the border into Bavaria, a former kingdom that extends as far as Passau, where the Danube becomes Austrian.

Aschaffenburg (K87) was a pleasant town to spend a complete day, buying food and smartening paintwork, while waiting for John to join us from London. A onetime lock cut, offering protection from the wash of passing traffic, is overlooked by the great Johannisburg Palace of the Bishops of Mainz, a seventeenth-century Renaissance structure in red sandstone with sturdy towers at each corner. Gutted by fire during the last war, it has been superbly restored, contributing to the grandeur of a riverscape where there is also a *Pompejanum*, a replica of the Roman villa of Castor and Pollux in Pompeii. Standing in its own vineyard, it was designed in the 1840s to the order of Ludwig I, the canal-building monarch of Bavaria. We returned to a favourite mooring on a public quay a little downstream of a yacht club that gladly supplied us with drinking-water. *Ketten-Schiff II*, one of two surviving Königliches Bayerisches chain tugs, is afloat nearby, converted into a restaurant/bar. Although her single funnel, machinery and superstructure have been replaced by a rather landlubberish bungaloid erection, the curiously 'hogged' hull remains intact. Built on the Elbe in Dresden, then brought overland in pieces to the Main, this species of steam tug relied on the sunken chain for upstream journeys only, using water-jet propulsion when returning from Bamberg to here.

Heidi and Wolfgang joined us for dinner. It was seven years since they had first cruised with *Avonbay* on the Canal de Bourgogne. We had a very happy evening, not least when they praised the 'dramatic' improvement in my German and then assured us that in our choice of Wildemann Restaurant we had selected by far the most prestigious eating house in town.

Speed limits exist on some parts of the river and in canal cuts; elsewhere, water skiing is permitted in specific reaches. As far as we could tell, no regulations prevent owners of small planing dayboats from behaving like demented Donald Campbells. We were aghast at the behaviour of numerous local sportsboats, roaring past in excess of 30 knots, throwing up washes far

OPPOSITE *Through the Main to the Danube.*

more uncomfortable and dangerous to a displacement cruiser than those of the 3300-tonne capacity pushtows regularly encountered. In one quite narrow, rock-lined section, five of these inconsiderates raced by, leaving our galley a disaster zone of broken glass. At sea, *Avonbay* would have been suitably prepared, but here we were not. Furious gestures from our flybridge resulted in three of them throttling back to receive a tirade of complaint. Among other things, I told them that such behaviour rates a £500 fine (or worse) on the Upper Thames. There is a strong possibility that they genuinely did not understand the problem, being people with too much money, a total lack of common sense and only the most rudimentary good manners. Such *Wasserschweins* ('water hogs') rarely summon sufficient courage to negotiate a lock and are disliked quite as much by 'real' German boaters. We could not comprehend how the water police could condone such actions until we noted them behaving in a similarly disgraceful way!

Sedately, *Avonbay* continued upriver, saddened rather than annoyed, and determined that nothing would spoil the pleasures of this exquisite waterway. Obernau, Wörth, Trennfurt, Gross and Kleinheubach and a scattering of lesser villages were all passed during a long hot day. We had our sights set on Miltenberg (K125), one of several jewels of the Main. This is justly a magnet for trippers and coach parties, for nowhere else were we to find such a wonderful collection of ornate timber buildings, some dating from the fourteenth century. At the centre of a sloping, cobbled market place stands a large stone fountain, built in 1583. Seen from the river, the twin towers of the Pfarrkirche rise to the protective walls of the Mildenburg *Schloss*, perched on the lower slopes of a tree-clad cliff. While by the late afternoon barge traffic had subsided to perhaps one ship every half-hour, the waterfront remained busy as passenger boats continued a lucrative trade far into a glorious evening. We lay on a deepwater mooring along a short section of wall beyond a stone gateway leading to the town bridge.

It would take much of a summer's cruise and fill a complete book to do full justice to all of this fantastic river. In our late July heatwave, we could wish for nothing more agreeable than to glide slowly up the valley, sometimes having brief conversations with lock keepers or the crews of barges. Unfailingly, it was the skippers of Dutch ships who were the most friendly, usually speaking good English and seeming to enjoy their summer travels as if they were there purely for the pleasure of it all. By mid-afternoon next day we had reached Wertheim (K157), situated on a bend at the confluence of the little River Tauber. Years before, we had explored the lowest reaches of this stream in the dinghy, but a more recent visit had been slightly alarming.

Several centuries ago, traders expected to be set upon by robber barons who terrorised many German rivers. During the 1960s and 1970s, when Jestyn (Lord) St Davids was running his children's boat club on the Regent's Canal at Camden Town, passing craft were frequently subjected to attacks by genial young pirates. But I had never anticipated *Avonbay* would be threatened in a similar fashion on the Main! I was steering inside, while members of our all-girl crew lazed on deck. Planning to dine at the Schwan Hotel, we approached the quay, where a gang of twenty youths sat on the grass surrounded by cans of beer. Even before we were alongside, one of these louts had jumped on board. No one gets on my boat uninvited: it would be a matter of seconds before we were swarming with them. I rushed outside, surprised the invader, and pushed him in the water – amid angry cries from his friends. Some, it appeared, were American servicemen. By backing off fast, we were safe from further molestation, but obviously could not now tie up within sight of this unpleasant mob. Dinner in a hotel had suddenly degenerated into omelettes cooked in our own galley! Half a kilometre upstream, beyond the ruins of a castle, a rowing club stage provided a barely adequate berth in rather shallow water. We hung up a riding light as a warning to any late-moving commercial traffic and agreed that we could

Half-timbering in Miltenberg's main square.

eat out after all. On returning in the dark, we found the boat quite safe, although her decks were thick with dead moths that had been attracted by the light. Worse, she was seriously aground. Knowing I could never sleep with hull and propellers grinding on the gravel bottom, we refloated *Avonbay* with difficulty and slipped gently downstream to the town centre, where all was now peaceful.

Members of the Wertheim/Bettingen yacht club have a headquarters basin in the countryside at K167. We pulled in to replenish water tanks and were told that ours was the first British cruiser ever to make a visit. Hospitality flowed in the clubhouse; they asked if we would like to exchange burgees, an arrangement rather more to their benefit than ours.

The next village that attracted our attention was Homburg (K171), off the starboard bow, with ruined castle atop an outcrop of bare rock. Mooring to the stony banks being ill-advised, we lowered the anchor and rowed ashore. Wine production is Homburg's chief preoccupation. Steep alleys with fountains and ornamental cascades provide access to a belvedere by the church. I have long considered that graveyards tell as much about the inhabitants of a foreign village as any other feature. This one was no exception. Immaculate scrubbed slabs of black polished marble were dotted with scores of candle lanterns, twinkling in the late afternoon.

Although barges lay along the sloping quay of Marktheidenfeld (K179), a safer halt for *Avonbay* was discovered next to a deserted maintenance boat on the opposite bank. Long regarded as home port to a large number of Main ships, the town provided us with a much-needed opportunity to restock the fridge. During our time in Germany we had eaten pork prepared in every possible manner, beef steak and occasionally veal and chicken. Apart from flocks of sheep, it was rare to see any animals grazing in the fields – yet joints of lamb seemed to be unobtainable. Drawing a blank at two butchers' shops, I approached the meat counter in a supermarket. Normally, it was merely necessary to point to what we wanted. Seeing no lamb, and not knowing what it was called in German, I had no alternative but to play out a mime accompanied by baa-ing noises. This prompted an amused reaction from the sales assistant and other shoppers, followed by the disappointing reply: '*Wir haben kein Lamm!*' This is one word that I am never likely to forget!

Rothenfels ('Red Cliff', K185), with bulbous-spired church and skyline *Schloss*, is followed by Lohr (K198), whose quay actually bears a sign welcoming pleasure craft – provided their draught is under 1.8 m. Gemünden (K211) offers possible moorings in the mouth of the Fränkische Saale by a camping site. We stopped briefly to enjoy the view over the river from the Scherenburg castle.

One unusual characteristic of these reaches is a series of quiet pools divided from the navigation channel by heaps of loose stones, suggesting that the river was once considerably wider than now. Shallow-draught boats can slide through gaps in the training walls; we passed several whose occupants had retreated for secluded sunbathing or fishing. Draw-off in the wake of barges can, however, briefly reduce water levels by a considerable amount.

Our first sighting of Karlstadt (K226) had been very early one morning. A rising sun flared beyond the high fortification wall, regularly punctuated by a series of tall, slender towers. This little town was so obviously worth a visit that on our next journey we attempted to enter a workboat basin, opposite, only to run hard aground. We next tried anchoring, but further consideration made this seem unwise for we were hardly clear of the channel where barges come sweeping through a bridge. Finally, a rowing club stage, upstream, provided a barely adequate overnight halt. To our delight, the local council had installed a splendidly central pontoon by 1992, right alongside the main

K.B.K.S.IV, *a surviving Main chain tug, now serving as a chandlery downstream of Würzburg.*

water gate. *Avonbay* pulled in here for lunch and found herself conveniently placed for the charming *Rathaus* square and some of the most accessible food shopping on the entire river. Every place on the Main that has no deepwater quay (and that includes the great majority of towns and villages) should follow Karlstadt's example. Much trade would result from passing pleasure craft.

That afternoon, two further locks brought us to the downstream outskirts of Würzburg (K248). Neither of two bunker stations near the commercial harbour was open in the early evening, so we continued to a quayside below the city bridge. During dinner on board, a friendly lock keeper arrived alongside by bicycle and suggested that we should moor elsewhere. Early next morning, from our new position close to a twin-jibbed eighteenth-century treadwheel crane opposite, we could appreciate how vulnerable we would have been as a succession of large barges edged towards the lock. Best moorings of all are reached by working to the higher level and turning into a short weirstream above the bridge. We, however, wished to return down-river to buy diesel from a chandlery established in one of only two remaining Main chain tugs. This example, *K.B.K.S. IV*, was built in 1916. Some years before, a nearby gas depot had conveniently filled our empty butane bottles, so avoiding discarding expensive French containers in favour of German ones.

On that earlier voyage, June had remained on shore to film while the rest of us negotiated the lock. Possibly not associating her with *Avonbay*, the keeper angrily demanded that she stopped shooting on the lockside, with implications that government structures were out of bounds to photographers. Ignoring his shouts until she had finished, she merely stepped back on board where it was possible to continue, unmolested – *Avonbay* being British territory, albeit mobile!

There is much to appreciate in this elegant city that experienced savage destruction during an Allied bombing raid in March 1945. Half a century later, restoration is virtually complete; stone figures of a dozen saints again decorate the ancient Gothic bridge. Each was rescued from the river bed, into which they were pushed by vandals in the final days of the Second World War. Long one of Germany's finest and most cultured cities, Würzburg reached a peak in the seventeenth and eighteenth centuries, when the vast Baroque Marienberg *Residenz* of the Prince-Bishops was constructed. Its gardens and lavish interiors, commanding a glorious view over the river, demand an obligatory visit. Equally richly ornate is St Kilian's Cathedral. Shops, museums and a *Rathaus* dating from 1200 are just a few of the attractions that will make most boaters want to linger.

Now nearing the heart of the Franconian vineyards, we worked through Randsacker Lock (K258) and were soon admiring a number of large pleasure cruisers gathered in the yacht club at Eibelstadt (K262.5). During the early eighteenth century, a notable physician named Beringer discovered many curious stone 'fossils' here, among them winged sea-horses, Hebrew letters, fish and smiling suns. Local inhabitants assisted him in uncovering ever more examples for his collection. A scholarly book on the finds was published, dedicated to the Prince-Bishop of Würzburg. Eventually the makers of these artefacts were forced to own up to their fraudulent activities. However, nearly 300 years later, Eibelstadt 'fossils' are much sought after.

Twin grey-stone villages, either side of a road bridge at K265, are respectively called Sommerhausen and Winterhausen, a situation so contrived that their names might have been selected by a local government committee for adjoining districts in a New Town! Sommerhausen was well known after the First World War for its artists' community. Today it has a 50-seat *Torturmtheater*, highly regarded throughout the region.

Our first visit to Ochsenfurt ('Oxford', K271) was in 1982, aboard Lord and Lady Harvington's *Melitina*. We arrived on Easter Saturday and, as navigation was to be suspended the next day, had ample opportunity to see how the festival was celebrated in this Catholic corner of Germany. On the boat, painted Bavarian eggs, rabbits and small birds hung from our Easter tree, a charming custom of decorating a branch of birch, alder or similar small-leaved plant. Each year since, *Avonbay*'s opening cruise has been enlivened by the need to find suitable green-budded material for this spring-time tradition. We have cruised with Easter tree on the Canal du Midi, at Toul, in Strasbourg, on the Lahn, the Moselle and the Upper Saône. That initial discovery of Ochsenfurt was further enhanced by a splendid con-fectioner's cake in the form of a Paschal Lamb, created from iced sponge and meringue, which was placed on the chart table.

While there is a yacht club harbour, an even better (free) mooring will be found on a public quay immediately upstream of the Alte Brücke. The Main has been bridged here since 1200, first in timber and from the early seventeenth century by a stone structure. The town was once a staging post on the trade route between the Baltic port of Lübeck and the Adriatic. The present bridge of many small, rounded arches was partly destroyed by the 'home team' in the final stages of the Second World War and the modern navigation span enlarged a few years after to accommodate the new breed of European inland ships. Seventeenth-century illustrations show the town built on a square plan, completely surrounded by walls. Much remains from this period, including huge entrance towers at each end of the main street. As befits the capital of the *Südliches Maindreieck*, Ochsenfurt's 'new' *Rathaus*, started in the late fifteenth century, is one of the finest buildings in Franconia, all the more special for its mechanical clock of 1560 housed in a pointed turret, grafted on to the centre of the slate roof. We gathered just before the striking of the hour to see Death emerge as a skeleton, invert an hour-glass and raise an arrow. Next a pair of councillors peeped out through mullioned windows, watching the *Bürgermeister*'s head nod in time with the mech-anism's striking. Two oxen engaged in battle with their horns and a maiden raised the Franconian coat of arms. Inside the building is preserved a replica of the seventeenth-century *Kauz* ('owl') drinking vessel; whosoever could consume its 3 litre capacity of wine in a single draught was entitled to have his name recorded for all time in the *Kauzen-Buch*. Two books were quickly filled, as the fame of this drinking contest rapidly spread.

Stopping for refreshment in a café/cake shop, we were politely but firmly told that our chosen table was reserved. Accordingly, we moved to another and within a few minutes an elegant and extremely elderly lady, wearing obligatory feathered hat, arrived to claim her habitual seat next to us. Sideways glances revealed that she was evidently fascinated by our conversation. I made a few remarks to her in German and so opened up a floodgate of reminiscence. She told of how she had been born in America 85 years earlier, emigrated with her family to Germany before the First World War, and had never managed to revisit her native country. We asked if she remembered any English. 'Certainly,' she replied and rapidly counted, parrot-fashion, in a pronounced American accent from one to twenty. Seemingly, this was the only English that remained. There was much I should have liked to ask, but we were defeated by a communication barrier.

Three kilometres upstream lies Frickenhausen, a walled village standing at the water's edge and surrounded on three sides by its famous vineyards. Since 1790 the Meintzinger family have been leading wine producers. The present generation also run a luxury hotel. As there was no mooring, we anchored briefly opposite the water-gate, where a row of flood mark plaques recorded some stupendous inundations. The prized Franconian wine of Frickenhausen is both excellent and expensive and is sold in a unique flattened bellied container known as a *Bocksbeutel*. Allegedly, these glass bottles are a modern substitute for billy-goats' scrotums. Even if production was once a fraction of its current level, any Bavarian he-goat with the slightest inclination towards self-preservation must have regarded the approach of adulthood with considerable worry!

Beyond a lock, Marktbreit (K277) and Segnitz are both charming towns with pretty waterfronts and stone towers. Pleasure craft moorings are to be found in a basin, immediately downstream of the road bridge. Marktbreit's Goldener Löwe of 1442 is said to be the second oldest inn in Bavaria; it is just one of many fine timbered houses near the town wall. We also noted a magnificent eighteenth-century circular crane, once used for unloading barges. In the days of basic sanitation, houses discharged directly into the Breitbach stream, but use of privies was banned by public edict for a period of three days when the nearby Prince's Castle Brewery was about to use water supplies for making beer! Segnitz was once populated by fishermen and barge families and has an impressive half-timbered *Rathaus*.

Now the river widened past extensive lakes formed from old gravel pits before reaching Marksteft (K281) with its renovated fortified church. Sulzfeld (K282) is another town ringed by walls and towers and was once associated with salt production. As a wine centre, it is today even better known for food-eating contests. The heart of this curious activity is the Zum Goldenen Löwen inn, where metre-long sausages are devoured. A record has been established for gorging $5\frac{1}{2}$ m of sausages in a single sitting!

After increasing worry that we would never find a suitable overnight stopping place, we discovered a perfect location in Kitzingen (K286), alongside a landscaped and central quay equipped with rings to which we tied. Unexpectedly deep, we were little affected by the wash of passing traffic. A short walk took us to the town centre, where a traditional Bavarian restaurant served one of the best dinners we had bought in Germany. John was delighted to find a cheerful red-nosed plastic gnome lurking in the window of a hardware shop. Happily clutching a concertina, this jolly creature could not fail to remind us of our musical marine engineer Jim! Duly purchased, the Gnome of Nuremberg (as he was subsequently named) awaited Mig and Jim in *Avonbay*'s bow cabin when they arrived in September to help us take the boat through the Rhine–Main–Danube Canal. Now installed beneath a bay tree on the Macdonalds' Grand Union Canal mooring at Cassio Bridge, Watford, *Der musikalische Gnom von Nürnberg* smiles contentedly at passing vessels, wistfully recalling the Bavaria of his youth and doubtless wondering if he will be invited to join the crew of *Elizabeth* when that mid-nineteenth-century converted narrow boat eventually sets out on her planned exploration of European waterways.

At Gerlachshausen (K300), 5 km of lock cut bypass more than twice that distance of natural river, a situation that has sadly removed all river traffic from several small villages. Some years earlier, while working through Wipfeld Lock (K316), the keeper's daughter Melanie took a special liking to us as she proudly displayed her latest acquisition: a powerful motorbike. She was a chatty young lady, fluent in English and eager for us to send her a selection of British pop music magazines. We complied with this request for what seemed to be a decent period, always anxious to forge friendships with people encountered on our travels. Now, six years later, there was no Melanie in evidence – but then, she never had been the kind of girl who would remain long in such a rural backwater.

Still the vineyards continued until we reached Schweinfurt ('Pigford', K332). Its ball-bearings factory prompted repeated bombing raids in the last war, resulting in much of the town being destroyed. By working uphill through the lock and turning into a weirstream, a useful quayside will be found just below the road bridge, close to an old crane, with green conical roof.

Upriver, the broad Main is dominated by the stepped gables of *Schloss* Mainberg. Rather than behaving like the higher reaches of most river navigations, this waterway achieves what is probably the greatest width in its entire course at the village of Untertheres (K348), with a long series of artificial rocky islets marking the starboard side of the fairway. Now evening was approaching. No pleasure boat moorings had appeared on the chart since Schweinfurt or were marked for a considerable distance to come. In all probability, we would have to lie at anchor, a nautical manœuvre that we had come to regard with distrust in regions frequented by large cargo ships.

It was therefore with considerable relief that we discovered a deserted quay outside an ancient brick-built warehouse in Hassfurt (K355). Designed as a fortified 'new town' in the thirteenth century, there remain three entrance gates and plenty of sixteenth-century architecture. One clue as to former industries is provided by a museum display of moulds used by chandlers and gingerbread-makers.

Shortly after we had finished dinner, a colourful Arab family arrived outside our saloon for an evening's fishing. The young father was immensely proud of his three small children and in quite passable English introduced them to us as Mary, Peter and Hassan: a curious collection of names for people from Afghanistan. As *Gastarbeiten*, they seemed to enjoy a somewhat precarious existence, living in a converted bus and undertaking casual labour when they could find it. They were among the most interesting encounters of our voyage up the river, but appeared to be dreadfully vulnerable in a country where distinctive foreigners are no longer universally welcomed on the labour market.

As night approached, a powerful and very affluent open sportsboat roared past our mooring, navigation lights blazing, its hull a sparkling streak of kingfisher blue. At the wheel, its yuppie owner was concentrating rather more on his girlfriend than his direction of travel. Having narrowly avoided sudden and violent contact with the bank, they silenced the engine and, blissfully unaware of anyone else, came drifting back downstream, tightly draped around each other.

We had planned an early start in order to reach Bamberg by lunchtime, and so spend 24 hours in our favourite Bavarian city. Ready to move by 7 am, the sky suddenly darkened as the blackest of clouds turned the clock back several hours. Distant thunder rapidly closed in until there was scarcely any interval between the jagged flashes of lightning and repeated crashes. For 20 minutes *Avonbay* lay at the very centre of the most violent storm I had ever experienced. Soon the decks were pouring with torrential rain that obliterated the shadowy landscape outside. A pair of laden barges came downriver, their searchlights unable to penetrate the thick gloom and obviously relying on radar. To think that we had seriously considered lying at anchor the previous night! Eventually the skies began to clear, and daybreak arrived for the second time.

Three final Main locks remained before we reached K384, where the unnavigable river branched off to the left. Ahead, the first 5 km of the Main–Donau Kanal brought us to the centre of Bamberg and a well-remembered mooring. *Avonbay* had travelled a considerable distance from the Rhine. We were now poised at the gateway to eastern Europe.

11 Rhine–Main–Danube Canal

Rhine is united with Danube. From the title page of a book on Ludwig's Canal, published in 1845.

In his masterly *World Canals*, Charles Hadfield describes the nineteenth-century Ludwig's Canal as 'Europe's most delightful canal'. Praise indeed. During our stay in Bamberg, I set off through the city on a bicycle to test this claim. Later, while waiting for the Grand Opening of the new Main–Danube Waterway, we were to explore much of the eastern part of the route by the somewhat more expensive method of hiring a taxi.

Ludwig's was not the first attempt to link waterways of western Europe with the Danube. Back in AD 793, Emperor Charlemagne ordered work to begin on the Fossa Carolina, little more than 5 km of ditch which would connect the River Altmühl with the Schwäbische Rezat. Centuries before the invention of navigation locks, this was a bold concept whose strategic value would have been considerable. But canal-building techniques had yet to reach their later sophistication. Water repeatedly flooded the workings and the labourers were moved to other tasks after just two months. Amazingly, 1200 years later, Charlemagne's ditch still holds water in a length that you can see near the village of Graben ('trench').

No further canal building was to be attempted in Bavaria's Frankisher Jura until Ludwig I ordered a survey in 1828. Work on the 172 km line started in 1836, beginning in the River Regnitz at Bamberg and rising to a height of 457 m above sea level near Nuremberg. Like the new canal we were about to navigate in *Avonbay*, Ludwig's was the highest navigation in Europe. Equipped with 100 stone-chambered locks suitable for 100-tonne capacity barges, it fell to the canalised Altmühl and eventually joined the Danube at Kelheim. Conditions on the Main and Danube were to discourage much long-distance traffic.

It was opened throughout in 1845 with a procession of vessels decorated with garlands and banners. In 1984 London antiquarian book dealer Ben Weinreb published a catalogue of more than 300 rare works and ephemera concerning inland waterways. Among these treasures were two Ludwig's Canal 'peepshows', each consisting of six exquisite coloured engraved panels: the viewer looked through a pair of circular windows to be treated in one case to a three-dimensional view down a staircase of locks, terminating in a distant representation of Nuremberg. The other version showed the scene on Opening Day. Each was fragile and difficult to display. Moreover, resembling a model theatre with multiple layers of scenery, they were virtually impossible to photograph for illustration purposes. Doubtless printed for Pfennigs, they were on offer at £650 and £485 respectively. I was tempted for a matter of seconds only, but my enthusiasm for the canal was fired. I determined to explore, one day, what remained.

Several travellers' accounts survive, all suggesting that traffic through Ludwig's Canal was never exactly brisk. Robert Mansfield's *The Water Lily on the Danube: A Brief Account of the Perils of a Pair-Oar during a Voyage from Lambeth to Pesth* (Budapest) appeared in 1853. *A Cruise Across Europe* by Donald Maxwell (1907) makes much of delays in Bamberg while permission was sought to navigate through to the Danube. He paid a total of about 27p for the use of all 100 locks and was quite unable to persuade any of the keepers to accept tips. The towpath was well maintained (*Walrus*'s crew were bow-hauling) and Maxwell comments as they climbed ever higher that it was as if 'the Wey and Arun Canal had lost itself upon a spur of the Alps'. Henry Rowland (*Across Europe in a Motor Boat*, 1908) missed the canal altogether, finding a mere 0.5 m of water in the Main above Frankfurt. *Beaver* was accordingly transported to the Danube on a cart: 'I was secretly glad. Since sailing from London we had passed through two hundred and twenty three locks. I never want to see another lock ... except in the Panama Canal.'

The next recorded passage is Negley Farson's *Sailing Across Europe* of 1926. By then, Ludwig's Canal was 'probably the most unknown and least-used waterway in the world. The German Consulate in London had never heard of it.' Arriving in Bamberg, Farson enquired how many pleasure craft used the route: 'There was a boat came through here in – let me see – 1905. And another only a few years ago,' said a canal official. They were charged 100 marks plus 10 Marks for their engine 'and 3 Marks also because you are foreigners'. In places, 'the weeds were so thick that the surface of the canal looked like dry land ... a veritable inland Saragasso Sea ... [it] will soon pass into history'. Probably the last passage by an Englishman (who was firmly of the opinion that he was the first!) was Merlin Minshall's curious epic of 1933, aboard a magnificent little Dutch barge named *Sperwer*. Reading his illustrated article in the *National Geographic Magazine* for May 1937, we learn nothing of the author's subsequent claim that he was employed as an anti-Nazi spy by the British government; and that he was investigating how best to block navigation on the Danube to prevent an annual 2 million tonnes of fuel oil and cereals reaching the Third Reich! Claiming to be the original of Ian Fleming's James Bond, Minshall was visited by Hermann Goering while the first Nuremberg Rally was in full swing nearby. He was obliged to fight a duel with pistols in Budapest and had a passionate love affair when a German spy called Lisa Kaltenbrunner was taken on board as mistress/crew (his young wife had jumped ship earlier in the voyage). For these lurid details, refer to his book *Guilt-Edged* (1975). One indisputable fact, supported by photographic evidence, is that Merlin Minshall did navigate Ludwig's Canal; whether he really escaped the threat of Nazi imprisonment

Canal builder Ludwig I of Bavaria.

by working himself through the final lock in Kelheim at dead of night and running downriver to Austria is for the reader to decide.

The canal attracted a record 196 000 tonnes of freight in 1850, but by 1936 this had slumped to 41 700 tonnes. The Second World War saw a massive resurgence of traffic with E-boats passing through to the Black Sea. Allied bombing in Nuremberg caused closure in 1944, and repairs had been carried out on the eastern half by 1947. Four years later restoration came to an abrupt end. Thereafter, all efforts were to be devoted to construction of the large-capacity R–M–D Canal. Many derelict waterways fill me with sadness, but I find it difficult to mourn the loss of Ludwig's Canal. Given the choice of a canal where, in its final years, both water and air draught were insufficient for *Avonbay*, or a brand new route capable of passing the biggest inland ships used in Europe, I know which I prefer – even if we did have to wait until September 1992 to reach the Danube.

Bamberg is a cathedral city whose ecclesiastical monuments dominate a hilly site beyond the River Regnitz. Earlier visits had confirmed this as one of Bavaria's most attractive towns, rich in ornate architecture and stylish shops. I cycled from our mooring at the Kettenbrücke – through the pedestrianised Maximilliansplatz, where a huge open-air market was doing good business – and reached a tangle of waterways formed from various channels and millstreams of the Regnitz. To the right, Little Venice is a jumble of onetime fishermen's houses. On the quayside is one of the characteristic mid-nineteenth-century Ludwig's Canal cranes, protected by a conical iron roof. While fully navigable from the through route via an electrically worked lock, it appears that all but passenger cruisers and local pleasure boats are banned. Rather a pity, I thought, for *Avonbay* would have looked very fine in front of the magnificent rococo *Rathaus*, set on an island, with curious half-timbered house projecting over a bridge cutwater next to the town gateway. Huge murals decorate one side of the old town hall and a painted cherub is fitted with a three-dimensional leg which he cocks over the edge of a stone pediment. Strong currents must have made entry to the canal anything but easy.

Expensive antique shops packed with unaffordable treasures, narrow twisting streets of ancient houses and everywhere the prospect of turning a corner to discover another little waterway, make this the most interesting part of town. During our last stay we had dined, somewhat financially ruinously, in the Böttingerhaus, an early eighteenth-century Baroque mansion, inspired by a Venetian palace. Now, in the heat of a late July day, I sought out a path alongside the river. On the opposite bank the classical columns of several large mansions were reflected in the clear water.

Soon I reached a lock connecting Ludwig's Canal with the river. Although the chamber was partially obstructed by young alders, the decayed wooden gates appeared quite as serviceable as those at the near-derelict Elvington Lock on the Yorkshire Derwent which I was to negotiate with a narrow boat several weeks later. But, judging from the state of the wood-decked iron

Bamberg's island Rathaus *on the River Regnitz.*

drawbridge, long fixed in a closed position at the upper end, it was many years since a boat had passed through. The original keeper's house, however, was well maintained as a private residence. For 20 minutes I cycled along the bank of the navigation, here absorbed into the Regnitz; ancient beeches hung over the water and at one point a rowing club and drinking establishment proved that boats have not entirely deserted Ludwig's Canal.

Years before, while I was standing in a Munich street, a group of German youths had called out 'Ludwig! Ludwig!' As the area was otherwise deserted, I concluded that they were addressing me. Subsequent pictorial research suggested that there was indeed a fleeting resemblance between myself and the eccentric (if not actually mad) King Ludwig II, grandson of the canal builder. A brief lifetime of hectic castle construction, commissioning boats in the form of swans (I share a mild fixation with this elegant water bird, derived in my case from St Hugh, Bishop of Lincoln, who kept one as a pet), and his drowning in frankly suspicious circumstances in Starnberg Lake in 1886 at the age of 41 are the bare bones of a fascinating story. The reclusive Ludwig II and his legacy of castles, none more fantastic than Neuschwanstein, may have been unpopular in his lifetime. After all, the castle-building mania threatened to bankrupt the kingdom of Bavaria. But today the Ludwig legend is perhaps the single most profitable feature of the region's tourist industry. Suddenly, in a grassy clearing near the canal, I came upon a larger than life bronze statue of the Swan King; it was unmistakably him, although I still felt compelled to get close enough to read the inscription beneath. So I was able to return to *Avonbay* to regale the disbelieving crew with an account of how I had come face to face with Ludwig himself!

So anxious were we to participate in the Grand Opening of the R–M–D Canal, that we planned to reach Nuremberg – temporary end of the line – seven weeks early. Months before, application for moorings until late September had been made to the grandly named No 1 Nürnberg Motor Yacht Club (there is only one!). Suitable details of our credentials accompanied this written enquiry. After all, there was little point in going unless we were accorded the status of Important British Yacht. When, after a long delay, no response was forthcoming, I pulled rank by appealing to my German publishers to confirm our booking. My friends replied that all was in order, but suggested that I should telephone Nuremberg 48 hours before arrival. Now feeding coins into a phone outside Bamberg's main post office, I was struggling with a conversation entirely in German with the yacht club harbourmaster. Such a procedure is not too awe-inspiring given eye-contact and gestures, but communication with this unseen Bavarian was hard work. 'And how long is your boat?' he asked, seemingly unaware that vital statistics had long ago been supplied in writing. 'Eleven metres? I think we have no space here for so large a ship!' Thinking quickly, I thanked Herr Hafenmeister, saying we were much looking forward to meeting him the next day. I then quickly replaced the receiver. None of this was reported to June and John – no point in being blamed for incompetence.

Bamberg to Nuremberg, the 65 km western portion of the R–M–D, is a fairly typical product of the 1960s. Widespread use of reinforced concrete for locks, bridges and bank protection creates a somewhat bleak landscape; even 20 years after this section was opened in 1972, in places it resembles an aqueous motorway. The seven 190 m-long locks, of which the deepest rise and fall 18 m, surprisingly lack floating bollards, necessitating frequent shifting of our lines as we rose towards the distant summit. On one occasion the incoming water, entering through ports directly beneath us, was so fierce that we were unable to hold on. Having lost control, we resorted to completing the manœuvre drifting in mid-chamber with short bursts on the engines as necessary.

On this hot Saturday afternoon each bankside path was alive with walkers, cyclists and fishermen. Some of the route is lined by fir tree plantations; elsewhere, there are broad views across undulating cornfields. While over-night moorings could have been found below a lock, the possibility of commercial traffic might have placed us in some danger. We therefore turned into the weirstream at K25, shortly before Forchheim Lock, and found ourselves at the idyllic headquarters of the MYC Forchheim. One of the members had worked as a nurse with the American forces in Nuremberg since the end of the war, spoke excellent English, fixed us up with a hotel for our final night in Germany, and levied a 15 DM charge for use of the club's facilities. Unfortunately we did not then know that Forchheim, just 1.5 km away, is a superb small town of half-timbered buildings with an intact medieval core where local kings were elected on at least three occasions. It was a very oppressive evening, almost unbearably hot and stuffy; and while swimming round the boat with detergent and sponge to make the hull look its best for our impending arrival in Nuremberg, a furious thunderstorm broke out overhead. After I had ascertained that there were many taller objects than *Avonbay* in the immediate vicinity and that we were unlikely to be struck by lightning, I thoroughly enjoyed floating in the warm water, while icy torrents of rain cascaded from above.

Having been informed that locks would close early on the Sunday after-noon, we presented ourselves at Forchheim Lock by 6 am, only to be faced by a 70-minute wait. VHF communication with the keeper confirmed a similar delay at the third lock, Erlangen, where we were not admitted until a Nuremberg-bound barge appeared from astern. Our Motor Yacht Club destination in the suburb of Gebersdorf was reached by 2 pm. In spite of earlier misgivings, there was ample space on a floating pontoon, where a pair of strikingly handsome (*they* obviously thought so!) young men in matching white shell suits with gold belts left their 1938-built steel cruiser to help us make fast.

We were not the first arrival in advance of the canal opening the following month: Charles and Phyllis had been waiting some time in their Cowes-registered Moody motor sailer *Barcarolle*, impatient to continue a cruise all the way to the Black Sea. The harbourmaster turned out to be welcoming and helpful, selling us an adaptor so that at long last *Avonbay*'s French-installed shore line could benefit from German electricity supplies. With 48 hours in hand, we worked hard on various minor refinements, cleaning, painting and polishing. Another form of entertainment centred on feeding giant carp, whose home waters we had invaded. Employing infinite patience and cunning, John managed to net a fine specimen that weighed several kilograms. Unfortunately he mistook our neighbours' congratulatory cries for strong disapproval and released the scaly monster before we had a chance to photograph it.

Random selection of a taxi driver to convey us to Nuremberg station as the first stage of our westward journey home to England was to have fortunate consequences. Andreas Knapek knew both Ludwig's Canal and the R–M–D intimately; as he drove us to the city centre we learned that he was a boatowner and regarded his job merely as a means of saving up for early retirement, when, like us, he could begin to explore the rivers and canals of Europe.

Back at the beginning of the year, a long correspondence had commenced with the R–M–D company and the navigation authority in Würzburg. Gradually it became apparent that little was being done to cater for private pleasure boats at the canal opening: indeed, for reasons of tight security we would be banned from navigating on *the* day: Friday, 25 September. Both bodies wished us well but were quite unable to confirm how far we might travel eastwards in advance of the official celebrations. Worse still, my request for a Press Pass – to cover the main events – was rejected in spite of my commission to produce a feature article for *Motor Boat & Yachting*. Just hours before our departure by air from London, a colleague who was not even planning to travel to Bavaria kindly faxed me the elusive application form. Two completed copies were duly transmitted to the canal company in Munich: one for me and the other for June, masquerading as Filmstudio Humphries. With no further questions asked, envelopes containing appropriate lapel badges awaited collection at the Press Centre in Nuremberg's *Meistersingerhalle*. Rarely had I worked so diligently to achieve this seemingly impossible result. At one stage it seemed as if the R–M–D were actively seeking to avoid all publicity!

Pressure of work sadly prevented John from joining June and me on a night flight back to the boat on 20 September. First impressions on reaching *Avonbay* in a taxi laden with provisions was that although we were obviously to form a convoy of cruisers, this would be a highly select collection of vessels. No sign of the anticipated swarms of craft from all parts of Europe, intent on being present at the birth of the world's most significant canal since Suez and Panama. I couldn't help thinking that had this event been taking place in Britain, the private boats would have been numbered in hundreds!

During the next few days a steady stream of cargo carriers and what appeared to be a sizeable proportion of the Rhine's passenger fleet passed our basin, all heading east. In addition to *Barcarolle*, our friends Caroline and Mike Hofman had journeyed from the Netherlands in their splendid Pedro Bora 41, *Van Hof*. Jean and Eric Stallard's trip in their motor sailer *Pulse* had begun off the French Mediterranean coast. Another long-standing friend, Freddy Solèr, arrived on a high-speed cruiser called *Calypso*, after negotiating the Rhine from Switzerland; he was soon to be joined by French hire-craft pioneer Michael Streat, whom we had first met on English canals more than thirty years before. And then there was the amazing Kjell. Kjell Ødegaard, recently retired from museum administration in Stavanger, Norway, was a supremely confident and relaxed boater, determined to reach Greece before the onset of winter in his little motorised sloop *Algenib*. He explained that his Christian name was pronounced 'Shell'; he played, moderately well, a battered trumpet and, slightly less well, a guitar. One night after the arrival of our guests Mig and Jim, we had him on board. Trumpet, guitar and Jim's concertina were played until the early hours, long after the rest of us had retired to bed. Kjell's main preoccupation was his planned arrival by water

1845 view of Ludwig's Canal in Erlangen.

at an Orkney folk music festival the following May, having by then sailed the Mediterranean, French canals and the North Sea.

Despite their name, retired Americans Susy and Jim Sink from Houston, Texas, had successfully crossed the Atlantic in their Nordhavn 46 motor cruiser *Salvation II*. Bound for the Black Sea, they were understandably concerned at the prospect of flying their stars and stripes in the 358 km of Danube wholly within war-torn former Yugoslavia. Tales of barges being shot at were actively circulating. A Berlin-based cruiser named *Komet* and several local vessels comprised the rest of our little fleet.

Rumours began to spread that we might be allowed to set sail on the Friday afternoon, so 24 hours earlier we erected *Avonbay*'s smart new varnished high-level mast, enabling her to be dressed overall for the first time in her 14 years. Including a shining gold flagpole bauble at the very top, this increased our air draught to 5 m, well within the published 6 m clearance of the canal's lowest bridges. Within minutes, other boats were putting up their flags; a keen sense of nervous anticipation was growing. Most of us gathered in *Van Hof*'s saloon one evening to watch a feature-length television programme on the R–M–D. Clearly, Bavaria was thinking about little else.

Time on our hands and nothing remaining to check on the boat, we commandeered Andreas's taxi for a whole day, destination Berching, a superb little medieval walled town chosen as the venue for the official opening ceremonies. Andreas had no intention of taking us there direct. Suddenly, he would swing off the autobahn, head into a forest, and come to a halt by yet another disused lock of the old Ludwig's Canal. Parts that remain are lovingly preserved as ancient monuments (although most locks are gateless, their chambers are better maintained than many that are operational on British canals); so are the attractive lock cottages, stone accommodation bridges and an impressive aqueduct spanning the Schwarzach River near Nuremberg. Towpaths are well surfaced and signposted as agreeable long-distance walks. Generally, the waterway is weedfree and must surely have a future for localised pleasure boating, especially where portions are linked to the R–M–D.

Eventually we reached Berching, an astonishing survival of Hansel and Gretel half-timbering, approached through four original town gates still fitted with massive protective oak doors. Colourful banners and streamers in the blue and white diamonds of the Bavarian flag hung from balconies. The canal had prompted a ten-day festival ranging in scope from fireworks to rock concerts; vast marquees for the consumption of beer to hot air balloons; string quartets to ox roasts; and street dancing to jousting from boats on the water. Everyone was determined to get in on the act, whether by dressing up as Robin Hood lookalikes or cashing in on a lucrative souvenir trade. Displayed in the window of a bank was a scattering of medals, struck to mark completion of the waterway. Supplies in bronze were exhausted while those of solid gold were much too expensive to tempt. We settled on examples of the silver version at 55DM each. One side shows Ludwig's Canal in 1846, while the other depicts the beautiful new Berching waterfront with its opening date. Further canal souvenirs included tee-shirts, a special postage stamp illustrating an undulating canal footbridge in the Altmühl Valley at Essing, picture books and posters. There were also billboard announcements by the Green Party, giving details of an anti-Canal protest rally – a concept that we considered ill-conceived and rather late!

Andreas joined the four of us for lunch in a town square restaurant and afterwards we started the drive back to Gebersdorf, laden with our trophies. One more canal site remained for our tireless guide to show us: a portion of the Mindorfer Line, an abortive section of the R–M–D Canal excavated in the late 1930s, south of Hilpoltstein. Certain lengths of channel are still water-filled and elsewhere in a grassy field are the stone piers of a road bridge that was never completed.

A brief visit to Nuremberg in August had encouraged us to want to see more, so while in town to collect our Press Passes there was ample opportunity to explore further. My 1887 Baedeker, *Southern Germany and Austria including Hungary and Transylvania*, comments: 'There is probably no town in Germany whose external appearance is still so mediaeval, or so well calculated to convey an idea of the wealth, importance, and artistic taste of a "City of the Empire".' Until 1806, when it was absorbed into Bavaria, Nuremberg was an independent imperial town. Severely damaged by Allied bombs in January 1945, it is now a modern industrial place. Nevertheless, extensive work has restored some 5 km of red sandstone fortification wall, punctuated by no fewer than 80 fat towers. Opposite the main railway station we entered a very commendable reconstruction of the medieval town at the Frauenthor to find ourselves in a jumble of narrow streets filled with craft shops, sausage houses and beer gardens.

Perhaps the most exciting time to visit the city is during the four-week run up to Christmas, when street garlands and floodlighting bring a taste of fairyland to the *Christkindlmarkt*. Dating from the mid-sixteenth century, this Christmas market attracts an amazing $2\frac{1}{2}$ million visitors. There are choir concerts, lantern processions and hundreds of stalls trading in everything from traditional wooden toys to decorations, *Lebkuchen* (honey and ginger-bread cakes) and mulled wine. It is perhaps worth remembering that many British Yuletide customs originated in Germany; and nowhere is there a more enthusiastic celebration of Christmas than in Nuremberg.

Most guide books contain little information on two sinister aspects of the city's recent past: Hitler's infamous Rally Grounds and the Nuremberg Trials. Doubtless, these are parts of their history that many of the half-million inhabitants would rather forget.

At the start of our drive back to the boat I asked Andreas, rather diffidently, if anything remained of the Third Reich monuments. Although his name suggested a non-German origin, it is always wise to mention the 1930s and their aftermath with a degree of caution. Saying nothing, he executed a U-turn and within minutes had halted at one end of the Great Road: more than 1 km long and 60 m wide, this is the uncompleted triumphal way from the old Congress Hall to the March Field. *Gastarbeiter* families were encamped on the crumbling edges, tending their barbecues, a concept that Hitler would scarcely have approved of. Nearby, in a vast concrete hall beneath the grandstands overlooking the Zeppelin Field, we discovered an audio-visual presentation of the chilling progress of Nazi rule. This show, entitled 'Fascination and Force', had been staged by the city council in an effort to 'come to terms with the rise and fall of National Socialism'. Familiar footage from Leni Riefenstahl's unforgettable *Triumph of the Will*, edited with shots of concentration camp victims, played on a bank of television screens to a small, silent audience, mainly comprised of young people.

Around us, the relics of Albert Speer's monumental structures were surprisingly intact, even if the giant gilded swastikas had long ago been torn down. A flooded pit is the only reminder of the never-finished German Stadium, designed as a horseshoe-shaped grandstand, 350 m × 150 m and with seating for 405 000. The New Congress Hall of 1935, again unfinished, is a massive four-storey building recalling Rome's Colosseum. Open to the sky, it was intended to be covered with a huge glass roof. Alarmingly, Andreas concluded our tour by driving up a ramp to first-floor level and taking us at high speed through the open colonnades – a feat that was both skilful and almost certainly illegal. Half-hearted current use of Nuremberg's Nazi monuments ranges from storage to football matches and automobile racing – all far removed from the Führer's original intentions. Restoration would undoubtedly be unpopular and yet there is somehow little point in total demolition.

Opening Day finally arrived. Close study of the official programme revealed a ten-hour list of events, in which, thanks to our Press Passes, June and I were entitled to participate. The morning was to be devoted to speeches before a huge gathering of VIPs and politicians in Nuremberg's *Meistersingerhalle*. Despite the presence of these worthies, including Richard Von Weizsäcker (President of the Federal Republic of Germany), Professor Dr Günther Krause (Transport Minister) and Dr Max Streibl (*Ministerpräsident* of Bavaria), absence of any mention of lunch suggested that it might be wise to skip this part of the proceedings. Next, the centre of action was Hilpoltstein Lock, at the west end of the canal's summit level, followed by a passenger ship flotilla to Berching. To be thus trapped on board seemed to offer poor photographic opportunities, so we decided once more to request Andreas to drive us to Berching to await the arrival of the waterborne guests. En route, we diverted to where the passenger ships halted briefly by the waterway monument, midway along the summit level. Fire hoses, aimed bank to bank, created a 'ribbon': cutting this was the symbolic opening ceremony.

Deeply worried by possible terrorist interference, the authorities had positioned security police at every road junction throughout a wide area. In all, 1 500 officers were deployed. Repeatedly, our Press Passes allowed us access to areas banned to the general public. Frogmen, patrol launches and helicopters checked every reach of the waterway. The German government was taking no chances. Already, many thousands of sightseers were in position as we selected a vantage point on the Berching road bridge and settled down to a two-hour wait before the first boats were expected to arrive. Fortunately, after several days of rain and cloud, the sun finally appeared and throughout the extended weekend we were blessed with the blue skies of a real Indian summer. There was plenty to entertain us: contingents of fire-fighters carrying ornate brass poles hung with colourful banners denoting membership of a specific local brigade; townsfolk parading in costumes straight out of the Middle Ages; a troupe of young cheer leaders, sporting feather hats and blue and white Bavarian outfits where narrow pelmets replaced skirts; and more than one brass band. For a waterway that had been under construction between Aschaffenburg and Passau for over 70 years at a reputed cost exceeding £1880 million, the show could hardly be described as extravagant. I enjoyed a long conversation with a German-Swiss waterways enthusiast who had regularly visited the canal works over a ten-year period: he was now taking several days' holiday in order to be part of the most historic canal event any of us were likely to witness.

To our dismay, dozens of unruly schoolchildren, dressed in the red, yellow and black tee-shirts of their national flag, were directed by police to stand immediately in front of our bridge parapet viewpoint. Each bore a stout stick carrying a single letter. When eventually herded into their correct sequence, these spelled out the message 'BERCHING GRUSST DIE GASTE AUS ALLER WELT' ('Berching welcomes guests from all over the world'), a laudable if rather exaggerated sentiment. One over-excited child insisted on waving a union flag in front of our camera lenses, doubtless oblivious of how appropriate this was: he had to be restrained with one hand, leaving the other free to take photographs.

Eventually, at 6 pm, the first of the VIP ships appeared. It was the magnificent *Regina Danubia*, recently built on the Rhine and now undertaking a maiden voyage before going into service on the Danube. Speaking some days later to her cruise director, I learned how this monster vessel, complete with interior marble staircase, had only just scraped under many of the canal bridges, doubtless assisted by the weight of her hundreds of passengers. We infiltrated areas reserved for guests, exchanged a few words with the affable *Ministerpräsident*, and suddenly realised that none of us had eaten for more than eight hours. The size and quantity of fireworks set up on the bridge promised a spectacular display, but we agreed that it was time to escape. What we wanted more than anything else was to return to *Avonbay* for a well-earned dinner.

Mig and Jim had been instructed to move up the canal with the pleasure craft convoy in our absence. The consensus had been that progress might be possible through one or two locks in the early evening. Now, our taxi was taking us through darkness and swirling mist to our flotilla's most likely overnight halt. Until that evening, I had never managed to lose my boat in more than forty years of inland cruising! Finding no sign of our friends below either Nuremberg or Eibach Locks, we concluded that they must still be waiting at the Gebersdorf Yacht Club. A fruitless journey there resulted in the normally cheerful Andreas issuing a string of Germanic oaths. He was tired and hungry, doubtless debating how much of his fare he could reasonably charge, and realised that his British passengers were fast becoming a considerable liability!

Had we foreseen this difficulty, a handheld VHF radio would have maintained contact with *Avonbay*. Sadly, we had not brought one with us. Mig and Jim's long canalling experience convinced us that unless they had both totally lost their powers of reasoning, they would only consider mooring at a lock in such circumstances. Further, progress must have been halted by lock closure for the night, therefore *Avonbay* and associated vessels would inevitably be lying on the *downhill* side of a lock approach. Wearily, we started the drive back towards Berching: Eibach, Leerstettin, Eckersmühlen and eventually Hilpoltsheim Locks. Still no sign. Shouted conversations with barge crews and canal staff suggested that our cruiser might perhaps have already reached the summit. Not a pleasing prospect, as June and I would thus be missing the chance of travelling a substantial part of the canal during this very special weekend. Bad tempered and increasingly worried, we alternated between autobahn and towpath until I suggested that we would have to seek a hotel for the night. Next morning, with lock keepers back on duty, it would not take long to telephone around and recover our missing 'home'. To our horror, Andreas rejected this idea: all accommodation in Greater Nuremberg was booked solid for a conference. We must therefore spend the night at his house. He was already hours late and it took little imagination to picture his wife's reaction when he returned close to midnight with a couple of unknown foreigners! As a last resort, I insisted that the uphill side of Eibach Lock should be checked – this was one of the few locations not yet investigated. There, with huge relief, we discovered a cluster of cruisers and a somewhat anxious Mig and Jim. They had actually seen our taxi near the lock hours before, but had been unable to attract our attention. In all, *Avonbay* had progressed a mere 5 km.

Next morning, I was out on the towpath before daybreak, but thick fog reduced visibility to under 50 m. Charles on *Barcarolle* and Mike Hofman were also awake; together we agreed to wait until conditions improved slightly. Even when the convoy did set out it was difficult to detect much of the presumably fine scenery on the pound to Leerstetten, as dense pine forests were wreathed in swirling whiteness. With all our lights switched on, total concentration was needed to keep the stern of the lead boat in sight, while at the same time attempting to stay clear of several laden freight craft that loomed up on their westward journey. A long wait ensued at Leerstetten Lock, a vast concrete cavern fitted with floating bollards to port. At the front, push-tug *Atlantis* filled the chamber with engine fumes. Seizing their chance to test the acoustics, Kjell and Jim provided a duet on trumpet and concertina, as we rose in a series of controlled surges 25 m to the next level. These deepest locks consume more than 10 million gallons of water during every 20-minute operation: about 60 per cent of supplies are released from sideponds, replenished in the downhill workings.

On board *Van Hof*, an aneroid barometer was running throughout passage of the canal, providing an ink tracing of changes in air pressure. Remarkably, every rise or fall through the locks was recorded on the sheet of graph paper, providing a fascinating 'profile' of the waterway ascending to the summit and falling by regular steps towards its eastern end.

Mid-morning brought clear skies and hot sunshine. Every town and village was *en fête*, decorated with flags and banners. Marquees dispensed foaming tankards of beer, delivered a dozen at a time by Amazonian serving wenches. Crowds thronged the banks, cheering and waving to the little European fleet as we passed. One onlooker applauded *Avonbay* with exceptional enthusiasm; I was pleased that we had taken so much trouble to polish the brass and paintwork and dress her with flags from stem to stern. After years of planning, delays, false press reports and even the suggestion that the R–M–D would never be completed, we could hardly believe that we were actually here, soon to reach the Danube. It was exciting and not a little emotional.

A party of sixteen Inland Waterways Association members were in Bavaria for the festivities. They included chairman David Stevenson and waterways consultant and writer David Edwards-May (co-author of two of my books published 20 years before). These friends were duly distributed between *Van Hof* and *Avonbay*, so that they could share in the unique experience of travelling with the very first private pleasure craft to cross the R–M–D's summit level. Among our contingent was my old friend Hugh Potter, editor of *Waterways World*. With the Hofmans writing a report for *Motorboats Monthly* and me taking care of *Motor Boat & Yachting* and *Canal & Riverboat*, the British boating press was to receive wide coverage. Curiously, the event appeared to be ignored by UK television and such brief national newspaper accounts as appeared in England were mainly discouraging, concentrating unfairly on environmental objections and a belief that the R–M–D can never operate profitably. Expert calculations suggest that to achieve success, the waterway must carry an annual 22 million tonnes of goods. With much anticipated traffic coming from the eastern Danube countries, there are fears that antiquated barges might cause catastrophic accidents in locks, should engines or gear boxes fail. However, traffic levels do not represent the whole story, for it is claimed that the R-M-D should be self-financing from a £23 million revenue produced each year by 55 hydroelectric stations working between the Rhine and the Danube.

June and I left *Avonbay* in the capable charge of our guests while we took to our bicycles to photograph the pound from Eckersmühlen to Hilpoltstein. This reach provided a foretaste of how very attractive a large freight waterway can become within a short time of its completion. If anyone fears that modern canals are a blot on the landscape, a visit to the eastern R–M–D would doubtless change that attitude. Yet, in spite of finding more than a million artefacts since building began in the Altmühl Valley, south-east Bavaria's leading archaeologist Bernd Engelhardt admits he would rather the canal had never been built!

Through the 406-m high summit and past the award-winning granite monument marking the watershed between east and west, darkness closed in as we made our first descent at Bachhausen Lock under the glare of floodlights. Unexpectedly, the pleasure cruiser convoy, now augmented by a dozen local boats, had been invited to jump a queue of perhaps three lockfuls of freight craft. Berching for Saturday night had suddenly become a reality. There, the new marina was already packed with sports boats. Searchlight directed ahead, we entered gingerly, amid a chorus of bankside shouts that draught was restricted to 1 m. *Avonbay* grounded, so we carefully reversed out to seek deeper moorings opposite the town's main gate. Until now, the authorities had been relaxed and helpful. Ahead, in the gloom, a police launch hovered, unlit except for a pair of red beacons at its masthead. 'Navigation into the town centre is *verboten!*' they bellowed, without any explanation that traffic had briefly been halted for yet another firework display. Further, they claimed that pleasure boats were forbidden to moor on the town walls. It had been a thrilling day, but a long one. I recalled other occasions when German water police had lacked the welcoming attitude that this situation demanded. None of us were prepared to be bullied by a boatload of officious youngsters in uniforms. One of our number conveniently forgot his fluent German and delivered a forceful speech to the effect that having travelled halfway across Europe to take part in the celebrations, we British expected a more congenial reception! By force of numbers and in the confusion of darkness, the convoy duly made fast at our chosen quayside. Defeated, the police launch's response was to surge past at high speed, throwing up a wash that threatened to deposit the smaller cruisers on top of the wall. And this from people who are employed to display an example of correct behaviour to other users! On subsequent reflection, we should have registered our official complaint; but its outcome might well have been rather different from what would have happened in similar circumstances back in England. Jim and his concertina vanished into the night to seek out a beer tent; the rest of us collapsed gratefully into bed.

Jollifications recommenced early next day, as fires in the streets of Berching were prepared for sausage roasts. Bells pealed as yet another brass band led a congregation of several hundred on their parade to church. Overhead, a hot air balloon drifted in the clear sky. On a preserved length of Ludwig's Canal, horsedrawn boat trips provided an evocative reminder of the past. A gentle amble through the streets came to an abrupt halt with news that the four remaining locks to Kelheim would close at 2 pm on this Sunday. While not in fact true, we were determined to reach the Danube by evening, as June was due to fly back to London the next day.

Leaving the rest of the British fleet behind, we joined a collection of German cruisers and enjoyed a long conversation with the English teacher owner of an electric dayboat as we waited for Dietfurt Lock. Water had been admitted to one section of the canal as recently as the previous July, so there was much raw earth and gravel in the valley of the Altmühl River. Rather than restrict landscaping of the new works to a narrow ribbon on each side of the

Avonbay suitably dressed for the canal opening.

waterway, a wide area was undergoing tree planting, creation of marshlands for wildlife and healing the scars in a wholly admirable fashion, all at an additional cost of £120 million. In Beilngries, boating enthusiasts thronged a brand new marina with waterfront restaurant. Later, several years had allowed the navigation to develop as a most attractive feature of the countryside. Already the easternmost section of the R–M–D is one of the most beautiful lengths of waterway in Germany. Several preserved lock keepers' houses remain from Ludwig's Canal and add considerable interest to the journey. Bridges have been architect-designed: the most memorable is an extraordinary undulating footbridge formed from planks of laminated timber at Essing. This has already achieved national fame through being featured on a commemorative postage stamp.

The two final locks before the Danube at Riedenburg and Kelheim unexpectedly remained in service for passenger vessels; we, however, chose to work ourselves through alternative tiny *Sportbootsschleusen*, just 4 m wide. At the first, an elderly Australian engineer watched the manœuvre with great interest, telling us that he was walking the entire canal. So nearly arrived at his objective, he refused our offer of a ride to the next lock.

Once towering above Ludwig's Canal and now crowning a limestone pinnacle high above the new waterway, *Schloss* Prunn is known as 'The jewel of the Altmühl Valley'. Dating back to the early eleventh century, the castle was restored by Ludwig I and is open to the public. Not far upstream are some Palaeolithic cave dwellings. We made a mental note that this was obviously an area for prolonged exploration during our next visit.

Jim was steering when, without warning, the boat veered towards a group of bystanders under a bridge. Frankly surprised that he seemed to be inviting these strangers on board without consulting us, I then recognised (with a little private embarrassment) David Stevenson and his IWA party. We organised an impromptu tea party and hurried on to Kelheim where they could disembark, ready to fly back to England.

Possible moorings in the concrete-lined cut below Kelheim Lock appeared somewhat congested with passenger boats, so we continued on, eager with anticipation at joining the mighty Danube. Deep in the heart of central Europe, it was almost impossible to believe that our brave little *Avonbay* had at long last reached this legendary navigation, the first motor cruiser in more than half a century to make the journey on her own keel! There was every excuse to celebrate with a bottle of German 'Champagne', bought for this purpose more than eight weeks earlier on the Rhine.

OPPOSITE *Hilpoltstein Lock, Rhine–Main–Danube Canal, has a rise and fall of 25 m. Avonbay is seen seeking a mooring, centre of the chamber. Floating bollards are installed on the left side only. Water enters in a series of fierce surges from a group of three side pounds constructed at differing levels to the right.*

12 *Danubian Epilogue*

Uncharacteristically carefree raftsman on the Bavarian Danube.
Early 20th century advertising card.

There had been a time when the Rhine sounded like a fairly terrifying waterway. However, our various *downstream* voyages had led us to the conclusion that its evil reputation had been somewhat embroidered in yacht club bars. But how would *Avonbay* fare on the Danube, with our maximum stillwater speed barely exceeding 10 knots? Lack of time and a reluctance to return westwards via Greece and the Mediterranean (our chosen relaxation is *inland* boating) means that we have no plans to travel all 2411 km from Kelheim to the Black Sea. Moreover, war-torn former Yugoslavia did not then constitute our ideal of peaceful cruising. Instead, an objective of Vienna and perhaps the Hungarian capital of Budapest seemed possible for our 1993 exploration: 761 km with 12 locks and some of the most glorious river scenery in Europe. But would we find the power to return against a current reputedly running at more than 10 knots? In May 1991 I joined June and John on a passenger ship cruise from Passau to Budapest and back; on that occasion, the stream frequently appeared to be making quite this speed. When it was time to attempt this run, there was a strong possibility that the return journey could only be made under tow from a freight barge.

Yet now, in late September 1992, water levels were considerably reduced and any flow in the through navigation was barely noticeable. A mystery had until recently surrounded 175 km of the uppermost Danube, between Kelheim and Ulm. Shown as navigable on certain charts, these reaches are totally ignored by Rod Heikell's newly published *The Danube, a River Guide*.

Equipped with 16 locks, about 22 m × 4 m, and used in its spectacular lower section by passenger craft, here is a cruising ground that seems to offer considerable scope. But investigation revealed bridges at Donauwörth, Offingen and Oberelchingen Lock respectively providing only 2.5 m, 2.4 m and 2.0 m air draught. Moreover, water depths seemed more suited to planing cruisers than heavy displacement craft like *Avonbay*. Finally, a bureaucracy devoted to limiting private boat passages to just five per week and a 136 hp restriction on engine power, all pointed to this being a length that perhaps we should avoid. Those determined to overcome the difficulties should apply to purchase a navigation permit from Stadt Ingolstadt, Postfach 2840, 8070 Ingolstadt (Tel: 0841 305 248).

We checked in at the Rammelmeyr family's impressive new marina at Saal/Donau, 2 km below the junction, where a winter berth had already been arranged. A 2290DM payment entitled us to six months of open-air storage ashore, inclusive of craning and pressure hosing the hull. In spite of our painstaking winterisation of engines and domestic water supplies, I accepted the yard's firm advice that boats should not be left afloat. Winters can be exceptionally severe, with half a metre of ice regularly building up in the harbour. This was hard to believe as we watched boaters wearing only swimwear and sun hats cleaning their boats' hulls on the hard-standing.

The brief visit to Bavaria was drawing to its close; we dined at an agreeable Italian restaurant overlooking the basin. Sadly, June departed next day by taxi, persuaded by Andreas that it was better value to have him make the return trip from Nuremberg rather than relying on a variety of taxis and local trains. The illusion that we were far from home was somewhat shattered when I telephoned her six hours later to discover that she had reached Wimbledon safely an hour before.

Mig, Jim and I had two free days before preparing the boat for her winter sojourn, so we agreed to run 33 km down the Danube to Regensburg (Ratisbon). All around us, trees were beginning to turn to gold. Autumn had arrived and the Danube was both placid and very beautiful. Clusters of deserted cruisers lay in a lagoon, the headquarters of the Kelheim Yacht Club. Later, there was a floating stage for the use of clients of a waterside restaurant. Compared with some German waterways, this part of the river seemed to be well furnished with pleasure craft facilities. Just before Bad Abbach Lock, we looked back to see a magnificent little tug bearing down on us, with tall funnel billowing black smoke while jets of steam issued from numerous pipes on her hull and superstructure. Like us, the 15 m-long *Gredo* had come here for the R–M–D opening and was also bound for Regensburg in order to make the acquaintance of a preserved Danube paddle steamer. Noting our enthusiastic interest, they handed us an information sheet. Built in 1916, she had been restored by a museum near Frankfurt. Those on board were equally divided into well-dressed passengers consuming tankards of beer while seated under an awning at the stern, and the crew, a collection of seriously grimy stokers and engineers. We accepted an invitation to view this archaic machine: I was alarmed to discover that visibility from the wheelhouse was for much of the time non-existent, thanks to swirling clouds of steam. Lacking direct controls, a telegraph system communicated with the engine room where a crew member changed speed and applied reverse. Heaps of coal lay stacked amid puddles of oil. This was an environment where no one could hope to remain clean for more than five minutes. My limited experience of steam craft had until this point been restricted to pretty contraptions of polished brass and mahogany, decorated with horn gramophones, picnic hampers and young ladies wearing Victorian costumes. *Gredo* was a very different kind of vessel: restored, certainly, but retaining much of the rugged character of a boat designed to work for her living.

Gredo's skipper came to look at our Danube chart. Quite correctly, he hesitated to plant his boots on our teak deck and gazed in wonder at *Avonbay*'s royal-blue saloon carpet. 'That doesn't matter,' cried Jim. 'Do come inside!' (We *Avonbay* regulars invariably remove our shoes before setting foot inside the cabin. But Jim has never been able to appreciate a carpeted area in which is located a trapdoor leading to 'his' engine room!) Rapidly I took the map outside, where it could be consulted without damage to our furnishings!

Darkness closed in well before Regensburg Lock. The two boats glided rapidly downriver, *Avonbay*'s navigation lights gleaming. *Gredo*, meanwhile, had started up her antiquated generator to power a string of fairy lights. The noisy whine of this machinery, coupled with the regular thumping of her steam engine and frequent joyous blasts on the whistle, were a heart-stopping combination, quite equal to an encounter with a veteran car or vintage steam locomotive.

Distracted by the glow of lights around us and unable to make out kilometre posts on the banks, we overshot the required righthand turn out of the through navigation where we needed to follow the original course of the Danube into Regensburg city centre. Switching on our searchlight, we swung round to face into the stream, found the correct channel, and hovered in a considerable flow while *Gredo* made fast to a high stone wall. Within seconds of mooring alongside her, I sensed that we had made a mistake. Blasts of scalding steam were being directed straight on to the paintwork of our hull. Our tugboat friends warned that they would be moving off at 6 am, although inevitably it was mid-morning before they finally departed. We decided to seek an alternative place to lie, against the opposite bank.

Rain fell almost continuously during our stay of two nights, an unwelcome if appropriate situation for a city named Regensburg (*Regen* = rain). In the grey light of morning, we discovered that our otherwise convenient and central berth, immediately downstream of the Eiserne Brücke, was obstructed by most unpleasant submerged sheets of piling which gnawed away at our paintwork in the wash of every passing boat. Several abortive attempts were made to find alternative accommodation; river levels were unusually low, leaving expanses of dry gravel. The current, however, remained fierce on this city channel and was racing dangerously fast through the many arches of the mid-twelfth century Steinerne Brücke. Originally this splendid structure featured three towers, recalling the famous Pont Valentré over the Lot at Cahors in south-west France. Only one now remains, alongside a huge old salt warehouse on the southern side. As the upstream navigation channel lies directly alongside the quay, it appeared most unwise to make use of a series of inviting mooring bollards here. However, what must surely be the best mooring in Regensburg was eventually located 300 m downriver.

Limited available time prompted exploration only of the more obvious attractions of this wonderful city: we plan to return in the future. Its history started in about 500 BC as the Celtic settlement of Radasbona. By the third century AD, the important fort of Castra Regina had been established by Roman Emperor Marcus Aurelius, while Regensburg's most powerful period came in the twelfth and thirteenth centuries, when it was granted the status of an autonomous Imperial City. Many medieval buildings remain, for Regensburg appears to have suffered little damage during the Second World War.

Until extension of the modern Rhine–Main–Danube Canal into these Danube reaches, Regensburg was effectively the upper navigation limit for all but the smallest freight barges. Now the troublesome Steinerne Bridge is bypassed by a new cut. We walked up the quayside to investigate the upstream navigation arch and decided that *Avonbay*'s return voyage to Kelheim would not include this route and the little *Sportbootschleuse* that lay well beyond. Passenger vessels regularly ploughing through the swirling water and the establishment of several large pleasure cruiser moorings in the next reach were insufficient reasons to subject our boat to an obvious and quite unnecessary danger.

Robert Mansfield describes the dilemma in his 1853 rowing boat account, *Water Lily on the Danube*:

> When we arrived at Ratisbon, we debated whether we should halt above or below the bridge. Most fortunately, we decided on the former; for the next morning, when crossing it, we found the rush of water through the arches so tremendous, that we could not have shot it in safety; and even if we had escaped being capsized by the waves, we must have been smashed, as immediately below there were a quantity of piles, which we could not possibly have avoided. The passage of the bridge is so awkward, that passengers coming by water from above, and going beyond Ratisbon, have to disembark here, as steamers cannot pass. It is a very picturesque old structure, and one would regret to see it pulled down; yet we could not but agree with the remark of Napoleon, '*Votre pont est très désavantageusement bâti pour la navigation.*'

Little has changed: I found myself totally in accord with Mansfield, 140 years after his visit. His lightly constructed pair-oar overcame the obstacle by means of a brief portage.

Remnants of towpath rollers suggested that a mechanical device had once assisted boats through the maelstrom. Local enquiry confirmed that an electrical haulage apparatus, working from the same 110 v DC supply as the town's tramway system, had operated until the demise of the trams.

Just before our departure, *downstream*, our American and Norwegian friends arrived by water. The river flow was now in excess of 4 knots, thanks to almost constant rain. Urgently, *Avonbay*'s crew called out a warning, indicating the only reliable mooring, alongside us. But intent on reaching the distant yacht club pontoons, just visible through the Steinerne Brücke's turbulent arches, they both insisted on trying their luck further upriver. Ignoring our emphatic advice as to where the sole navigation arch lay, hard on the port side, *Salvation II* headed for the second arch (in spite of clear prohibition notices fixed above), narrowly avoided a head-on collision with an understandably angry down-coming passenger boat, and promptly grounded on a gravel shoal on the far side of the bridge. Somewhat mortified, they managed to turn their sizeable cruiser in the swift current and eventually made fast, with our help, to the very quayside I had pointed out 20 minutes earlier. Notwithstanding all these problems, I suspect that Regensburg's medieval bridge was in fairly good-natured mood that day; obviously, it is best avoided by all sane pleasure boatmen. Negley Farson had no choice in 1925 (*Sailing Across Europe*); he decided to save money on a pilot's fee and shot the rapids without disastrous consequences: 'I got a fleeting glance of Ratisboners hanging over the bridge with their mouths open.' Merlin Minshall was attempting to evade the Nazis and had rather less time to work out a strategy when taking *Sperwer* through in 1933:

> I started up the engine. Got up the anchor. Breathed a quick prayer to Saint Christopher and slipped the final mooring line.
>
> At that exact moment a man who had just joined the crowd of onlookers, leaped off the quayside and landed on my feet. He then tried to grab the tiller. *Sperwer* was already gathering speed. I had no time to ask the man who he was. He might well have been one of Goering's boys of the Abwehr come to arrest me. If he was he'd chosen the wrong moment. One fractional error with the tiller and *Sperwer* and her owner would be a complete write-off.
>
> There was only one thing to do. Remove the man, whoever he was. I didn't have time to pitch him overboard, so, clutching on to the tiller with one hand, I raised the other and gave him the classical Karate chop one and a half inches below the mastoid.
>
> He fell like a poled ox, and even before he'd hit the deck, the sky went black. I had managed to slot *Sperwer*'s thirteen foot beam bang into the centre of the only navigable arch. The bows tilted down at thirty degrees for the plunge and out of the corner of my eye I saw finely tooled masonry whipping past my ear. Then the bows reared up as the stern was sucked down into the after trough of the mill-race and we were through.
>
> I heard a faint cheer from the bridge and at the same moment a movement from my passenger. At least he was alive. It was going to be just too bad if he was also a member of the Gestapo.

Thankfully, in 1992 no such problems faced the crew of *Avonbay*.

We set out to explore what had to be Regensburg's leading attraction. She lay on permanent moorings on the far side of the river: the Navigation Museum, housed in a Danube paddle steamer named *Ruthof*. When built for Bayerischer Lloyd in the city's Ruthof Dockyard during 1922–3, this elegant twin-funnelled vessel was considered to be the ultimate in Danube towing ships. Some 61.55 m overall, with a maximum beam of 16.62 m across the paddle boxes and working on a 1.37 m draught (little more than *Avonbay*'s), she enjoyed a successful career until running on to a wartime mine at Érsekcsanád in June 1944. For the next 12 years, she was a sunken wreck until being salvaged for reconstruction and taken into the service of a Hungarian shipping company under the new name of *Érsekcsanád*. Her working life came to an end during the mid-1970s. Anxious to preserve the last remaining Bavarian paddle steamer, enthusiasts of the Arbeitskreis Schiffahrtsmuseum raised funds for purchase and restoration of the vessel in 1979. Four years of painstaking work enabled *Ruthof* to go on permanent display. Although no longer capable of moving under her own power, the 800 hp two-cylinder main engine, boilers and steam-driven auxiliaries once used for working capstan, towrope winch and steering have all been reinstated. Parts of the crew accommodation remain, while other areas of the ship are devoted to displays of models and photographs, all arranged with a professional flair that would arouse the interest of the least technically minded visitor. We spent an enthralling hour examining this remarkable survival from stem to stern, with Jim all the time explaining her workings. I then paid an obligatory visit to the sales kiosk to purchase various technical books and postcards.

'And how many days have you taken to reach here from England?' asked the attendant, when we pointed out our little ship on the far shore. I paused before replying 'A little over seven years!' to the astonished man, who clearly suspected my German was at fault until I explained how *Avonbay* had been wandering through mainland Europe since leaving her homeland in 1985.

Nearby, *Regina Danubia*, star of the R–M–D celebrations, was staging an Open Day for local townspeople. Hoping to avoid a reprimand as we tiptoed across acres of new carpet in our rather muddy shoes, we were accosted by a rotund young man in a black beret. He introduced himself as Rainer Ehm, director of the Shipping Museum. Intrigued to meet a group of British inland waterways enthusiasts, he returned with us to *Avonbay*, bearing further publications filled with pictures of Danube barges in various stages of destruction. 'This is quite normal on our river,' he said. 'It has always been most dangerous!' We asked which time of the year would be safest to attempt a voyage down to Vienna and Budapest. 'March and April bring the worst currents, when the snows are melting,' Rainer answered, 'but always navigation can be difficult.' This depressing news confirmed my suspicions.

Rainer told us that he was a lawyer, while we lunched with him at the Historische Wurstküche, the Historic Sausage Kitchen, where we were seated at long tables under an awning by the Steinerne Brücke. Much of the credit for *Ruthof*'s restoration seemed due to his efforts. 'We have vintage marine engines in store all over town,' he told us. 'Soon, when we have more display space, they can go on public view.'

That evening, making a circuitous progress through alleys and courtyards to dinner in the *Ratskeller*, we passed through the Cathedral Square. Occupying a prominent corner site was a brightly illuminated store bearing the legend 'Hutkönig'. Investigation proved this to be a very large emporium devoted to nothing but hats. Of hundreds in window displays, I was immediately attracted by an unusual conical, wide-brimmed creation in thick grey felt, decorated with coloured braid and a large curled feather. Essentially Bavarian, with faint overtones of Jack and the Beanstalk, I decided I wanted this strange hat. The moment I said so, Mig and Jim mercilessly encouraged me. We returned the next morning to examine the thousands of items of stock arranged in several rooms on two floors. I don't particularly like wearing hats, but the sheer quantity was almost hypnotic. They ranged from nautical caps to the kind of headgear beloved of the well-equipped *Bürgermeister*. Nothing, though, appealed quite so much as the grey cone of the previous night; without even the slightest notion of where I might sport this curiosity, I was quite unable to avoid purchase. The silver clasp and feather were not included, so I could augment my pleasure by selecting a suitable example from several drawerfuls produced for my inspection. Mig came away with two slightly more useful hats. Jim, normally the most hat-conscious one of us all, was spoiled for choice and sensibly saved his money.

'You must be the biggest and best hat shop in Regensburg,' I tactfully suggested to the proprietor as he operated various strange devices that pressed, stretched and otherwise treated hats for the discerning buyer. 'Mein Herr,' he replied gravely, 'we are the best hat shop in the whole of *Deutschland*!' It appeared that my chosen item was traditional wear of a *Wildmann*, some form of forest dweller, hunter or fur-trapper. Once back on the boat, I wore it for much of that day but have yet to summon up the courage to put it on again!

An uneventful run brought us back up the still placid Danube to Rammelmeyr's marina. Caroline and Michael Hofman were there with *Van Hof* and joined us for a final meal ashore. Down came our decorative flags and we spent a frantic morning preparing *Avonbay* for her long winter of solitude. It would be six months before the first of three planned return visits to this part of central Europe, when we expected to drive over to Prague and devote time to an extended exploration of the great river that leads to the Black Sea.

Postscript

Sadly, *Avonbay* was defeated by the capricious River Danube. We returned, as intended, over Easter 1993, found that all was well, de-winterised the engines and enjoyed a brief return cruise up the Main–Danube Canal to Riedenburg. Then it was time for an eagerly awaited overland journey by car to the magnificent city of Prague; this naturally included a lunchtime cruise by passenger boat on the Vltava, through the heart of the Czech capital.

To our dismay, first sighting of the Danube at Kelheim, when we came back in mid-July, showed it to be badly flooded. It took 48 hours, while preparing the boat, for me to decide reluctantly that a downstream voyage would verge on the suicidal! Of seven ladder rungs on the Rammelmeyr quayside, only two now remained exposed. And the water was still rising, gushing past the marina entrance at an estimated 10 kph. Travelling by hired car to refill our three gas cylinders at the Tega depot in Regensburg's Siemenstrasse, the torrent through the restricted arches of the Steinerne Brücke was of real ship-wrecking proportions – more than 1 m fall between up- and downstream sides. Flood warnings were being broadcast on the local radio station. Already the quays and streets of Passau were said to be awash. Had we attempted a downriver run, it would scarcely have been enjoyable, while there remained a positive doubt that conditions would be any better for our return some weeks later.

So, the decision was made to head westwards, back towards the Rhine, an exercise that began with fighting the Danube's current for just 2 km. Navigation buoys were half-submerged in the torrent. Each of these two kilometres lasted a worrying ten minutes, running both engines at unac-customed maximum speed. We had emerged into still water above Kelheim lock when the port engine suddenly died. Unable to diagnose the cause, I summoned a rescue boat from Rammelmeyr's, to tow us back to the marina. Thereafter, a farcical chain of events included our saving the rescue launch when it almost sank; the expensive removal of our engine for workshop rebuilding, only to discover that the gearbox had been at fault (we carried a spare); and a leisurely cruise to Frankfurt, during which the 'rebuilt' motor revealed newly-created problems, VHF radio and echo-sounder both expired and we received a visit from the *Wasserpolizei* when a commercial fisherman registered an official complaint that we had broken nets he had strung across the entrance to a harbour at Hasloch (River Main, K151). This time, the police were extremely understanding, especially when we told them that the nets' floats had been blue instead of the regulation yellow! 'It is the fisherman that we must now prosecute. We are sorry you have been troubled!'

Passsage down the Main was otherwise an enjoyable discovery of towns previously neglected. Gradually, our Danube disappointment faded; what now mattered more was anticipation of cruises yet to come on the varied – and never dull – inland waterways of Germany.

APPENDIX 1

Cruising in Germany

The network

There are approximately 7130 km of interconnected inland waterways. Easiest entry, for a boat on its own keel, is from the French canal and river system, near Mulhouse or Strasbourg; alternatively, via the Saar at Saarbrücken (from about 1996) or the Moselle, downstream of Sierck-les-Bains. Otherwise, the lower Rhine may be reached from the Netherlands, or at various points along Germany's North Sea and Baltic coasts. Except where brought overland by trailer, some use of the Rhine is unavoidable. Unless highly powered, craft should plan to travel downstream on this generally swift navigation.

Maximum dimensions

Many routes in Germany are equipped for very large commercial freight vessels, whose length, beam, water draught and air draught are almost certain to exceed these measurements in private pleasure craft. Among a small number of lesser routes, now reserved exclusively for leisure use, are the River Lahn and navigations in former East Germany, especially north and south of Berlin. *Avonbay* has only rarely experienced size restrictions, with a length of 11 m, 3.4 m beam, water draught of 1.3 m and air draught of 3.2 m. If in doubt, dimensions of individual routes should be checked in the appropriate chart books or annual *Weska* (see Appendix 2).

Hire cruisers

On account of many German navigations being heavily used by large commercial vessels and a resultant requirement for pleasure boatmen to hold some form of qualification, Germany's hire-cruiser industry has been slow to develop. Matters are rather different in the east, and a short time after reunification a number of possibilities were being offered. Here, at least, competence requirements are only demanded if they are needed in the helmsman's own country: no qualifications are needed by British holiday-makers. By 1993 the following companies were offering modern boats, similar to those long operated in Britain and France. Choice is likely to be expanded during the coming years. All should be able to cope with enquiries in English.

Where operating on routes in the west, a Competence Certificate may be required. See under 'Regulations' on p. 186

Amadeus Yachtcharter, D & F Riegel, Wilhelm-Hammann-Strasse 45, 6087 Worfelden (*Mainz/Rhine/Main*)

AME-Müritz-Charter, Müritzstrasse 11, 0-2060 Waren (*Mecklenburg Lakes*)

Arche Noah Yachtcharter, Heidrun Bergmann, Stieglitzweg 18, 7332 Eislingen (*Neckar*)

Aqua Cruising Berlin, W-R Kruhl, Fährallee 35, 0-1186 Berlin (*Berlin*)

Barone Yachting, Unterlinden 11, 7800 Freiburg (*Mecklenburg. Dahme. *Bingen/Rhine*)

Bodingbauer Yachtcharter, Zapfweg 18, 8000 München 60 (*Mecklenburg Lakes. Havel*)

Boots-Charter Potsdam, Otto-Grotewohl-Strasse 60, 0-1580 Potsdam (*Potsdam*)

Bootshandel & Yachtcharter, H. Schlief, Theodor-Storm-Strasse 10, 8501 Feucht (*Mecklenburg*)

Andrew Brock Travel Ltd, 10 Barley Mow Passage, Chiswick, London W4 4PH, England (agents for Locaboat Plaisance) (*Mecklenburg Lakes*)

Chartertours K. Hennings, An der Alten Werft, 2990 Papenburg/Ems (*Berlin*)

Deutsches Reisebüro Dertour, Emil-von-Behring-Strasse 6, 6000 Frankfurt 50 (*Berlin, Brandenburg, Mecklenburg, *Moselle, Lahn*)

Donau Charter Dieter Pramschüfer, Erlbach 25 a, 8411 Bernhardswald (*German Danube*)

Freibeuter Yachtcharter, Waldstrasse 18, 7615 Zell am Harmersbach (*Germany*)

Frey Yachting Hanau, Pestalozzistrasse 26, 6454 Bruchköbel (*Mecklenburg Lakes. *Main, Moselle*)

Friesland Boating, de Tille 5, 8723 ER Koudum (Fr), Netherlands (associated with Kuhnle-Tours) (*Mecklenburg Lakes*)

Funboat, In der Eisel 38, 6530 Bingen (*Elbe, Mecklenburg. *Rhine*)

HJM Jacht-Charter, H. P. Lüllau, Dresdner Strasse 27, 6307 Linden/Hessen (*Lahn*)

Interboat-Vertrieb, Holzhafenufer 4, 2000 Hamburg 74 (*Mecklenburg Lakes*)

Jachtcharter Domingo, Erika Thiele, Ahornstrasse 5, 6540 Nannhausen (*Moselle, Saar, Lahn*)

Kähler und Wruck, Mietbootreederei, Alsterchaussee 38, 2000 Hamburg 13 (*Mecklenburg Lakes*)

K&K Lahncharter, Ahlerhof 18, 5420 Lahnstein (*Lahn*)

Kuhnle-Tours, Nagelstrasse 4, 7000 Stuttgart 1 (*Mecklenburg Lakes, Havel, Dahme*)

Kutscher KG, Boots-Service, Nieverner Strasse 2, 5427 Bad Ems (*Lahn*) (*Motor dayboats, suitable for overnighting at hotels.*)

Lahn–Mosel-Yachtcharter, R. Herde, Emser Landstrasse, 5420 Lahnstein (*Lahn*)

Loreley Yacht Charter, Postfach 1452, 5414 Vallendar (*Moselle*)

Marina-Yacht-Charter, Scharfe Lanke 109–131, 1000 Berlin 20 (*Berlin*)

Regenbogenflotte, Hausbootcharter, Solitüderstrasse 78, 2390 Flensburg (*Mecklenburg Lakes*)

Schermer Yachtcharter, Tel: 04546/244; Fax: 512 (*Mecklenburg Lakes. *Elbe–Lübeck-Kanal*)

Schiffswerft Rechlin, Bereich Marina Claassee, Boeker Strasse 1, 0-2085 Rechlin (*Mecklenburg Lakes*)

Sea Line Yachtcharter, Fa. Könneke, Südstrasse 16, 3204 Nordstemmen (*Rhine*)

Ulrike Bauer Yacht Charter, Am Weiher 9, 8035 Gauting/München (*Mecklenburg Lakes*)

Yachtcharter Geistmann-Brand, Heldeweg 4, 6966 Seckach (*Mecklenburg Lakes*)

Yachtcharter Herde, 5420 Lahnstein (*Lahn, Moselle*)

Yachtcharter Pohling, Hans Miller, Eichenweg 17, 5416 Hillscheid (*Moselle*)

Zur Guten Fahrt, Dieter Öchsner, Brückentorstrasse 24, 8702 Kürnach/Würzburg (*Main*)

The following companies are likely to enter the east German hire cruiser business some time after 1994:

Blakes Holidays Ltd, Wroxham, Norwich, Norfolk NR12 8DH, England. Tel: (06053) 2911 or 2917 or 3221 or 3224.

Crown Blue Line, 8 Ber Street, Norwich, Norfolk NR1 3EJ, England. Tel: (0603) 630513. Fax: (0603) 664298.

Hoseasons Holidays, Sunway House, Lowestoft, Suffolk NR32 3LT, England. Tel: (0502) 501010.

Hotel ships

These offer luxury cruises on all the major river navigations, with optional shore excursions. There are regular sailings on the Rhine, Elbe, Moselle, Main and Danube; occasionally on the Neckar and Rhine–Main–Danube Canal. Details from the German National Tourist Office.

Day-tripping vessels

These are widely available on most routes, especially the Rhine, Greater Berlin, Elbe near Dresden (historic fleet of steam-powered vessels), etc. For details, consult local tourism offices or the annual directory *Kursbuch Personenschiffahrt* (see Appendix 2).

Canoes/rowing boats

These are widely noted on many rivers, the Rhine included! Sailing canoes may be hired at most boating centres in the Mecklenburg Lakes, eg Fürstenberg.

Trailed boats

These are subject to the same regulations as other pleasure craft. Numerous launching sites are available at yacht clubs and commercial marinas (see chart books). They are ideal for reaching distant locations or for exploring a waterway in one direction only.

Inland cruisers

Many privately owned motor boats in Germany are high-speed, planing craft, easily able to combat the Rhine current. If unable to contemplate a crossing of the English Channel on your own keel, it is well worth considering having your boat transported to mainland Europe. Costs will start to seem quite reasonable if you are planning a journey of several months or intend to leave the boat abroad for a series of holiday trips. I have seen just one British canal narrow boat on the Rhine: providing these fall within the 15 tonnes displacement rule (see 'Regulations' on p. 186) and are fitted with a fairly powerful engine, they should be suitable for German inland waterways, especially the quieter, less commercial routes. But do not underestimate the wash that can be produced by freight traffic and (even worse) speeding pleasure boats. One leading transport expert, making regular deliveries between the UK and various Channel ports along the French and Belgian coasts, is Ray Bowern, Mobile Tel: (0860) 729522 (see display advertisement).

The above remarks are valid if you already own a craft specifically designed for inland use only. I would, however, generally advise against purchase of such a vessel for European waterways.

Seagoing motor cruisers and motor sailers

This is easily the most realistic choice, for these boats are well able to cope with the sometimes rough conditions. *Avonbay*, sleeping six, is close to the perfect answer for Germany. Hulls up to 14 m overall can normally be handled comfortably by two people, especially if fitted with twin engines and/or a bow thruster to improve handling at locks or moorings.

Motor sailers should not be so deep-draughted that their keels regularly make contact with the bottom, especially when tying up. Carrying a recumbent mast is not really a problem unless it overhangs the bow and stern by a considerable amount.

Present trends favour construction in GRP (plastic) or steel: each material has drawbacks, but of the two I favour the greater strength of steel. A study of the advertisements in the British, French and German boating magazines will produce many suitable craft, but do check carefully on the air draught. Astonishingly, this figure is rarely quoted by manufacturers or brokers. Buying secondhand and then spending money on modifications and improvements is perhaps the most sensible approach. Always employ a marine surveyor who will be able to provide detailed reports on condition and suitability for the purpose. Such boats *must* be less than 15 tonnes displacement, if you are to navigate without professional help (see 'Regulations' below). It is surprising how many sizeable cruisers have registration papers that confirm their tonnage as a fraction under 15! *Avonbay* weighs 10.62 tonnes, both according to her documents and also when measured while suspended from a crane.

Converted barges

Few, if any, Dutch barges or similar ex-freight craft will be under 15 tonnes. A typical 20 m example is likely to be nearer 60. Thus, while an excellent choice for French, Belgian and Dutch canals and rivers, these boats are impracticable for German waters unless you (a) hold the required qualifications, or (b) wish to employ a qualified skipper.

Regulations

In Germany, every aspect of boating is subject to strict rules. Most are not difficult to comply with, but a few must be taken very seriously if you are to avoid having your vessel impounded and consequent prosecution. The boat itself must be fully seaworthy, with machinery, fire extinguishers and other equipment conforming to certain standards. In practical terms, requirements for British waters such as the Upper Thames are more than sufficient; also, the fact of your having arrived in German waters should in itself suggest that satisfactory standards have been maintained.

Registration papers (Small Ships Register or Part 1 [Merchant Shipping Act, 1894]: the Royal Yachting Association will advise on procedures) are needed to supply details of the boat, dimensions, tonnage and owner/s name and address. In addition to passports for all on board, insurance documents (with generous third party cover) must be carried. Ask your broker if any additional premium is payable for German inland use. Young people are not permitted to be in control of a boat if under the ages of 15, 18 or 21 (depending on the particular waterway). The person in overall charge *must carry a Royal Yachting Association Helmsman's (Overseas) Certificate of Competence.* If you belong to a recognised yachting club or similar, the procedure is for your application form to be signed by an officer of that club. Otherwise, consult the RYA for details of where you can take a practical test. Certificates are issued free to Association members, which is a valid reason for joining; details from RYA House, Romsey Road, Eastleigh, Hampshire SO5 4YA, England. Tel: (0703) 629962. Overseas readers are also advised to follow this course of action. Possession of the Certificate (or at least something equivalent) is vital; checks are made fairly frequently by the German water police.

The Certificate *is valid for all craft up to 15 tonnes displacement*, as indicated on the Registration document. Repeat: some boats that at first sight would appear to be in excess of 15 tonnes are recorded as slightly less on their paperwork. If you cannot comply, you might consider taking a course in

German, normally lasting several years and resulting in the granting of a Patent. But there are few pleasure boatmen whose native tongue is English who will want to embark on this!

East Germany appears not to demand qualifications of foreign boaters, provided there is no such requirement in their own country. This explains the current rapid growth of hire craft on the Mecklenburg waterways.

Copies of the (German language) regulations for the Rhine (*Rheinschiffahrtpolizeiverordnung!*), Moselle, Danube and other waterways must be carried on board, even if you cannot understand them! (See Appendix 2.) I have never been asked to show mine to an official. Equally, craft over 10 m overall are said to have to fly a special navigation flag at the bows, similar in concept to the Belgian *drapeau de navigation*, and signifying that they are under way. This device is a white square with a horizontal red stripe. I cannot ever recall seeing one, except on the German Danube.

Customs and VAT

Following the dismantling of trade barriers throughout the European Community in January 1993, it now appears that a national of any of those 12 countries has full rights to keep and use his boat within the EC without payment of any taxes other than navigation tolls or licences. This assumes that Value Added Tax has been paid, normally in your country of origin; it would be wise to carry documentary proof that this is the case. The requirement is waived on craft over a certain age. The RYA will be able to advise. The position relating to non-EC nationals seems rather different, but in practice prolonged visits are likely to be allowed as in the period pre-1993. In cases of doubt, seek advice from your own Customs/Taxation departments.

Tolls and payments

Most German boaters belong to a club that is affiliated to the ADAC, a national umbrella body. This makes a sizeable annual payment to the waterways authorities' finances, in return for 'free' pleasure boating. Non-Germans are not expected to make any contribution. A few exceptions will be encountered (eg when a pleasure cruiser uses a Moselle lock unaccompanied by passenger or commercial craft); and in other rare cases such as working through a lock after normal operating hours (eg in Berlin).

Tipping lock keepers does not seem to be a matter of course, although a can of cold beer or other small gift will sometimes be appropriate. At large commercial locks, our only keeper contact is usually by radio telephone.

Moorings

This is a thorny subject! Often banks on both rivers and canals are of unfriendly rock or sloping stonework. Pleasure craft using freight routes should only tie up where it is expressly stated that they may do so (see chart books). Normally, this will be in basins or arms off the through route, many of which are managed by yacht clubs or commercial marinas. Overnight charges will not always be requested; a typical cost in 1992 was 1DM per metre of boat length. We always attempt to use town quays, workboats or (with permission) lock approaches, having first ascertained that we are in no danger from commercial craft. It is normal practice to display a white anchor light during hours of darkness, unless of course you are lying secure in a marina.

Avonbay's European cruising (now in its eighth year) is achieved by making arrangements for long-term moorings, preferably with a commercial boatyard or for shorter periods of several weeks with a yacht club. This latter option is usually much cheaper, but requires the establishment of a friendly relationship with a conscientious member who can keep an eye on the boat during our absence.

During 1993, overnight mooring charges began to appear at certain marinas and quaysides in the east. Fees, however, are mostly very reasonable. Moreover, the choice of suitable places is often wider than in the west. In both areas, avoid tying to passenger boat jetties unless you have checked with a reliable source that no craft are likely to call.

Boat handling and locks

We can assume that boat-handling skills will have been acquired elsewhere. In Germany it is important to remember that many routes are devoted to freight transport; pleasure craft are tolerated provided they do not interfere with the waterway's trading function. Both cargo and passenger vessels have priority over cruisers at locks and must be allowed to enter first. Frequently, there will be a space at the back of the chamber for small craft. We find it helpful to note the lock's usable length in the cruising guide and that of craft (painted on their superstructure) as they enter. Keepers relay instructions via a public address system and less often by hand signals. Colour lights, red and green, show when you may enter. Locks on the Lahn are fitted with 'semaphore' signal arms. Most useful of all is VHF radio contact. Channel numbers are normally posted on the bank several km farther back or appear in the chart books. Radio is not yet widespread in the east. When your turn comes to enter a lock, do so with a minimum of delay and secure to a bollard as quickly as possible. We keep engines running so as to maintain control when the water is entering fiercely. Often, mooring bollards are placed so far apart that a small boat can reach only one. In this case, use a single rope, as short as possible, attached to a centre point on the boat. If time allows, fix bow and stern lines also. Where deep locks necessitate shifting mooring lines from one bollard to another, up to a dozen times, never tie the ropes: you may need to change them quickly. This also applies to floating bollards, which sometimes reach the end of their travel while the water level continues to rise or fall for up to 0.5 m.

If leaving a lock astern of heavy commercial traffic, wait, securely tied, until the wash from the barge has subsided, otherwise you will lose control in the resulting swirl.

Fast-flowing rivers should only be navigated within the limitations of your engine power. It is vital to be able to turn to face the current and then pull into the side to stop. Always keep a suitable anchor rigged in case of engine failure.

Night navigation is best avoided, especially on rivers such as the Rhine. Unfamiliar waters are potentially dangerous in the dark; in any case, you are presumably cruising in order to appreciate the scenery. Daylight hours are sufficiently long for all pleasure boating.

Equipment

Echo-sounder, VHF radio and radar are useful navigation aids. We have lately installed radar as an insurance against suddenly encountering fog. When early morning visibility on the Moselle was unexpectedly reduced to a few metres, we rapidly became disorientated, could not see approaching traffic, and were far from a suitable mooring.

Lines long enough for all expected mooring purposes should be kept ready for use. Enough fenders to protect topsides in locks or when tied up are vital. Even the big barges hang short lengths of timber over their vulnerable quarters. It is neither necessary nor seamanlike to drape the hull with a collection of car tyres, canvas sheets or horizontal wooden planks. Published sources that advise otherwise are advertising an inability to handle a boat correctly. Attractive pleasure craft disguised as rubbish containers will not elicit admiration from other competent boaters. In addition to a stout rubber D-section fender all round the gunwhales, *Avonbay* uses just four inflated fenders each side. These are invariably lifted on deck when not required.

A dinghy is a most useful acquisition, but is best stowed on deck or, better still, hung in davits. This allows contact with the shore when at anchor, and also serves as filming boat, bathing float, plaything for younger crew members and, not infrequently, allows us to explore shallow backwaters.

Long boat hooks (for grabbing mooring buoys, taking depth soundings or pushing off should you accidentally ground), swimming ladder, mooring stakes (with heavy hammer) and small fishing net are all useful. The latter can be invaluable for recovering objects blown overboard and for passing gifts (eg a bottle of wine) to the helpful crews of other boats.

While most cruisers have insufficient deck space to carry a small car, a miniature motorbike – or, in our case, a pair of bicycles – is much appreciated on shore/shopping expeditions. Heavy loads of food, gas bottles or, *in extremis*, jerry cans of fuel, can be transported on a folding trolley.

Hoses are frequently available at water-filling points, but not invariably. We carry two 30 m lengths, with connector, of the type that packs flat on to a reel. Several tap fittings may be necessary. The most useful sort is a rubber push-on joint, fixed with jubilee clip or butterfly screw.

A really powerful horn, of the kind that cannot be confused with a car hooter, is necessary, together with a searchlight for discovering suitable moorings if you should be caught out by the onset of darkness. Do carry a selection of more obvious engine spares such as drive belts, fuel filters, injectors, gaskets, fuses, water pump components, light bulbs, etc, together with service manuals for all machinery on board. As a safeguard against breakdowns, compile a list of agents for your make of engine/s in Germany.

Navigation signals

These mainly conform to European waterways standards. Explanations appear in most of the chart books.

Hours of navigation

Lock-operating times vary from waterway to waterway and with the time of the year. Summer hours are typically 5 am–9 pm on larger routes, Monday to Saturday. Sundays and public holidays may bring afternoon or even all-day closures. Details appear in the chart books. For a nationally comprehensive list, obtain the *Schleusenkalender*, published every spring by *Boote Magazine*, Grosse Bleichen 5, 2000 Hamburg 36. Tel: (040) 353461. Fax: (040) 354770.

Occasional stoppages for maintenance work may close a route for periods varying from days to months. Advance details are available from:

Wasser-und Schiffahrtsdirektion Nord, Hindenburgufer 247, 2300 Kiel.
Wasser-und Schiffahrtsdirektion Nordwest, Schlossplatz 9, 2960 Aurich.
Wasser-und Schiffahrtsdirektion Mitte, Am Waterlooplatz 5, 3000 Hannover.
Wasser-und Schiffahrtsdirektion West, Cheruskerring 11, 440 Munster.
Wasser-und Schiffahrtsdirektion Sudwest, Stresemannufer 2, 6500 Mainz.
Wasser-und Schiffahrtsdirektion Sud, Worthstrasse 19, 8700 Würzburg.
Bundesverband der Deutschen Binnenschiffahrt e.V., Westhafen, 1000 Berlin 65.
Wasser-und Schiffahrtsdirektion Ost, Poststrasse 21–22, 0-1020, Berlin.
Wasser-und Schiffahrtsamt Magdeburg, Aussenstelle Wittenberge, Bern.-Remy-Strasse 15, 0-3010 Magdeburg.
Wasser-und Schiffahrtsamt Magdeburg, Aussenstelle Halle, Wilhelm-Külz-Strasse 22, 0-4020 Halle.
Wasser-und Schiffahrtsamt Brandenburg, Beetzsee Ufer 3, 0-1800 Brandenburg.
Wasser-und Schiffahrtsamt Eberswalde, Hans-Beimler Strasse 1, 0-1300 Eberswalde-Finow 1.
Wasser-und Schiffahrtsamt Berlin, Aussenstelle Fürstenwalde, Mühlenbrücke 2, 0-1240 Fürstenwalde.
Wasser-und Schiffahrtsamt Eberswalde, Aussenstelle Zehdenick, Am Voss-kanal, 0-1434 Zehdenick.
Wasser-und Schiffahrtsamt Lauenburg, Aussenstelle Grabow, Karl Marx Strasse 31, 0-2804 Grabow.
Wasser-und Schiffahrtsamt Lauenburg, Grünstrasse 16, W-2058 Lauenburg.

Speed limits

Frequently, there are no speed limits (eg the Rhine and Main), except in lock cuts or other restricted areas. Where limits are imposed, the maximum is shown on bankside signs or in the chart books.

Flags

You will want to fly your country's ensign, not necessarily for nationalistic reasons but more to advise lock keepers and other users that you may not comprehend their instructions. In many cases, our flag is not readily visible to keepers as *Avonbay* enters locks. To avoid a barrage of distorted German over the public-address system, we additionally fly a pilot-jack at the bows to denote our country of origin. This consists of your national flag (in our case the union flag) on a white ground. Its use in these circumstances has been approved by both the Flag Institute and the Ministry of Defence. Expect to receive curious and/or critical comments from fellow countrymen, unaware of its official acceptance.

Technically, a 'Navigation Flag' should fly on the bows of craft more than 10 m in length (see 'Regulations' on p. 186). When in German waters, it is customary to hoist a courtesy flag (small German ensign) on the starboard yardarm. This might well be replaced by the attractive Bavarian flag when on appropriate southern navigations. Where the waterway is the line of a national frontier (eg Moselle in Luxembourg), two courtesy flags are in order. Flag enthusiasts can briefly use three simultaneously on the Rhine at Basle and on the Moselle, where Germany, France and Luxembourg meet!

Language

In west Germany, English is spoken by many of the more affluent pleasure boaters and at yacht clubs. Perhaps 20 per cent of lock keepers and shop staff, especially younger ones, are moderately fluent. Restaurant and shop personnel in tourist centres have an embarrassingly comprehensive command of the language compared with the reverse situation in England. In the east, for four decades Russian was taught as the first foreign language, so English speakers are rarely encountered. The best prospects are schoolchildren or those who were PoWs with the British or American forces during the Second World War.

Because I can speak French, I found basic German surprisingly easy to master. An extensive vocabulary is the key to success in this context. Instruction tapes or videos are useful; individual tuition or evening classes even better. Our 12 hourly classes improved my very elementary knowledge considerably. Even if you do not go to this trouble, a few phrases such as 'Good morning', 'Please', 'Thank you' and 'Goodbye' at least demonstrate a degree of willingness. Practise a selection of short sentences which cover the more obvious boating situations. It's all easier than you might imagine!

Fuel, gas, water and electricity

Diesel fuel is readily available at tax-inclusive prices throughout the west and is not particularly scarce in the east. Waterside petrol pumps, however, are rare. Expect to carry supplies from road garages. Bottled gas (propane/butane) is nothing like as widespread as in France, except for the more expensive Camping Gaz. Fittings and regulators are the same as in most European countries, but differ from British patterns. Obviously empty bottles will only be exchanged for full ones of the same brand. The best sources of supply are fuel stations that cater for barges. We have discovered depots on the Main at Würzburg and in Berlin/Spandau, where empty containers are filled while you wait. Doubtless there are other similar places.

Drinking-water is usually obtainable at locks, marinas and yacht clubs, but expect to make a small payment. Commercial harbours sometimes have slot machines with water issuing under considerable pressure. Overnight charging of boats' batteries is possible at most marinas: shore sockets are of a different design to those used in France. Payment is normally required.

Sanitation

In the absence of facilities for emptying sewage-holding tanks, overboard discharge is the norm. Try not to do this too obviously in a crowded marina!

Shopping and restaurants

Unless your German is good, self-service supermarkets are easier to use than village shops. Food quality is excellent in the west, with a massive variety, especially of sausages. Pork is consumed in huge quantities. Credit cards are less acceptable than in the UK or France. Use cash or, for large purchases, Eurocheques. Most shops close on Saturday afternoons, Sundays and public holidays. We found none of the anticipated food shortages in the east. Prices are lower (especially in restaurants), but choice is more limited.

Eating out is one of the more pleasurable aspects of boating in Germany. The national drinks are beer and white wine. Costs need not be excessive: although the portions served frequently are! Unless you are extremely hungry, it is ill-advised to order a starter. A single course is often all you can comfortably eat. Even that may be too large for the plate and served *halb und halb*: half now, the other half when you have finished!

Telephones

By mid-1993, great advances had been achieved with modernising the east German telephone system. In most cases, there should now be little difficulty in establishing contact with the UK and other 'western' countries.

Cruising times and distances

A few statistics relating to *Avonbay*'s progress will serve as an idea of what can be achieved. For much of the time we adopted a leisurely pace, allowing several hours on most days for exploration ashore. These breaks are included in the times listed below; periods where the boat remained stationary for prolonged sightseeing are not. Because of its rapid flow, the Rhine was navigated rather quickly, while our eagerness to reach east Germany and a lack of scenic interest prompted us to pass through the Mittelland Canal without delay.

Chapter	Waterway	From/To	Distance (km) (one way)	Locks	Time taken (days)
1	Rhine	Basle–Netherlands	708	10	5
2	Neckar	Mannheim– Plochingen	201	27	6
3	Lahn	Lahnstein–Dehrn	65	12	3
4	Moselle	Koblenz–Apach	242	13	6/7
5	Rhein-Herne	Duisburg–Ruhrort– Henrichenburg	47	6	$1\frac{1}{2}$
	Dortmund-Ems	Henrichenburg– Bergeshövede	82	1	$1\frac{1}{2}$
	Mittelland	Bergeshövede–Rühen	256	2	$3\frac{1}{2}$
6	Mittelland	Rühen–Rothensee	62	1	1
	Elbe	Rothensee–Havelberg	90	—	1
	Havel	Havelberg–Berlin	148	6	$2\frac{1}{2}$
7	Berlin Waterways	Berlin Circuit	c141	4	3
	Dahme	Schmöckwitz–Wolzig	32	1	1
8	Havel-Oder/ Müritz-Havel etc	Spandau–Waren– Templin–Rheinsberg	c194	16	6/7
9	Potsdamer Havel/ Elbe-Havel	Potsdam–Elbe	c70	4	2
	Wesel-Dateln	Dateln–Rhine	60	6	$1\frac{1}{2}$
10	Main	Mainz–Bamberg	384	34	8/9
11	Rhine-Main- Danube	Bamberg–Kelheim	171	16	3
12	Danube	Kelheim–Regensburg	36	2	$\frac{1}{2}$

Selected Bibliography

The following publications are all relevant to journeys described in this book. The dates given are those of the latest editions. (* Denotes publications where the text is in German; only those works containing maps or statistical information of use to English-speaking readers have been included. Most can be purchased from the author by mail order at Shepperton Swan Ltd, The Clock House, Upper Halliford, Shepperton, Middlesex TW17 8RU, England. Tel: (0932) 783319. A regular list of secondhand and out of print titles can also be provided.)

General

Castles on the Rhine. Stollfuss, Bonn, 1985.

The Guinness Guide to Waterways of Western Europe, by Hugh McKnight. Guinness, London, 1978. Includes some west German routes.

Inland Waterways of Europe, by Roger Calvert. George Allen & Unwin, London, 1963. East and west Germany included.

Insight Guides, APA Publications, 1980s/1990s. Excellent value, fully illustrated in colour. Titles include *Berlin, Cologne, Düsseldorf, Frankfurt, The New Germany, The Rhine*.

* *Kursbuch Personenschiffahrt*. Annually. Jaeger, Darmstadt. Lists all inland passenger boat services.

Legends of the Rhine, by Wilhelm Ruland. Stollfuss, Bonn, 1985.

Michelin Green Guide, Germany. Michelin, London, regularly updated.

* *Regulations for Shipping* (*Rheinschiffahrtpolizeiverordnung* etc), Inland Shipping Publishers, Duisburg. *Rhein, Mosel, Donau, Binnenschiffahrtstrassenverordnung* (for other waterways). Appropriate volumes must be carried on board.

Through the German Waterways, by Philip Bristow. Adlard Coles Nautical, London, 1988. Describes west Germany only.

Waterways in Europe, by Roger Pilkington. John Murray, London, 1972. West Germany only.

* *Weska* (annually), Inland Shipping Publishers Duisburg. Comprehensive directory of all German waterways with dimensions and much other useful information.

World Canals, by Charles Hadfield. David & Charles, Newton Abbot, 1986. Good coverage of historical waterway development.

Maps and chart books

* *Karte der Wasserstrassen in Deutschland und den Beneluxländern*. Petersohn, Düren, 1992. Excellent large map with all German routes, locks/distances, connections to neighbouring countries.
* *Bootsfahrten auf der Saar*. Vol. 1, Saarbrücken–Mosel; Vol. 2, Saarbrücken–Canal de la Marne au Rhin, by Karl Conrath. Saarbrücken Druckerei, Saarbrücken, 1983/4.
* *Die Donau, Kelheim–Jochenstein*, by Wolfgang Banzhaf. Verlag Rheinschiffahrt, Bad Soden, 1992. Charts of the German Danube.
* *Gewässer in und um Berlin*, by Jürgen Strassburger. Edition Maritim, Hamburg, 1991. Large map and booklet, waterways of Greater Berlin.
* *Die Lahn*, by Karin Brundiers and Gerd Fleischhauer. Verlag Rheinschiffahrt, Bad Soden, 1982.
* *Main, Main–Donau Kanal*, Karin Brundiers and Gerd Fleischhauer. Verlag Rheinschiffahrt, Bad Soden, 1993.
* *Mosel Handbuch, Koblenz–Neuves-Maisons*, by Karin Brundiers and Gerd Fleischhauer. DSV-Verlag, Hamburg, 1985.
* *Der Neckar*, by Karin Brundiers and Gerd Fleischhauer. Verlag Rheinschiffahrt, Bad Soden, 1984.
* *Ost-Deutschland Binnen von Elbe bis Oder*, by Henry Nagel. Nagel, Wislikofen, Switzerland, 1991. Very full guide, with maps, to all east German routes.
* *Rhein/Mosel Atlas*. Verlag Rheinschiffahrt, Bad Soden. Massive ring-bound chartbook for all of each river. German and French text. Includes Saar.
* *Rhein-Handbuch*. Vol. 1, Basel–Koblenz; Vol. 2, Koblenz–Lobith, by Karin Brundiers and Gerd Fleischhauer. DSV-Verlag, Hamburg, 1988.
* *Schiffahrtskarten der Binnenwasserstrassen der DDR*, Wasserstrassenaufsichtsamt der DDR, Berlin, 1985/9. 5 vols. Detailed hardback chart coverage of all east German waterways.
* *Sportschiffahrtskarten Binnen*, Vol. 1, *Berlin & Märkische Gewässer*, 1991; Vol. 2, *Berlin & Mecklenburger Gewässer*, 1992; Vol. 3, *Oder & Peene*; Vol. 4, *Elbe, Lower Havel etc*, in preparation. Nautische Veröffentlichung Verlagsgesellschaft Scheidt & Co, Arnis. Excellent large-scale chart books, covering all east Germany.
* *Wasserwander Atlas*, Vol. 1, *Märkische Gewässer* (Elbe–Oder, excluding Berlin); Vol. 2, *Mecklenburger Gewässer und Boddengewässer* (Mecklenburg Lakes etc). Tourist Verlag, Leipzig, 1990. Very detailed charts. Key in English/German/French/Russian.
* *West- und Norddeutsche Binnenwasserstrassen*, by Karin Brundiers and Gerd Fleischhauer. DSV-Verlag, Hamburg, 1989. Vol. 1 includes Rhein–Herne, Wesel–Dateln, Dortmund–Ems etc; Vol. 2 Mittelland and Elbe Seiten Canals.

Cruising and travelogues

Across Europe in a Motor Boat, by Henry C. Rowland. Appleton, New York, 1908. Rhine and Danube.

The Annie Marble in Germany, by C. S. Forester. Bodley Head, London, 1930. Exploration in east Germany by outboard dinghy.

The Bride of the Rhine: 200 Miles in a Mosel Row-Boat, by George Waring. Osgood, Boston, USA, 1878.

Camping Voyages on German Rivers, by Arthur A. MacDonell. Stanford, London, 1890. Werra, Weser, Neckar, Rhine, Moselle, Main, Elbe, Danube.

Canoe Errant, by R. Raven-Hart. John Murray, London, 1935. Includes Saar, Moselle, Rhine, Danube, Lahn, Elbe, Havel, Mecklenburg Lakes.

A Cruise Across Europe, by Donald Maxwell. Bodley Head, London/New York, 1907. Rhine, Main, Ludwig's Canal, Danube.

Guilt-Edged, by Merlin Minshall. Bachman & Turner, London, 1975. Includes chapters on a 1933 voyage, Rhine, Main, Ludwig's Canal, Danube.

The Improbable Voyage, by Tristan Jones. Bodley Head, London, 1986. By ocean-going trimaran, North Sea to Black Sea, via Rhine, Main, Main–Danube and Danube.

Leontyne: By Barge from London to Vienna, by Richard Goodwin. Collins, London, 1989. The book of the television series. Rhine, Main, Danube.

The Life of the Moselle, by Octavius Rooke. Booth, London, 1858.

The Log of the Griffin, by Donald Maxwell. Bodley Head, London, 1905. Sailing boat down the Rhine from Switzerland.

The Log of the Water Lily, during three Cruises on the Rhine, Neckar, Main, Moselle, Danube, Saône and Rhône, by Robert Mansfield. Hotten, London, 5th edn 1877. Rowing boat cruises of the 1850s.

Our Cruise in the Undine: The Journal of an English Pair-Oar Expedition through France, Baden, Rhenish Bavaria, Prussia and Belgium, by 'The Captain' (Edmund G. Harvey). Parker, London, 1854. Includes Rhine and Neckar.

Our Wherry in Wendish Lands, from Friesland through the Mecklenburg Lakes to Bohemia, by H. M. Doughty. Jarrold, London, 1892, reprinted, Ashford, Southampton, 1985.

Sailing Across Europe, by Negley Farson. Century, London and New York, 1926 and reprints. Rhine, Main, Ludwig's Canal, Danube.

Small Boat series, by Roger Pilkington. Macmillan, London. Titles include *Bavaria*, 1962; *Germany*, 1963; *Luxembourg*, 1967; *Moselle*, 1968; *Northern Germany*, 1969; *Lower Rhine*, 1970; *Upper Rhine*, 1971.

Steam Voyages on the Seine, the Moselle, and the Rhine, by Michael J. Quin. 2 vols. Colburn, London, 1843.

A Thousand Miles in the Rob Roy Canoe on Rivers and Lakes of Europe, by J. Macgregor. Samson Low, London, 1866 and reprints. Rhine, Main, Danube and Moselle.

Up the Seine and Down the Rhine, by M. A. Lloyd. Imray, London, 1938. Family cruising in a small motor boat.

Yankee Sails Across Europe, by Irving and Electa Johnson. Norton, New York, 1962. Includes Rhine.

Index

Page numbers in **bold** refer to illustrations

Alf 52
Altmühl R **127**, 171–3
Anderten 82
Andernach 18, **57**
Annie Marble in Germany, The 70, **72**, 88
Apach 69
Arneberg 89
Aschaffenburg **62**, 139, 140, 145
Assmannshausen 13
Augsburg 139

Bad Abbach 175
Bad Ems 34–6
Bad Essen 80
Bad Wimpen 29
Balduinstein 40
Bamberg 155–60
Basle 5, 6
Bech-Kleinmacher 69
Beilngries 173
Beilstein **43**, 50
Belgium 75, 138
Berching **61**, 132, 164–7, 170
Bergeshövede 79–80
Berncastel 63
Berlin 71, 96–108, 126, **131**, 135
Bingen 11–13
Bonn 18, **60**
Boppard 16
Brandenburg 94–5
Britzer Zweikanal 101
Bürgel 143
Burg Eltz 45–6, **49**
Burton, Sir Michael & Lady Henrietta 96, 106, 135

Camping Voyages on German Rivers 23–4
Canal de la Marne au Rhin 6
Cannstatt 30–1
Canow 117
Chain tugs 23–4, 139, 145, **149**, 150
Charlemagne 155

Charlottenburg Verbindungs C 105
Cochem **46–7**, 48, 50
Cologne 18–19, **57**, 66
Cruisers, choice of 185–6
Cruising French Waterways 9
Czech Republic 87–8

Dahme Wasserstrasse **61**, 100, 102–3
Danube R **134**, 140, 174–81
Dausenau 36
Dietfurt 171
Dietkirchen **41**, 42
Diez **39**, 40
Dortmund-Ems C **70**, 75–9, **130**, 137–8
Doughty, H M 70, 71, **72**, 110, 113, **115**, 118
Dresden 86, 88
Duisburg-Ruhrort 20–1, 73
Düsseldorf 19

Eberbach 28
Eibelstadt 150–1
Elbe-Havel C 94, 136–7
Elbe Lateral C 83
Elbe R **85**, 86–90, 137
Elde-Müritz Wasserstrasse 119
Emmerich 21–2
Erlangen 161, **163**

Farson, Negley 156, 178
Flags 108, **171**, 191
Forchheim 161
Forester, C S 70, **72**, 88, 110, 115–16, 120
Frankfurt-am-Main 141–3
Freikörperkultur (FKK) 113
Frickenhausen **134**, 152
Fürstenberg 116

Gebersdorf 161–2
Gemünden 148
Genthin **61**, 137
Gérard, Charles 73
Giessen 33, 42
Gondorf 45

Gorbachev, Mikhail 71, 126, 135
Grand Canal d'Alsace 4–5
Grevenmacher 68
Guilt-Edged 156–8, 178

Hadfield, Charles 155
Halfar, Norman 106
Hamelin 80–1
Harvington, Lord 5, 151
Hassmersheim 29
Hassfurt 154
Havelberg 91
Havel-Oder Wasserstrasse 107–8
Havel R 90–5, 108–17
Heidelberg 23–6, **56**
Heilbronn 29–30
Hennigsdorf 107
Henrichenburg **70**, 76–8, 137–8
Hilpoltstein 166, 169, **172**
Hire cruisers 182–4
Hirschhorn 27, 28
Hitdorf 19
Hitler, Adolph 16, 83, 165
Hofman, Caroline & Michael 163, 164, 168, 180
Hollerich 37–8
Homburg 148
Hornberg 29
Hotel ships 184

Iffezheim 7
Ingolstadt 175
Inland Waterways Association 169, 173

Kannenburg 112
Karlstadt **ii**, 149–50
Kelheim 173–5
Kitzingen 153
Klink 120
Koblenz 17, 33, 44–5
Köpenick 101
Krotzenburg 140, **141**

Lahn R 16, 32–42, **58**
Lahnstein 33

Laurenburg 38
Leerstetten 168–9
Lehnitz 107
Liebenwalde 109–10
Life on the Moselle, The 53–4, 66
Limburg 40–2
Linz 18
Lobith 22
Lorch 12
Loreley 13, **58**
Lüdinghausen 79, **130**
Ludwig I 155, **157**
Ludwig II 160
Ludwig the Bavarian 13
Ludwig's C 139, 155–60, **163**, 164, 173
Ludwigshafen 9
Luxembourg 67–9

MacDonnell, Arthur 23–4
Machnow 101
Main R 11, **60**, **133**, **134**, 139–54
Mainz 11, 140
Mannheim 9, 24
Mansfield, Robert 156, 177
Markbreit 152
Marktheidenfeld 148
Maximum craft sizes 182
Maxwell, Donald 156
Mecklenburg 109–25, **128**, **129**
Milow 92–3
Miltenberg **133**, 146, **147**
Minden 80–2
Minheim **59**, 63
Minshall, Merlin 157–8, 178
Mirow 118–19, **128**
Mittelland C 80–6, **87**, **89**, **129**, 137
Molkenberg 91
Mondorf 18
Moorings 187–8
Moselle R (Mosel) 43–54, **59**, **60**, 63–9
Muggelsee 104
Münster 79
Müritz (lake) 120–2, **128**
Müritz-Havel Wasserstrasse 114–19

Nassau 36–7
Navigation, hours of 190
Neckar R 23–31, **56**
Neckar-Donau C 24

Neckarrems 30
Neckarsteinach 27–8
Netherlands 22
Neuburgweier 8
Neue Mühle 102
Neumagen **60**, 63–4, **65**
Niederfinow 108
Niegripp 88, 137
Nierstein 10–11
Nuremberg (Nürnberg) 139, 165–6

Obernhof 38
Oberwinter 18
Ochsenfurt **60**, 151–2
Offenbach 142–3
Our Wherry in Wendish Lands 70, 71, **72**, 110, 113, **115**, **126**

Passenger craft **ix**, **57**, 184
Pfalz 13, **55**
Pilkington, Roger 75, 80–1
Plauer See (Berlin) 94, **126**
Plochingen 31
Poland 108
Potsdam 95, **130**, 135–6
Prague 87–8, 181
Prunn **127**, 173
Pritzerbe 93

Quin, Michael 50–2

Rathenow 92, **93**
Ravensbrück 116
Regensburg 176–81
Regnitz R 155, 158
Regulations 186–7
Remich 68
Rheinfelden 5
Rhein-Herne C 75–6
Rheinsberg **109**, 124–5
Rhine R **ix**, 1–22, **55**, **57**, **58**
Rhine-Main-Danube C **127**, **132**, 139–40, 154–73
Riedenburg 173
Rooke, Octavius 53–4, 66
Rothensee 85–6, **87**, 88, **89**, **129**, 137
Rüdesheim **1**, 11–12
Rühen 84–5
Ruhr 19, 20, 75–6
Russian troops 112, 116

Saal/Donau 175, 180–1

Sailing Across Europe 156–7, 178
St Aldegund 52
St Goar 12, **14–15**, 16
Schwebsange 68
Schweinfurt 153
Slow Boat Through France vii, 5
Small Boat Through Germany 75, 80–1
Spandau **61**, 99, 106–7
Speyer 9
Spree-Oder Wasserstrasse 103
Spree R 99, 106
Steam Voyages on the Seine etc 50–2
Stolzenfels 16, **17**, **58**
Storkower C 103
Strasbourg 6–7
Stuttgart 24, 30–1
Sülfeld 83
Sulzfeld 152–3
Switzerland 5, 24

Tangermünde 88–9, **90**
Teltow C **96**, 100–1
Templin 113, **115**
Traben-Trabach 54, 63
Trier **53**, 64–7
Tries 48
Tulla, Johann 6

Ulm 174
Untertheres 153

Vltava R 87, 181

Wanne-Eikel 75–6
Wannsee 99, 106
Waren 122–3, **128**
Wasserbillig 67
Water Lily on the Danube, The 156, 177
Wends 118
Wertheim **133**, 146–7
Wesel-Dateln C 138
Weser R 80–2
Wolfsburg 83
Wolzig 103
Worms 10, **11**
Würzburg **149**, 150

Zehdenick 110
Zell 52–3
Zwingenberg 28

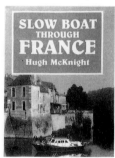

If any of the following words mean something to you

Luxemotors Moorings Craning

Steelwork *AXS* Drydock Tjalks

Rope **spares** Klippers Oil

Shackles **pumps** Brokerage Pontoons

Fridges Lifevests

Haagenaar Paint **Antifreeze** Gearboxes *Steilsteven*

Mechanical work Anchors *Klipperaaks* Chain

Boat transport Fenders Marine Toilets

Insurance A.G.F. Canal charts

Conversion work Electrics Heating Hire craft Importation

Information Electronics Plumbing

Winter covers Dry storage

Surveys Canal books Dutch steel cruisers

Second hand boat equipment Fibreglass

then we are here to help you

H2O

Port de Plaisance
21170 Saint Jean de Losne
France
Tel: (33) 80 39 23 00
Fax: (33) 80 29 04 67

We are a company in central France specialising in all aspects of canal boats: Brokerage (always about 30 boats for sale on site), moorings on modern pontoons with water and electricity, all repair and maintenance services, chandlery, showers, laundry

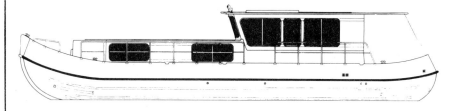

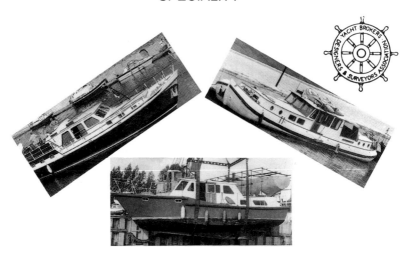

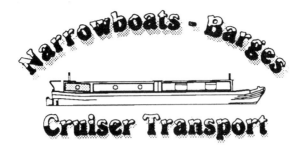

Rhythmuswechsel

Auf der Liberté wird Streß zu einem Fremdwort

„… hetzen, jagen, schneller sein, nervös werden, sich beeilen, unter Druck stehen, keine Zeit haben, Fast-Food, Quick-Lunch, Schnellkochtopf…

*D*ie meistbenutzten Vokabeln aus ungeschriebenen Managertagebüchern sind inzwischen jedermann sehr geläufig. Im Gästebuch der Liberté tauchen solche Begriffe nicht auf.

Bei uns ist mehr von *„… Entspannung, gelöster Atmosphäre, ungezwungenem Beisammensein, Genuß und Beschaulichkeit…" die Rede.*

MS *Liberté*

*W*er uns das ins Gästebuch schreibt?

Wer auf der Liberté an Bord geht, um für ein paar Tage Terminhetze und hektische Betriebsamkeit über Bord zu werfen?

*E*s sind Gruppen bis zu 12 Mitgliedern, die mit der Liberté in aller Ruhe auf europäischen Wasserwegen entlang schippern; eine mehrtägige Spazierfahrt unternehmen, vorbei an stillen Winkeln und idyllischen Landschaftsbildern. Auf verträumten Seitenärmen und Kanälen gibt die Liberté den Blick auf viele verborgene Sehenswürdigkeiten frei.

Liberté-Reisen · Postfach 1228 D ·69140 Neckargemünd ·Telefon 0 62 21/ 80 45 46

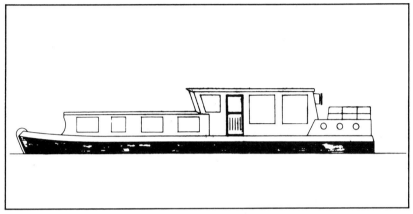

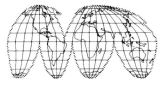